IMAGES
*of America*

# SOUTH BOSTON

## VOLUME II

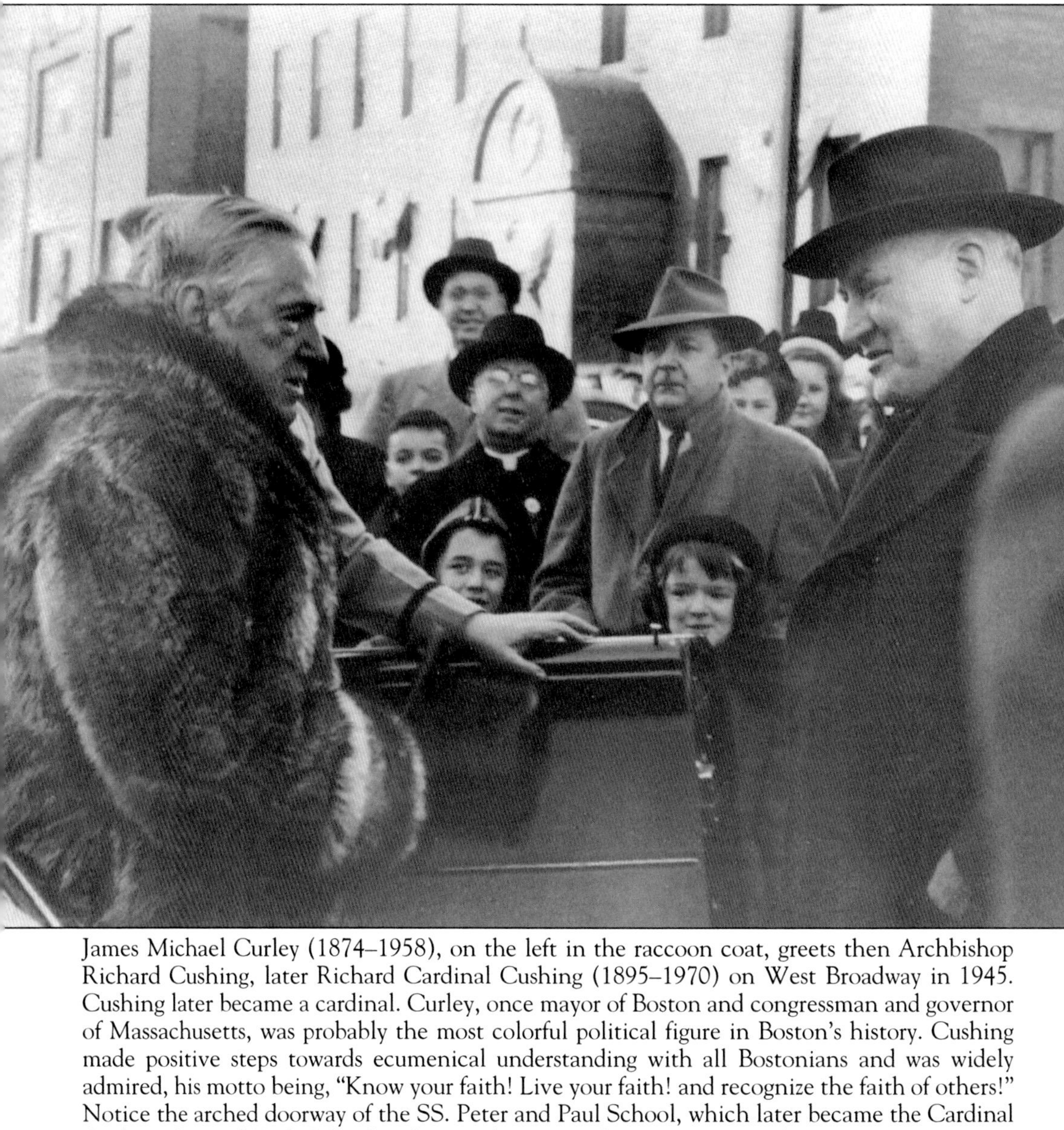

James Michael Curley (1874–1958), on the left in the raccoon coat, greets then Archbishop Richard Cushing, later Richard Cardinal Cushing (1895–1970) on West Broadway in 1945. Cushing later became a cardinal. Curley, once mayor of Boston and congressman and governor of Massachusetts, was probably the most colorful political figure in Boston's history. Cushing made positive steps towards ecumenical understanding with all Bostonians and was widely admired, his motto being, "Know your faith! Live your faith! and recognize the faith of others!" Notice the arched doorway of the SS. Peter and Paul School, which later became the Cardinal Cushing Central High School and now is known as the Notre Dame Education Center.

*On the cover:* In 1907, members of Division Five of the Boston Elevated Railway pose for a group photograph in the North Point Carhouse at City Point in South Boston. Almost every man was a resident of South Boston and lived within walking distance of the carhouse.

IMAGES of America

# SOUTH BOSTON

## VOLUME II

Anthony Mitchell Sammarco

ARCADIA PUBLISHING

ISBN 978-0-7385-6423-4

Published by Arcadia Publishing
Charleston, South Carolina

Printed in the United States of America

For all general information contact Arcadia Publishing at:
Telephone 843-853-2070
Fax 843-853-0044
E-mail sales@arcadiapublishing.com
For customer service and orders:
Toll-Free 1-888-313-2665

Visit us on the Internet at www.arcadiapublishing.com

*In honor of Dr. William J. Reid, retired headmaster of the South Boston High School and president of the South Boston Historical Society.*

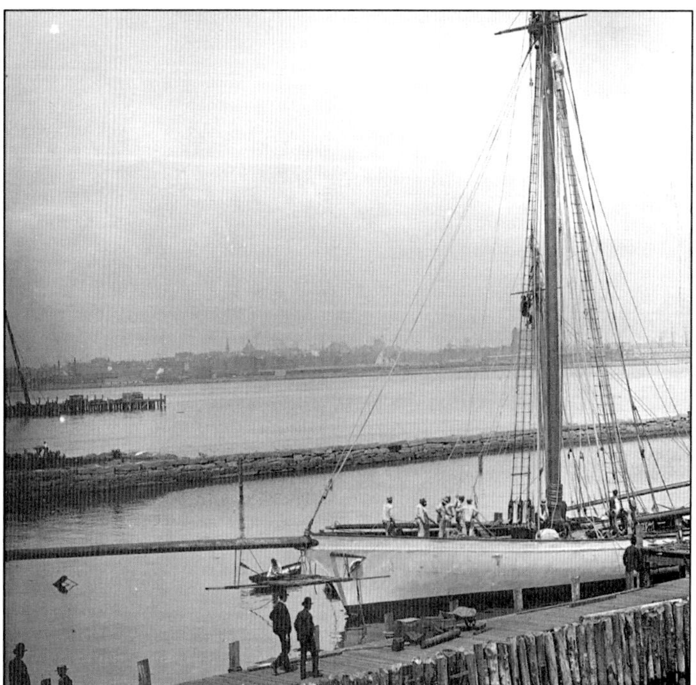

The America's Cup defender *Volunteer* is being fitted out at Lawley's Shipyard at City Point, South Boston, in 1887. The ship, which was designed by Edward Burgess, is aflutter with activity, as bystanders watch from the dock in the foreground. The ongoing filling in of the Commonwealth Flats, the area north of West First Street, can be seen across the water. The many newly created acres of new land was used primarily for commercial purposes.

# Contents

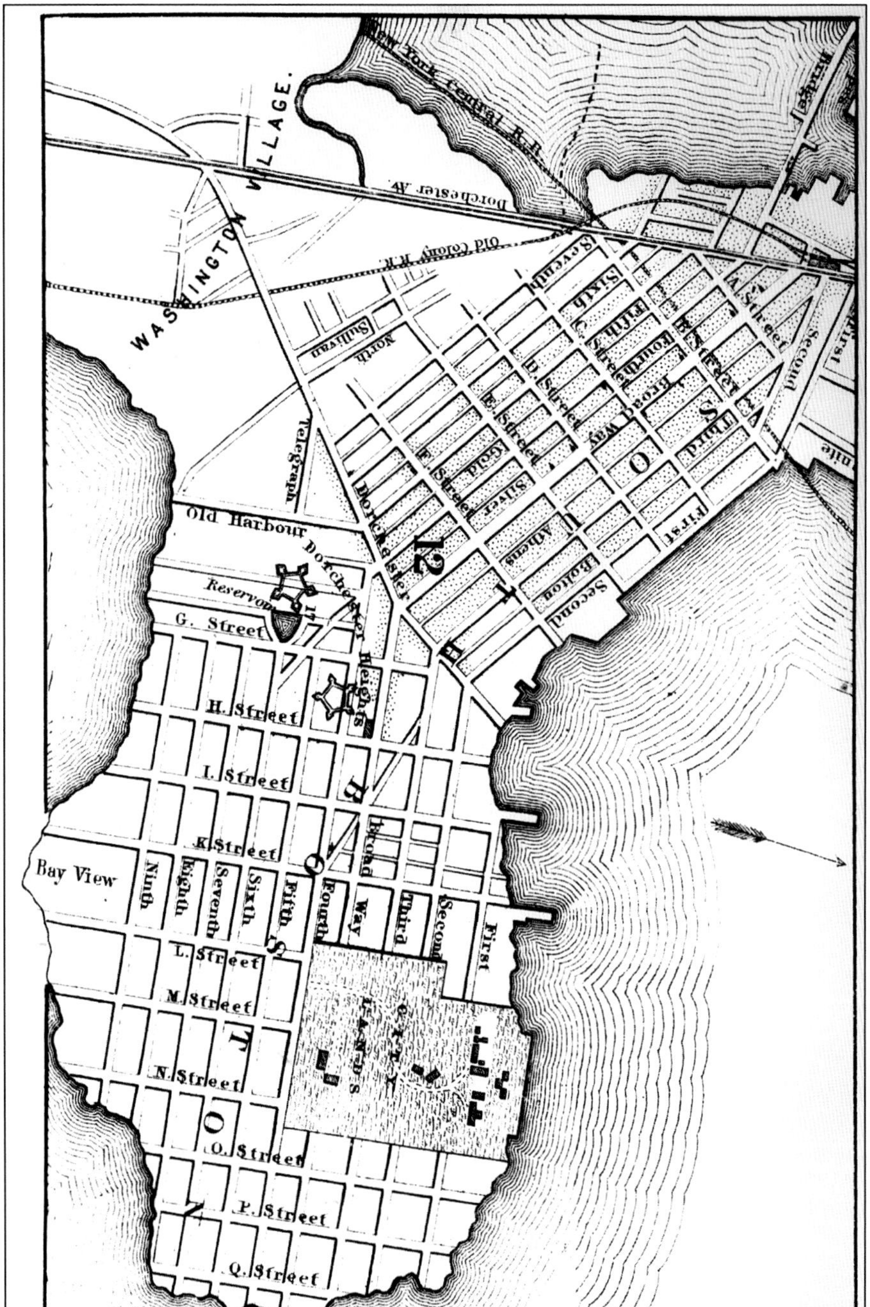

South Boston was laid out by Mather Withington (1758–1831), a noted surveyor, who created an urban street grid divided by Dorchester Street. The streets running from east to west utilize a number, and those running from north to south begin with a letter of the alphabet. Drawn in 1859 for the *Boston Almanac*, this map detail shows that most of South Boston had already been laid out by the mid-19th century, though much of Washington Village (annexed from Dorchester in 1855 and now known as Andrew Square) remained undeveloped until well after 1880.

# Introduction

South Boston was once a part of Dorchester and was annexed to the town of Boston in 1804, 18 years before it was incorporated as a city. Known as "Mattapanock" by the Neponset tribe of Massachusetts Indians and as "Great Neck" by the Puritans who had settled Dorchester in 1630, this roughly 560-acre peninsula remained undeveloped pastureland until the first decade of the 19th century.

By 1800, the close proximity of Great Neck to Boston propelled speculative developers to begin purchasing land and to advocate for the annexation to Boston of this prime real estate. These speculators and developers included Judge William Tudor, Gardiner Greene, Jonathan Mason, Harrison Gray Otis, and Joseph Woodward (1758–1838). Woodward was considered the "Father of South Boston" and successfully petitioned the state legislature for an act of annexation, which passed on March 6, 1804. The immediate effects of the annexation were to see an increase in land values, almost tenfold in some cases, and an increase in population from 35 residents in 1804 to 17,786 in less than five decades.

The close proximity to Boston and the increased accessibility as a result of the South Boston Bridge (later known as the Dover Street Bridge), erected in 1805, and the Federal Street Bridge, completed in 1828, made South Boston a convenient and desirable place for both residential and commercial development. "Its growth has been rapid and steady." Following 1804, numerous houses of both brick and wood were built in the area closest to the bridges and industries, such as iron foundries, glassworks, breweries, distilleries, and shipbuilding concerns were established. These industries required skilled workers, many of whom moved to South Boston to be close to these newly established mills and factories. This influx of new residents brought people from all walks of life, religious backgrounds, and political groups. Subsequently, churches were established for a wide range of religious beliefs, among them St. Augustine's Chapel on Dorchester Street. Erected in 1819 in the Gothic Revival style, this brick chapel designed by Charles Bulfinch was surrounded by a consecrated burial ground for the early Catholics of Boston. Within three decades, South Boston's accessibility by foot, horse-drawn omnibus, and later the streetcar along Broadway and Dorchester Avenue brought to the community numerous immigrants whose European background mirrored those of the city. By the time of the Civil War, one out of every three Bostonians was of foreign birth.

With the wide expanse of open land, Boston built the House of Correction and the Home for the Feeble Minded at City Point. The Perkins Institution for the Blind relocated to the former Mount Washington House in 1839. The establishment of these institutions in South Boston might not have been appreciated by the residents of the 19th century, especially the prison, but they became an important aspect of South Boston's continued development. At the beginning of the 20th century, the prison was moved to Deer Island and the city lands were partially developed for Marine Park and a playground at City Point. During the first three decades of the 20th century, South Boston became a densely built up neighborhood of Boston with a wide spectrum of residents, reflecting many nationalities, religions, and economic groups.

By the start of the 20th century, South Boston's population had doubled from 30 years earlier and was composed of representatives of numerous immigrant groups who contributed to the unique distinctiveness of South Boston. Already with a large population of Irish, South Boston had Albanians, Polish, Lithuanians, and "Down Easters" making the former Dorchester Neck their home and a thriving nexus of cultures. Churches, schools, institutions, and social groups were formed and each had a decisive impact on the continued development and increasing diversity of the neighborhood. With ease of transportation from streetcars and later buses, as well as the Dorchester Tunnel (now known as the Red Line) having stations at Broadway and Andrew Square, many new residents found that South Boston was not just a convenient place but also an attractive and safe place in which to raise a family. With numerous attractions at City Point, such as the Head House, designed by Edmund March Wheelwright, the old aquarium, designed by William Downer Austin, and the superb view from Castle Island, South Boston has offered a wide spectrum of quality city life to Bostonians for over a century.

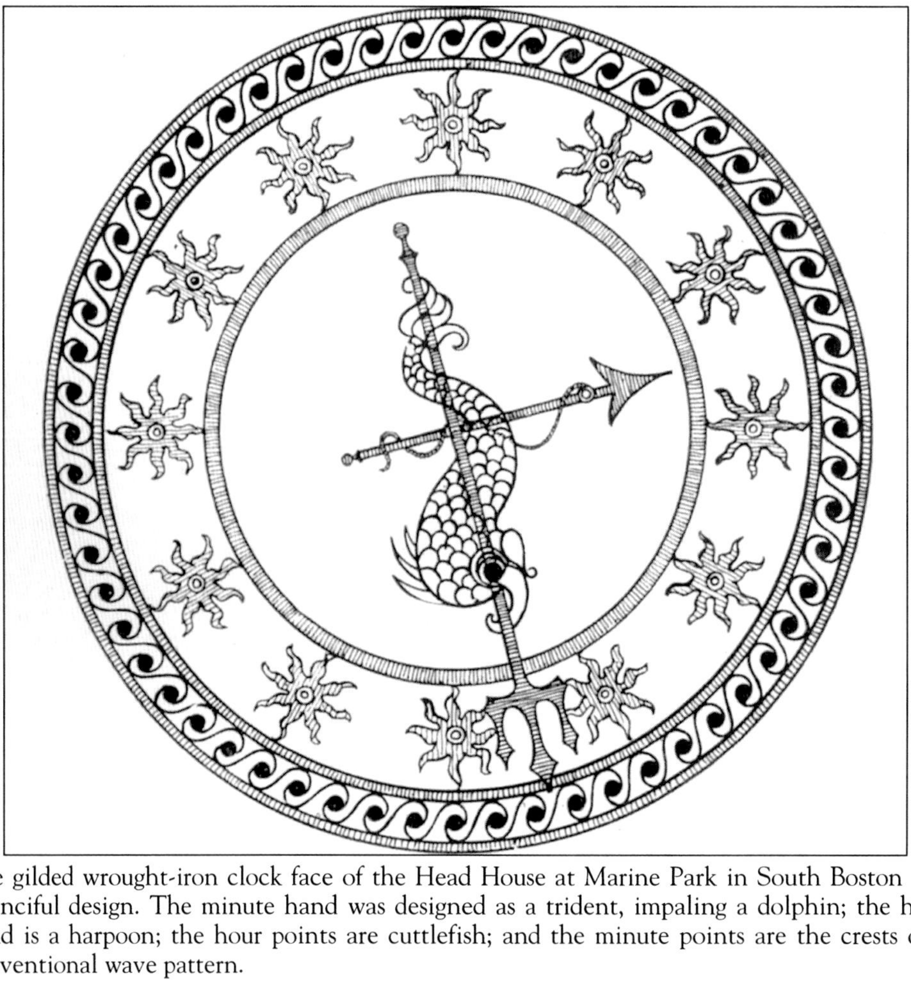

The gilded wrought-iron clock face of the Head House at Marine Park in South Boston was a fanciful design. The minute hand was designed as a trident, impaling a dolphin; the hour hand is a harpoon; the hour points are cuttlefish; and the minute points are the crests of a conventional wave pattern.

# *One*

# Early South Boston 1804–1859

The first 55 years of South Boston's history began on March 6, 1804, when the Massachusetts Legislature allowed for the annexation of Dorchester Neck to the town of Boston. Following a riotous discourse between representatives of the town of Dorchester and the promoters of the annexation, the culmination was that the selectmen of Boston laid out "Streets, Public Squares, and Market Places as they shall judge necessary for the public accommodation." Streets were laid out on a grid plan by the noted surveyor Mather Withington, and new buildings were swiftly erected. The attractive panoramas from Leek Hill, Nook Hill, Pow Wow Point, and Dorchester Heights attracted many people, but the erection of the elegant Mount Washington House on Broadway was an attempt to attract summer visitors to the peninsula. This palatial hotel, complete with piazzas overlooking the ocean and fireplaces in every room, was connected to Boston by an hourly omnibus, which brought guests to enjoy the cool summer breezes. Though advantageous, the hotel failed and was quickly remodeled for the Perkins Institution for the Blind, recently removed from Pearl Street in Boston. The new streets were built up with brick and wood-framed dwellings and were embellished with trees by the Shade Tree Society, whose premise was that streets should be "graced with flourishing and beautiful shade trees." The first five decades of South Boston's history and development were swift, decisive, and economically beneficial—so much so that by 1855, there were 1,978 houses in South Boston, with a greater increase in new housing "than in any ward of the city."

In the period between 1804 and 1859, South Boston was transformed from lush pastureland to a productive ward of the city of Boston, with citizens who strove to found such institutions as the Mattapan Literary Association, Lyceum Hall, the South Boston Samaritan Society, and the Hawes Free Evening School. These early years proved a solid foundation for the later 19th-century development.

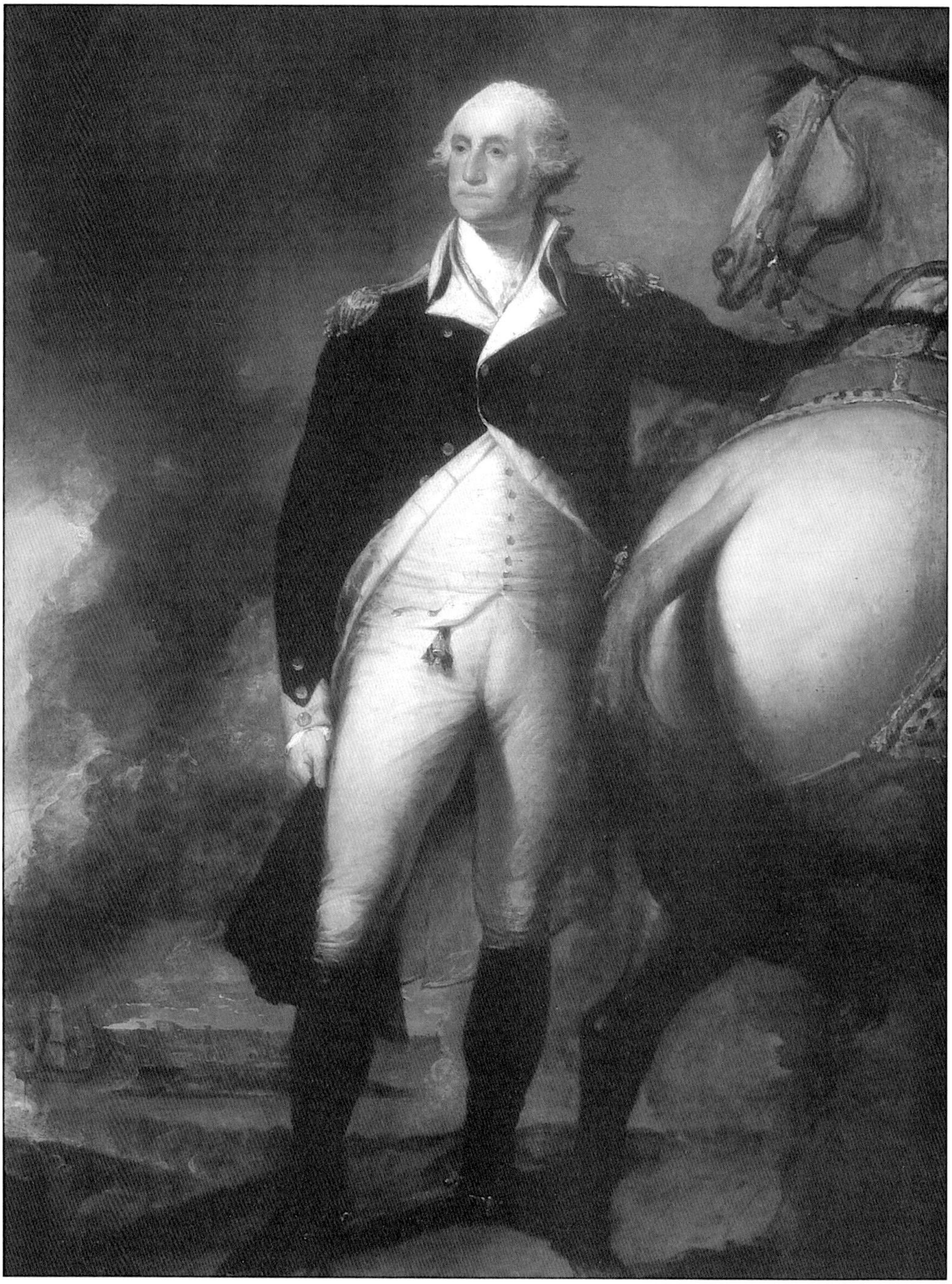

Painted by Gilbert Stuart in 1806 on a monumental canvas, *Washington at Dorchester Heights* shows the man who liberated Boston on Evacuation Day—March 17, 1776. This dramatic painting was commissioned by Samuel Parkman of Boston and shows the "Father of Our Country" at Dorchester Heights, now South Boston. The breastworks were constructed on the evening of March 4, 1776, and successfully routed the British. The password suggested by Gen. John Thomas, for whom Thomas Park is named, was "St. Patrick," which was an appropriate one, considering the day. (Collection of the Boston Museum of Fine Arts.)

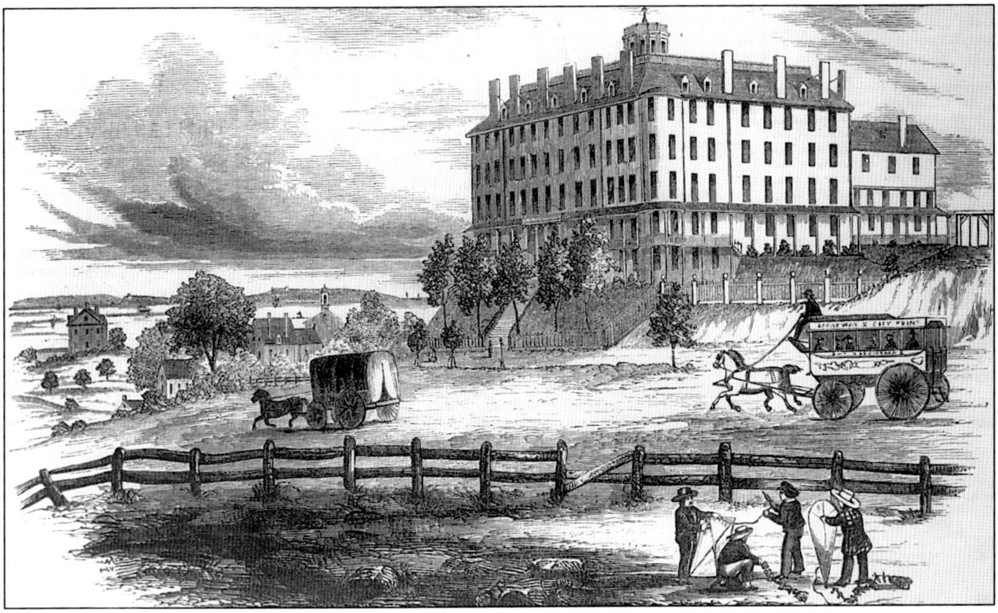

The Mount Washington House was an elaborate hotel built on East Broadway, now the site of the South Boston Municipal Building, overlooking the harbor. A horse-drawn omnibus, run by the Warren Line, can be seen on the right. The bus connected Boston to South Boston via Broadway and City Point. (Courtesy of the Boston Public Library.)

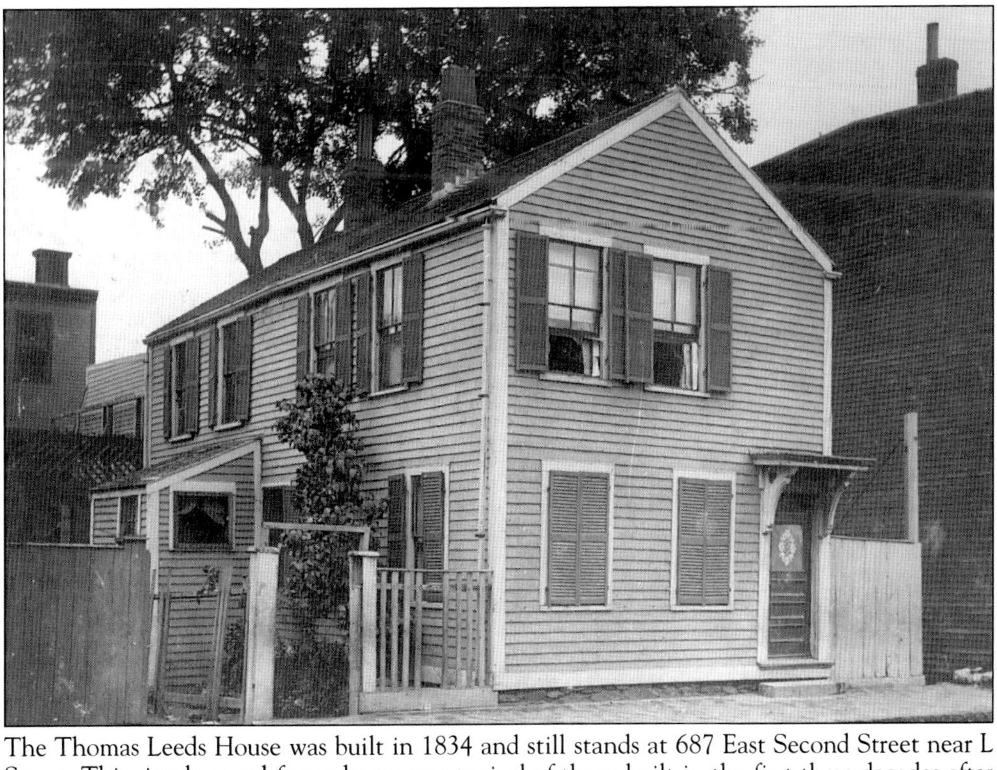

The Thomas Leeds House was built in 1834 and still stands at 687 East Second Street near L Street. This simple wood-frame house was typical of those built in the first three decades after Dorchester Neck was annexed to Boston. (Courtesy of the Boston Public Library.)

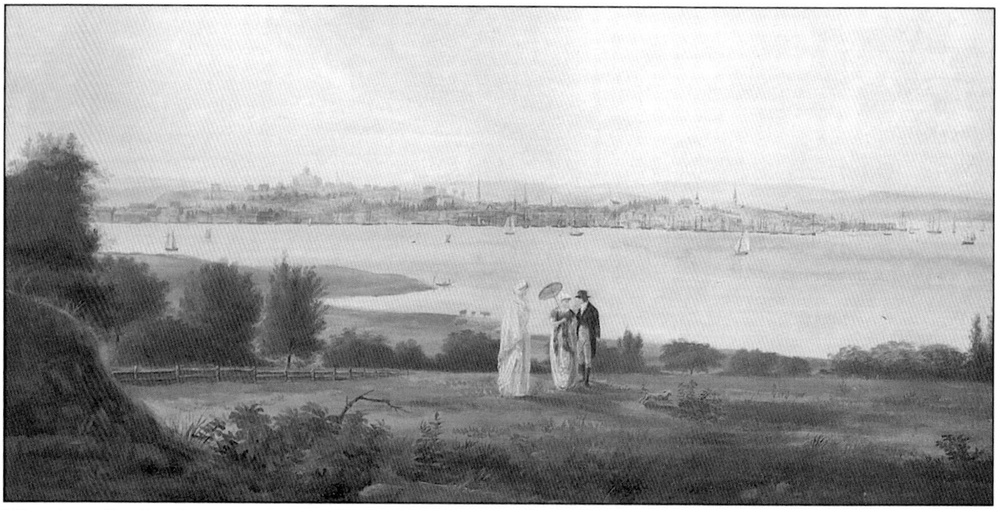

This bucolic landscape scene is known as *Boston from the Road to Dorchester*; it was painted by John L.B. De Woiseri in 1809. The peaceful pastureland of South Boston gently descends to the harbor, and Boston, capped with the Massachusetts Statehouse, can be seen in the distance. James Hayes said of South Boston in 1835 that it "would be hard to surpass as a residential section. The broad, green fields, the straight streets . . . the magnificent scenery in and around South Boston, the activity and the general contentment of the people, were all that one could wish for." (Collection of the Bostonian Society.)

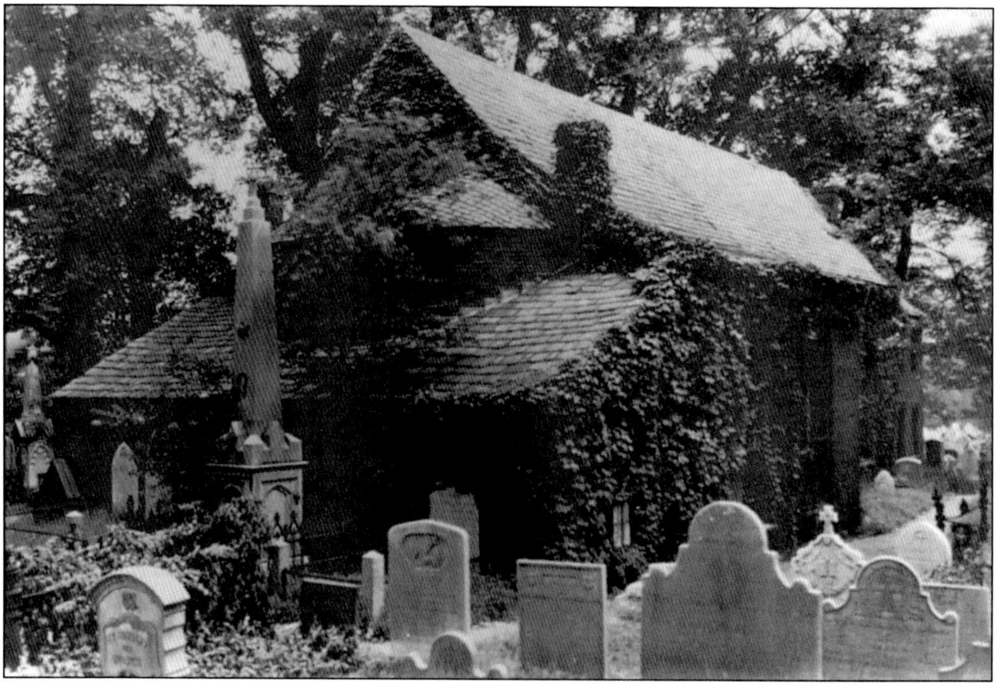

St. Augustine's Chapel was built in 1819 on Dorchester Street between Tudor and West Fourth Streets. The cemetery that surrounds the Gothic chapel is the oldest Roman Catholic cemetery in New England. Bishop Jean Louis de Cheverus purchased the land in 1818 for a chapel to house the remains of Rev. Francis A. Matignon (1753–1818), the late pastor of the Church of the Holy Cross in Boston. (Courtesy of the Boston Public Library.)

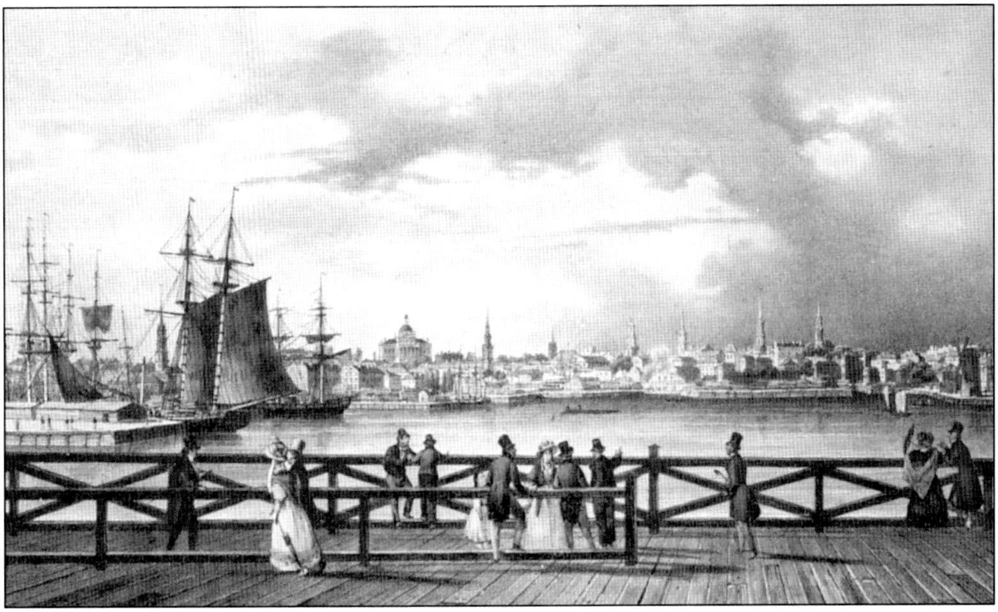

The South Boston Bridge, colloquially known as the "Bridge of Sighs," was a wooden pile bridge built to connect Boston to the recently annexed South Boston. People promenade along the bridge, and Boston can be seen across the area known as the South Cove. Often, courting couples would rendezvous on the bridge, hence, the name Bridge of Sighs.

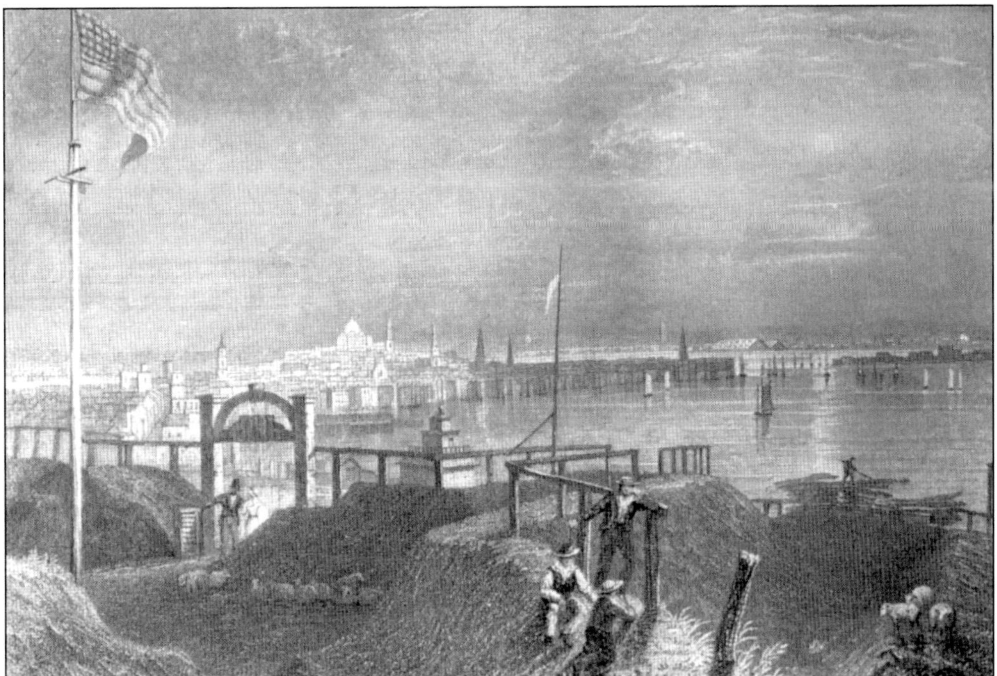

Boston, seen from Dorchester Heights in South Boston, was but a short distance by either foot or carriage. A U.S. flag waves in the breeze on the hill, which was fortified during the American Revolution by the patriots, who successfully routed the British from Boston on March 17, 1776—Evacuation Day.

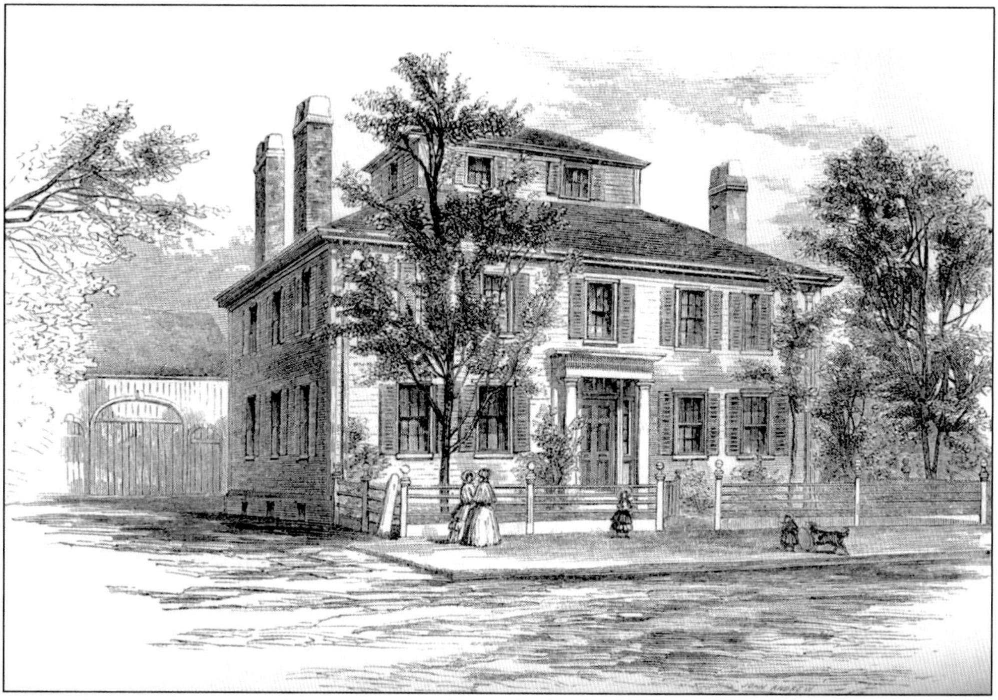

Early houses built in South Boston were of wood, such as this elegant Federal house with a lantern cupola, located on West Broadway between Dorchester and E Streets. It was the home of Capt. Noah Brooks (1782–1852), a noted shipbuilder, of whom it was said that "No person took a more active interest in the community than he." Brooks succeeded Samuel Knight as manager of Lincoln & Wheelwright and also served as a member of the Boston Board of Aldermen in 1825.

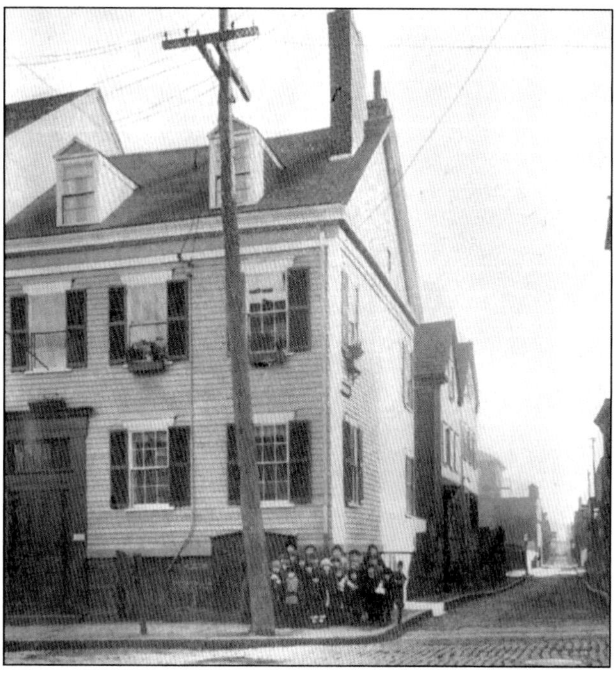

This small, wood clapboard row house was built at the corner of A and Athens Streets, *c.* 1830. This style of house predominated in South Boston before 1840. Another well-preserved example of this house style, complete with green sun blinds, can be seen at the corner of E and Athens Streets.

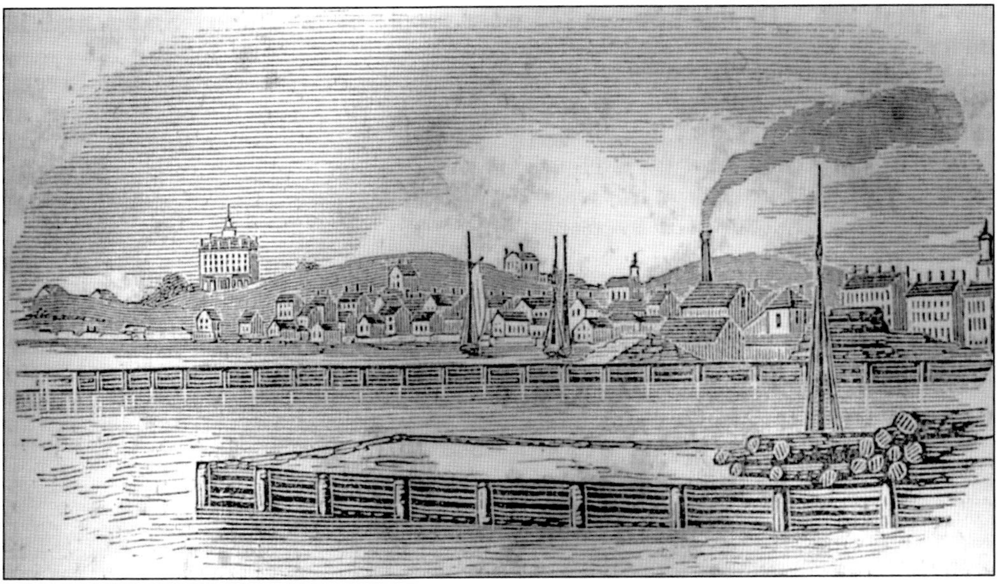

This etching of South Boston in 1839, done by John Warner Barber for his book *Historical Collections of Every Town in Massachusetts*, shows the northern part of the ward with the Perkins Institution for the Blind, formerly the Mount Washington House, on the left, and the Suffolk Glass Works on the right. By 1839, South Boston was "rapidly increasing in population and wealth."

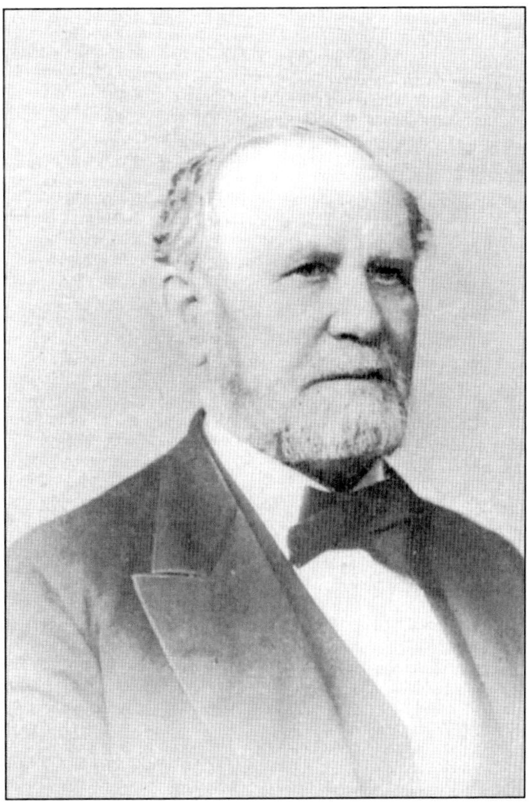

Benjamin James (1814–1901) was "active in real estate circles, and . . . built 123 houses" in South Boston in the 19th century. He was a member of the lumber firm of B. and G.B. James, Pope and Company, which had yards, docks, and mills on First Street. James served as a member of the Massachusetts House of Representatives and the Boston Board of Aldermen. It was said of him that "there is no one who is dearer to the people than the venerable Benjamin James."

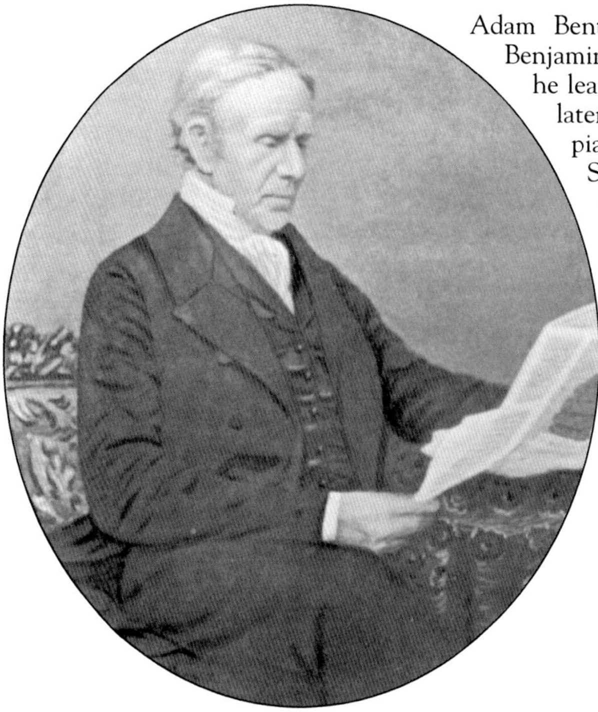

Adam Bent (1776–1857) was apprenticed to Benjamin Crehore of Milton Village, where he learned the trade of piano making. Bent later become a leading manufacturer of pianos in Boston. He was married to Sukey Foster Blake, who was related to two early families on Dorchester Neck. They were among the founders of the Hawes Place Society, the first church in South Boston. Bent lived on East Fourth Street near Q Street (now Farragut Road). Bent Court off Columbia Road was named in his memory.

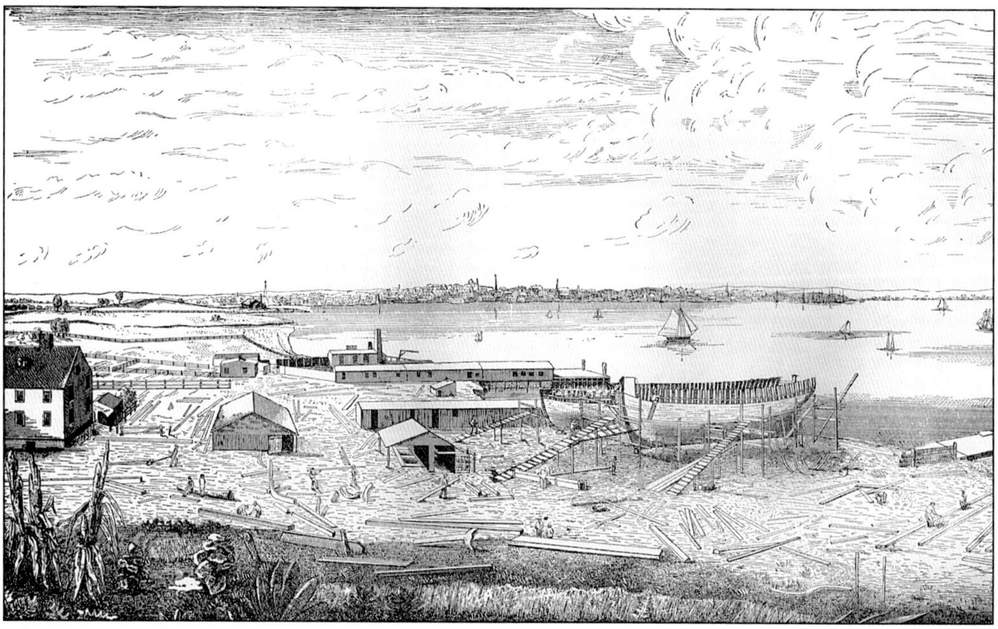

The etching *Ship Building in South Boston* was done in 1820, looking east from Leek Hill. The hull of a ship is being constructed on the right, Samuel Kent's house is on the far left, and a ropewalk is in the center. Shipbuilding began in South Boston when Lincoln & Wheelwright began a shipyard between Dorchester and F Streets, at the foot of Leek Hill, with Samuel Kent as superintendent. Other shipbuilders in town, including Baker & Morrell and the E&H Briggs Yard, continued until the harbor proved too shallow and many of them moved to East Boston.

Timothy Hannon (1819–1891) was a major developer in South Boston, who during "his active business life cut down a major portion of the high hills which made South Boston so unfit for travel in former years, grading the streets and using the soil to fill in First Street and the adjoining territory." Employing 100 men and laborers, Hannon also cut through Story Street and used the soil for filling the new Strandway and Marine Park.

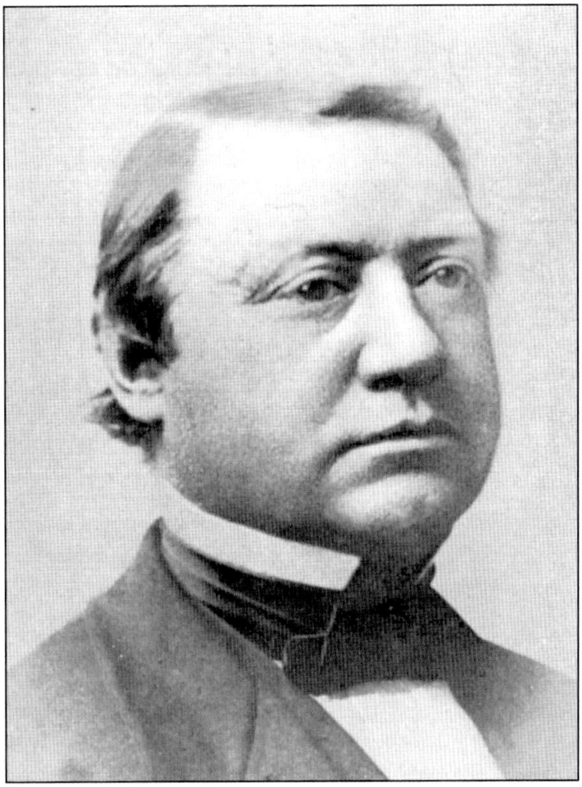

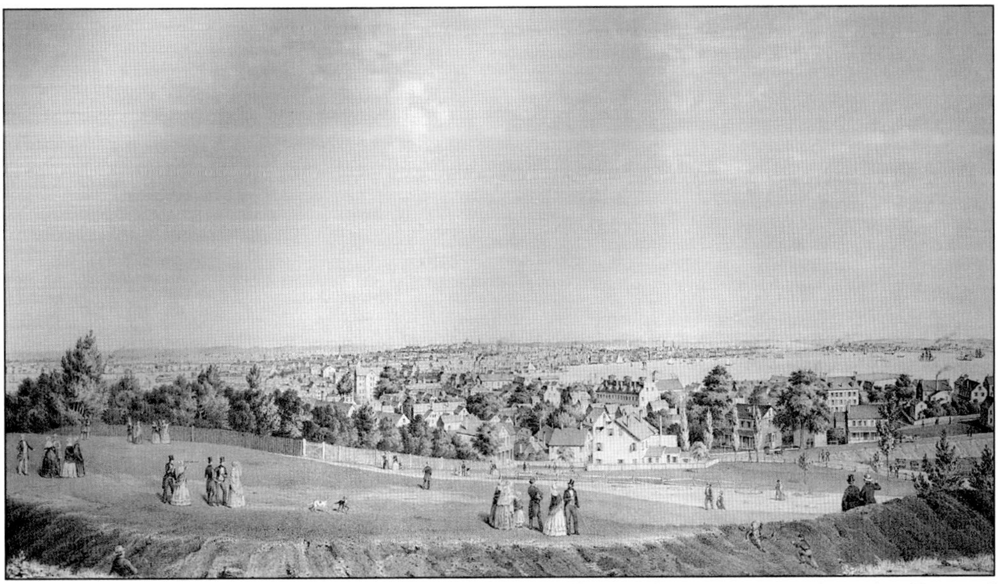

The lithograph *View of Boston, from Telegraph Hill, South Boston* was done by Bernard Spindler in 1854. The gently sloping field in the foreground led down to Dorchester Street, and the extent of the building boom in mid-19th-century South Boston can be seen in the distance. Notice the large number of freestanding wood houses at this time and the woman in the foreground with a telescope enjoying the panoramic vistas. (Courtesy of the Boston Athenaeum.)

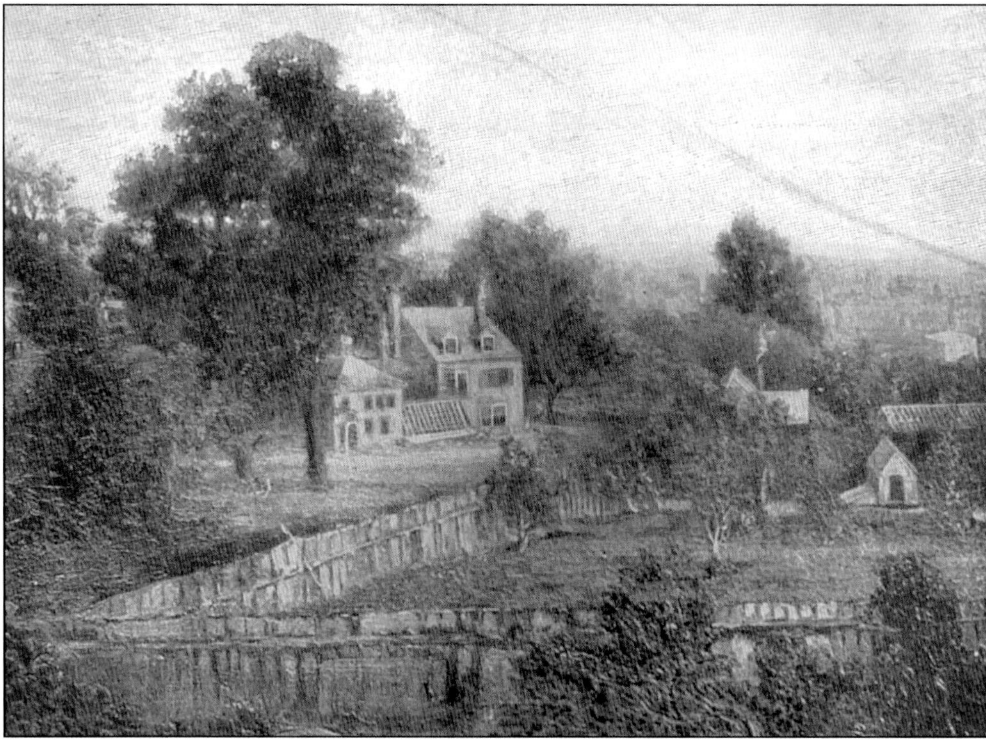

The Howe House, known as Green Peace, was originally built by Thomas Bird on Bird's Lane, Dorchester Heights, South Boston, within walking distance of the Perkins Institution for the Blind, where Dr. Samuel Gridley Howe was the superintendent. Notice the glass conservatory adjacent to the house, where the Howe gardener raised flowers during the winter months.

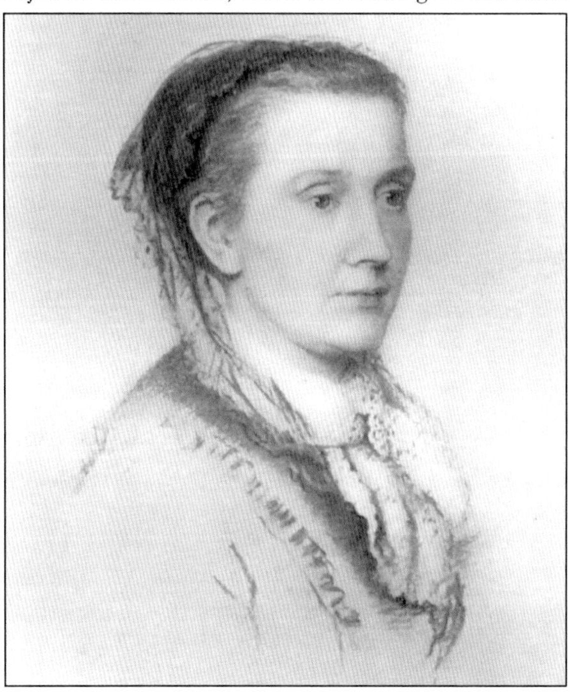

Julia Ward Howe (1819–1910) was the wife of Dr. Samuel Gridley Howe, director of the Perkins Institution for the Blind. While a resident of South Boston, she wrote the words to the "Battle Hymn of the Republic," at the request of Pres. Abraham Lincoln. The beginning stanza, "Mine eyes have seen the glory of the coming of the Lord," was sung to the tune of "John Brown's Body," the inspirational song of the Second Infantry (Tiger Battalion). A brilliant woman, she once said that she might have chosen as her personal motto "I have followed the great masters with my heart." A noted suffragist in later life, she served as first president of the New England Women's Club.

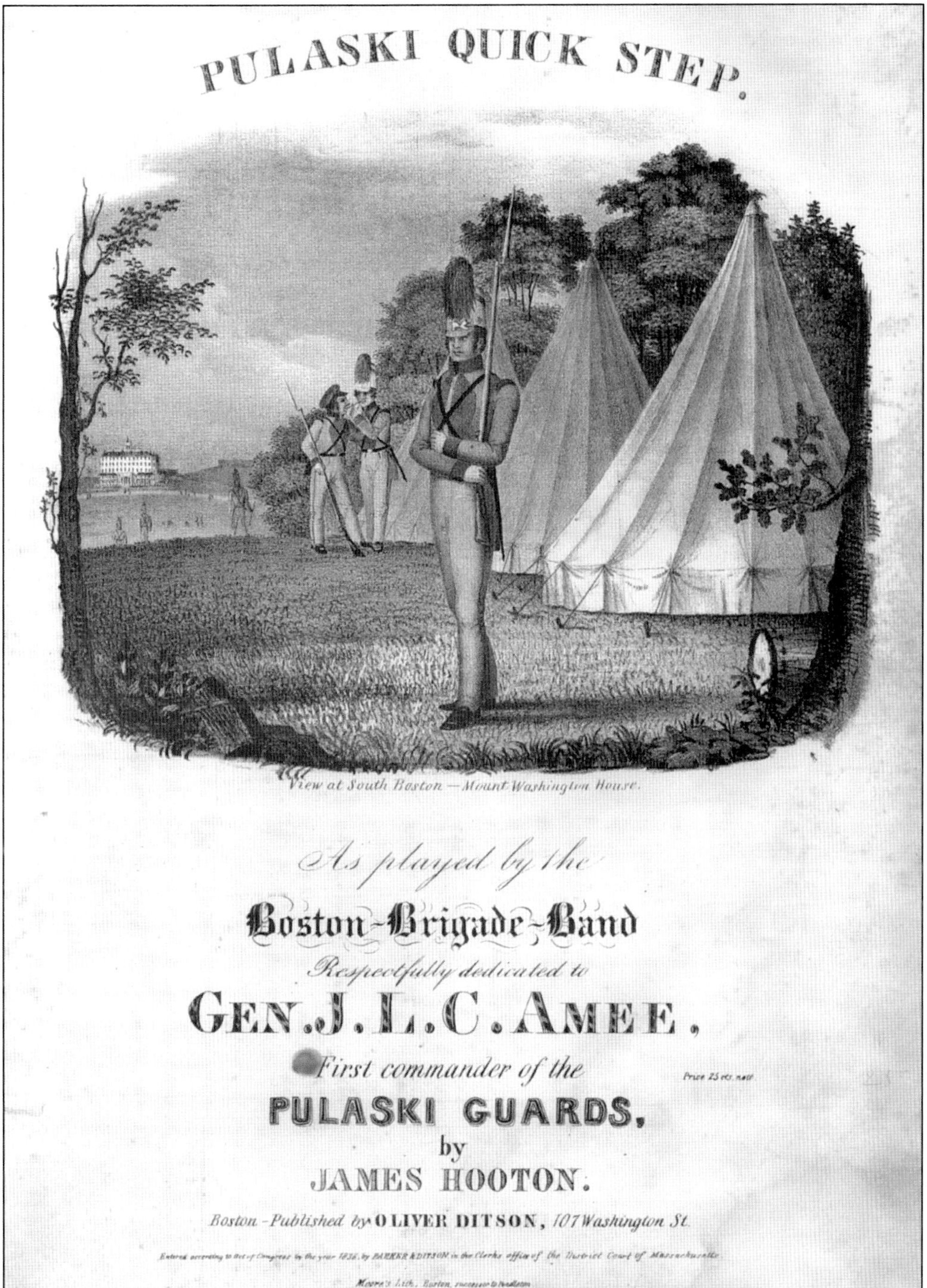


The "Pulaski Quick Step" was a musical composition written in 1836 by James Hooton and dedicated to Gen. Josiah L.C. Amee, the chief of police and first commander of the Pulaski Guards of South Boston. The cover shows a uniformed member of the Pulaski Guards, which was chartered in 1836, in front of a tent. The Mount Washington House, later the Perkins Institution for the Blind, can be seen on the left.

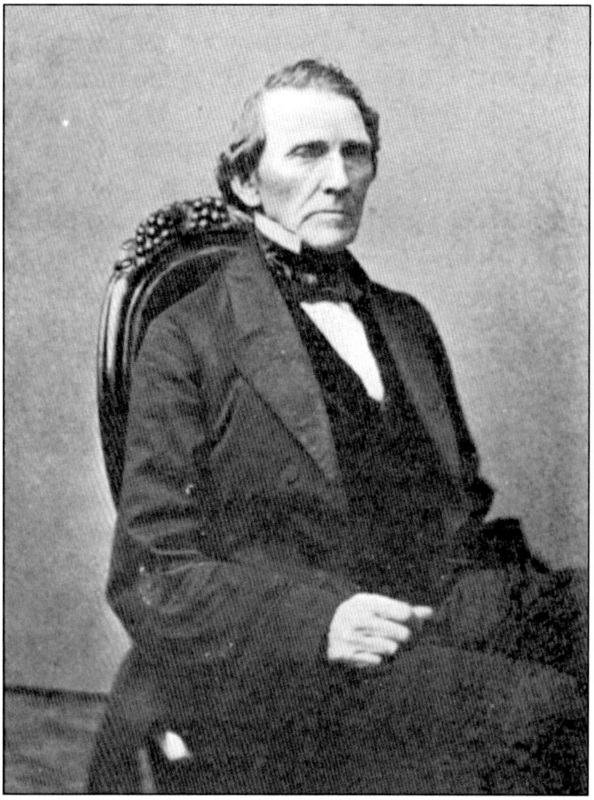

Luther Felton (1790–1868) was a well-known distiller and founder of Felton & Son, a major supplier of rum for use in the Crimean War. He lived at the corner of East Broadway and G Street. Before his death, he "planted many of the large elm trees which to-day grace the streets of South Boston with their majestic arms."

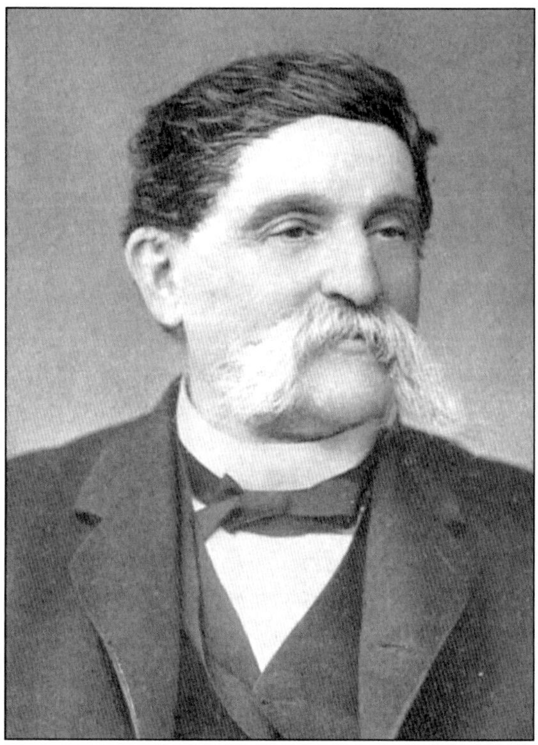

Gridley J. Fox Bryant (1816–1899) was a noted architect who once lived in South Boston and who designed and built the Mechanics Building on West Broadway in 1836. He said that the Mechanics Building "was my first triumph; from that I date my professional success." A prolific architect, he also designed Boston's Old City Hall and the Charles Street Jail, all built of the granite that his father Gridley Bryant successfully quarried in nearby Quincy.

John Souther (1816–1911) was probably the most important engineer ever to live in South Boston, where his "sterling integrity as a man, and his practical knowledge of the details of business, render him particularly well fitted for the position which he occupies." President of the Globe Locomotive Works, he invented the Souther Steam Shovel, which allowed for the filling in of Boston's Back Bay with soil from Needham. He also dredged Fort Point Channel to City Point, deepening the harbor and also filling in 25 acres north of First Street, the area known as the Commonwealth Flats.

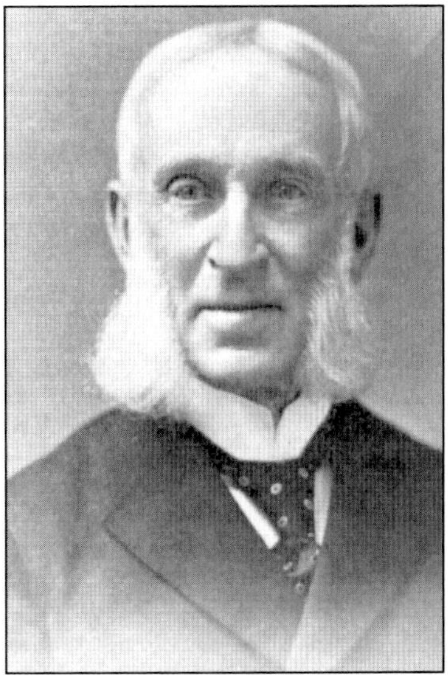

The Suffolk Glass Works, with its enormous smokestacks, was on West Second and B Streets in South Boston. The industry not only thrived but also expanded with the influx of skilled glassblowers, gaffers, and laborers who mass-produced flint glass.

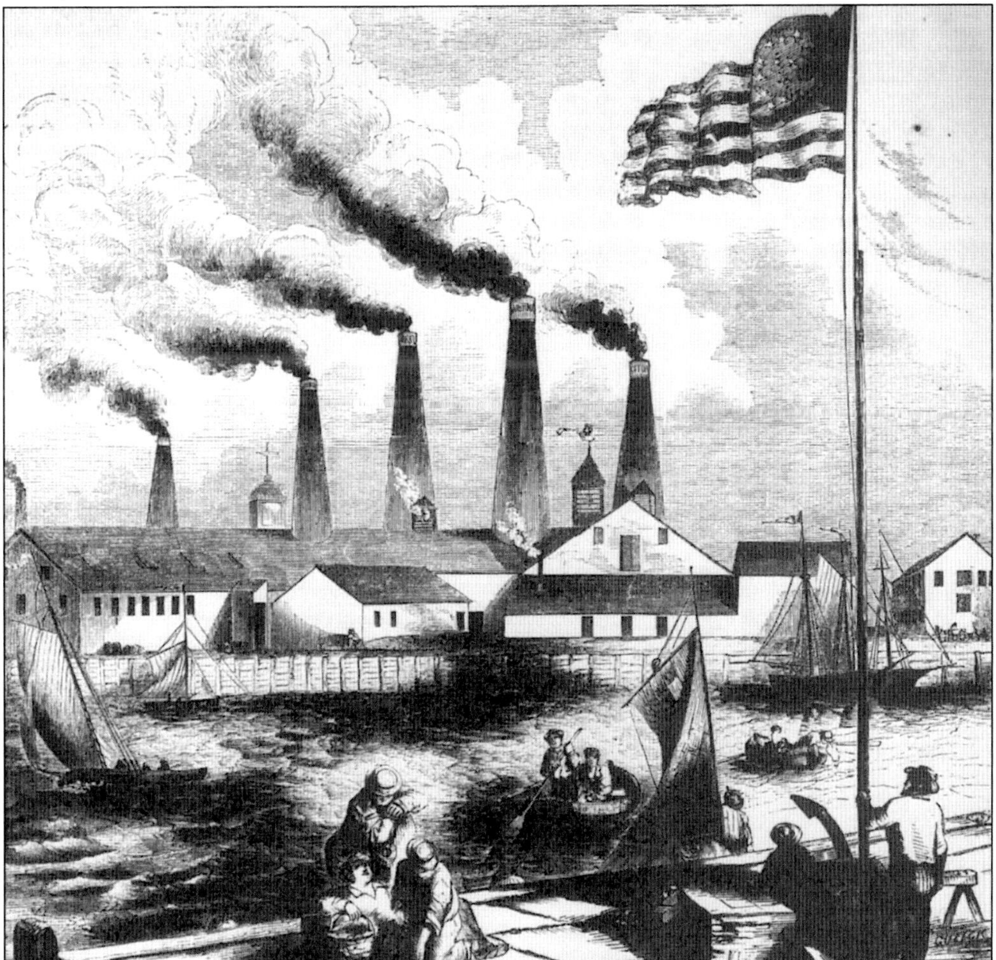

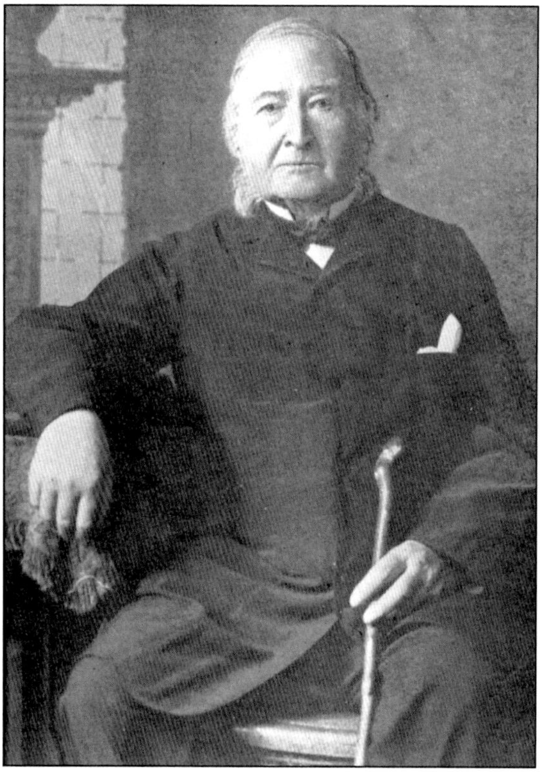

William Cains (1814–1907) lived at 557 East Fourth Street in South Boston and was known as the "Great Old Man of South Boston." He was the son of Thomas Cains, who founded the Phoenix Glass Works at B and West Second Streets in 1811 and who was considered the "pioneer glass manufacturer of flint and ground glass in the United States," after his arrival from Bristol, England.

The Phoenix Glass Works was known for the numerous fires that destroyed the business—which each time was resurrected, like the proverbial phoenix rising from the ashes. In the center the glassworkers, wearing a top hat, is William Cains. Other glassworks in South Boston included those of Andrew Jones, the Mount Washington Glass Works, the American Flint Glass Company, and the Suffolk Glass Works.

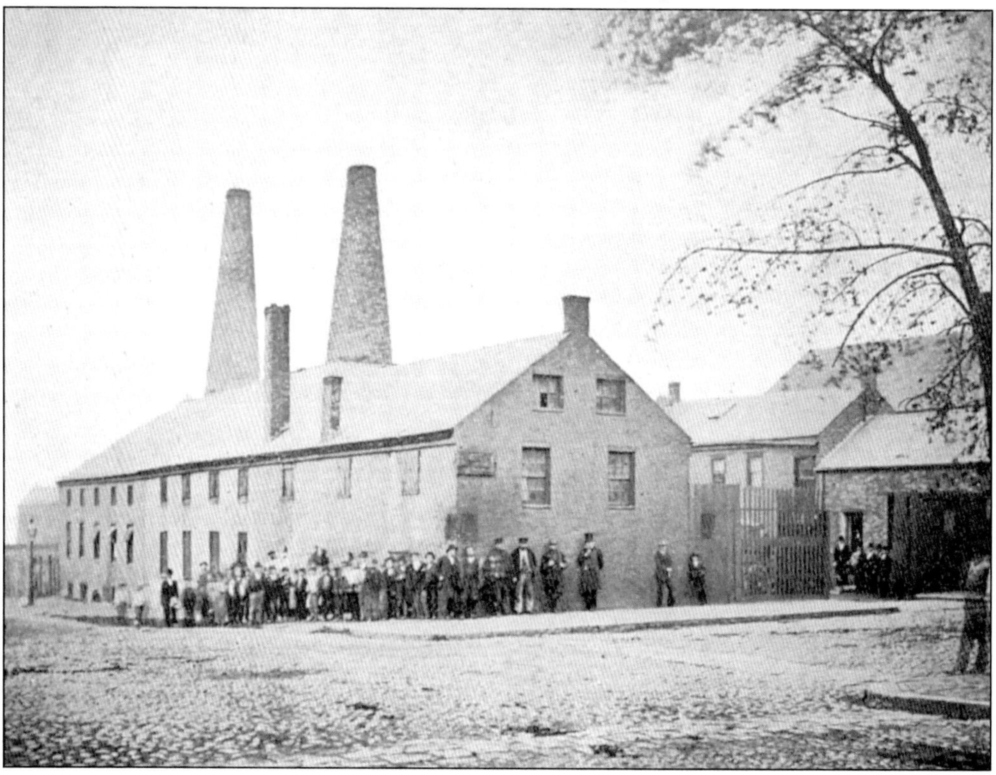

*Two*

# South Boston 1860–1945

It was said that by 1900, South Boston had a population of 70,161, which was one eighth of the entire population of Boston—a tremendous growth since being annexed to Boston in 1804. It was also said that "the people of the district, themselves, make the reputation of that section, whether it be good or bad; therefore upon the residents depends the good name of their community."

At the start of the 20th century, South Boston had not only a good name but also a wide diversity of people who accomplished much, were friendly, loved their home and community, and had "a general spreading of good feeling." Further, it was said that from "a religious, social, educational, political and business standpoint, the future of South Boston is bright, and the prospects are for an even more prosperous and happy people and community. Let each one do his or her share in aiding the district to reach this utopian state. And our community will enjoy then, what it so much deserves, peace and contentment."

By the early 1900s, South Boston's population was double what it was 30 years earlier, but "the greatest change in the population, next to its great increase, was its cosmopolitan character, and at the close of the century natives of nearly every foreign country were residents." Residents included not just the Irish, whom many assume are the only ethnic group in South Boston, but also Armenians, Albanians, Canadians, English, Germans, Italians, Lithuanians, and Poles. Truly, South Boston in the 20th century could be considered a league of nations.

"There's something about it, permit me to shout it,
Southie Is My Home Town!"

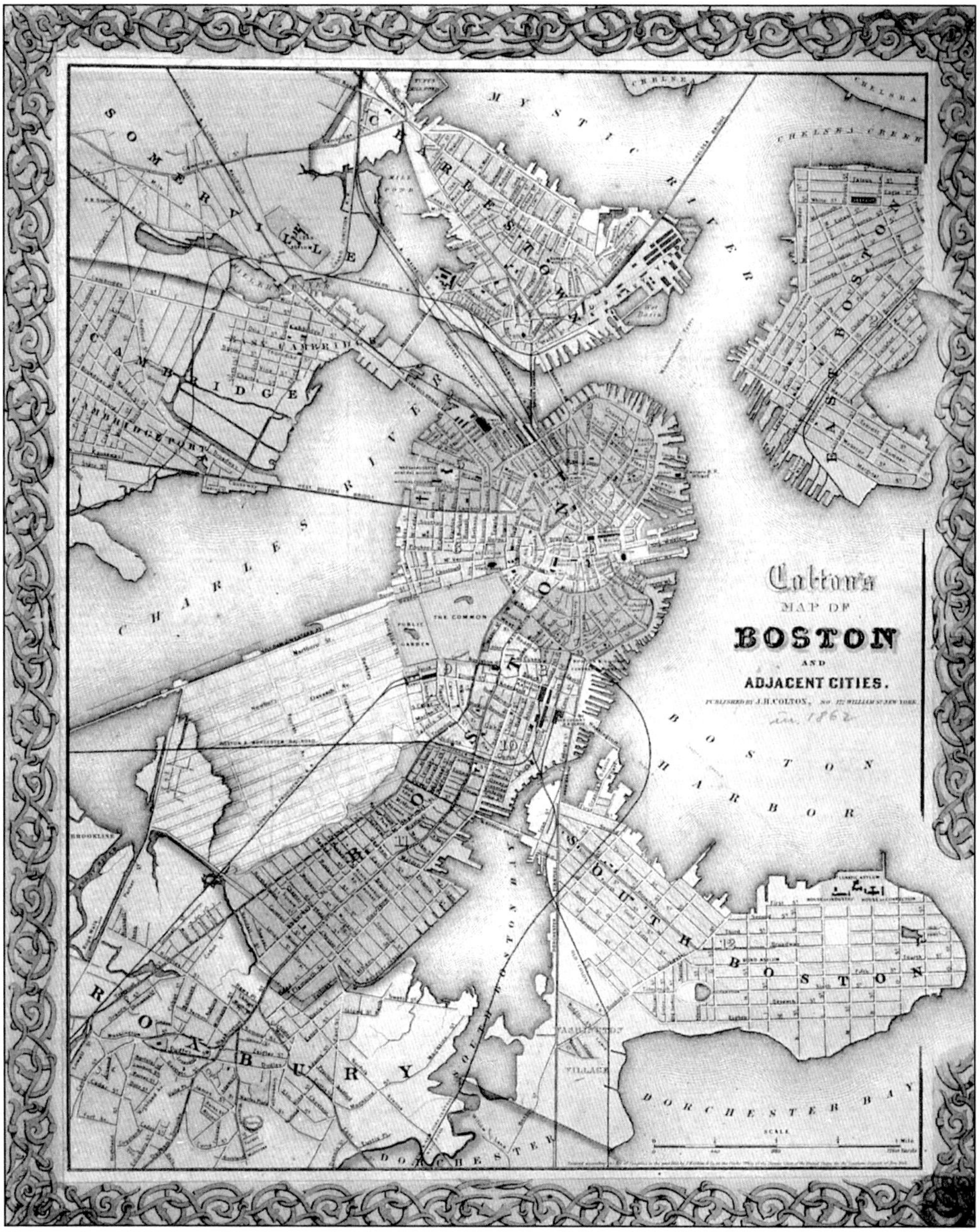


Colton's 1855 *Map of Boston and Adjacent Cities* showed how dramatically the city's topography had changed by the mid-19th century, through the development of South Boston and East Boston, the filling in of the South End, and the beginnings of the filling in of the Back Bay of Boston. In just over the five decades since South Boston was annexed to Boston, the street grid plan was already well established with a tremendous growth in population and increased immigration from Europe.

The South Boston Municipal Court was built in 1868 at the corner of Dorchester and West Fourth Streets. The Honorable Robert I. Burbank served as the first presiding judge. The fashionable Second French Empire building served as a courthouse, police court, and Engine Company 1 Firehouse. This c. 1907 photograph shows the building with signs for various military groups, including the Grand Army Hall; Gettysburg Commandery No. 19, United Veterans Union; Washington Post 32, Grand Army of the Republic; and the Major O'Connor Camp No. 4, Spanish War Veterans. Recently converted to condominiums, the building is still impressive, although much of the Victorian detail, including the fanciful copper weather vane, has been lost. (Courtesy of Paul A. Christian.)

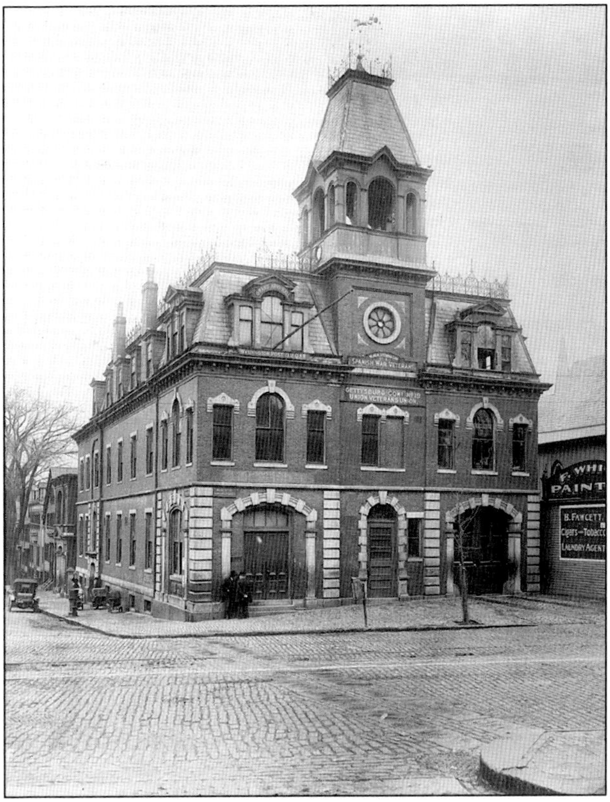


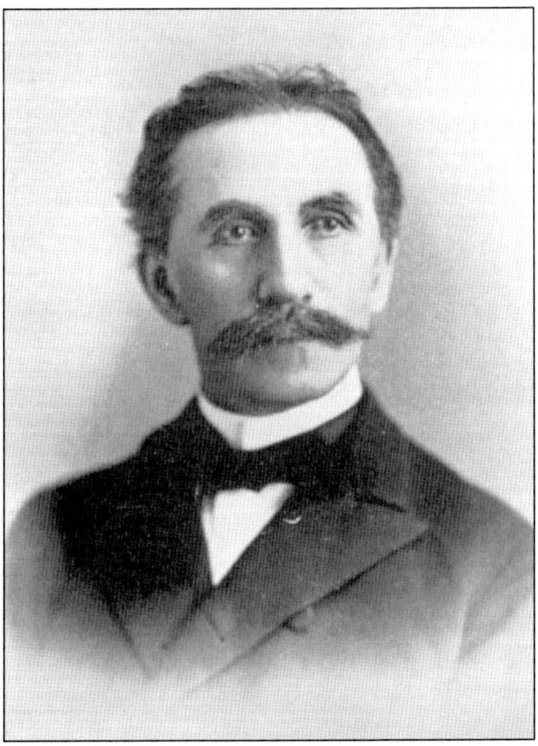

Judge Joseph D. Fallon (1837–1917) was appointed in 1875 as the first special justice of the South Boston Municipal Court by Gov. Thomas Talbot. In 1893, Fallon became justice of the court. It was said of him that during his "long service he was in accord with the broadest men among his associates, supporting and advocating every advance made or proposed in the administration." Described as a "thorough, but considerate, fearless and kindly judge," he lived at East Broadway and N Street.

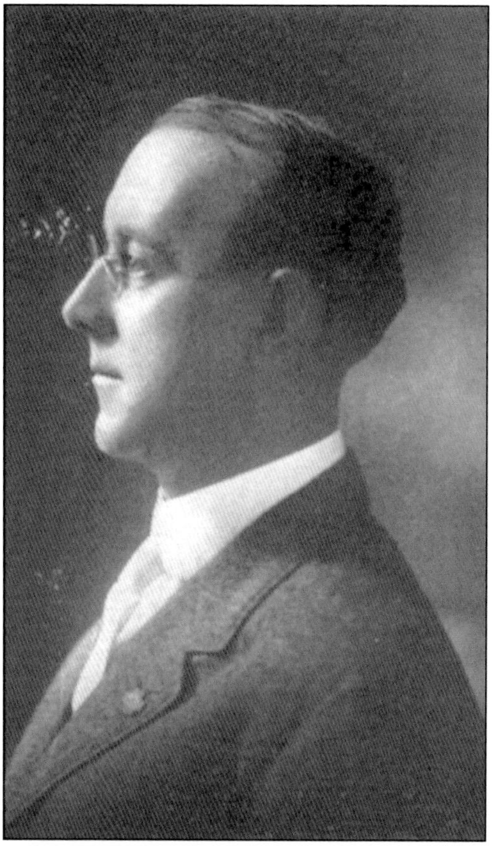

Judge Edward L. Logan (1875–1939) was appointed justice of the South Boston Municipal Court in 1907. He was a decorated veteran, a state representative, a state senator, and a member of the Boston Common Council. Logan International Airport in East Boston was named in his honor.

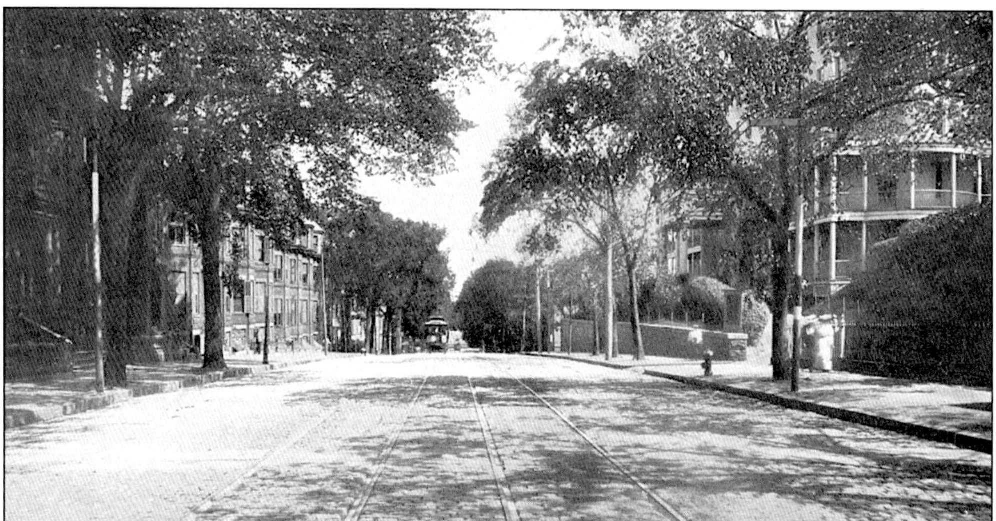

East Broadway, looking toward H Street, was built up in the 1870s with a row of brick town houses on the left. The streetcar tracks in the foreground were the prime reason for the rapid development of South Boston, as they allowed accessibility to town in a timely manner. On the right, a portion of the Perkins School for the Blind, now the site of the South Boston Municipal Court, can be seen.

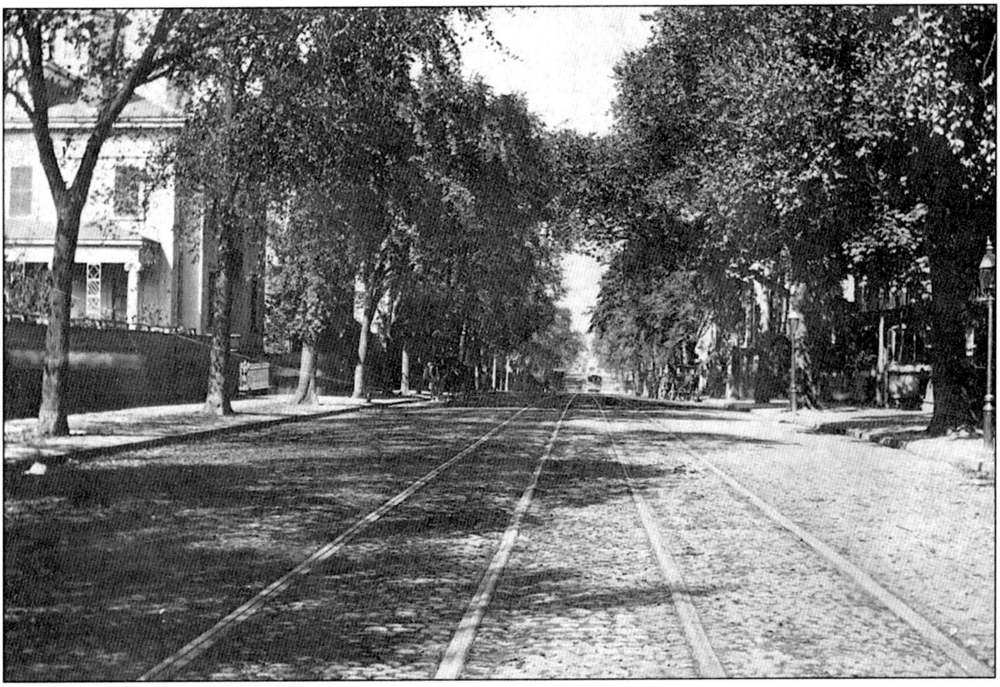

East Broadway, looking west from Farragut Road, has been a bucolic section of City Point since the Shade Tree Society set out trees along Broadway in the mid-19th century. The Shade Tree Society was founded in 1853 with Samuel Leeds as president and Isaac Adams and Samuel Hill as vice presidents. It was said that the "benefit to South Boston by this organization cannot be estimated by the amount of money collected and expended, or the number of trees set out by it during its existence."

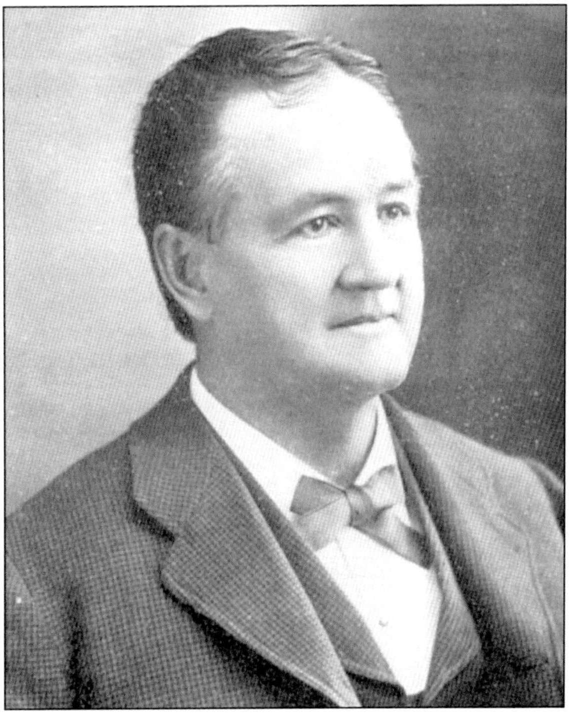

John Hogan was said to possess "a thorough knowledge of the value of real estate properties; the smallest tenement house and the largest business block are easily within the scope of his keen judgement and can be appraised by him with accuracy." He was also "one of the originators of the idea of selling houses on easy monthly payments, thus enabling those of moderate means to occupy a home and at the same time pay for it."

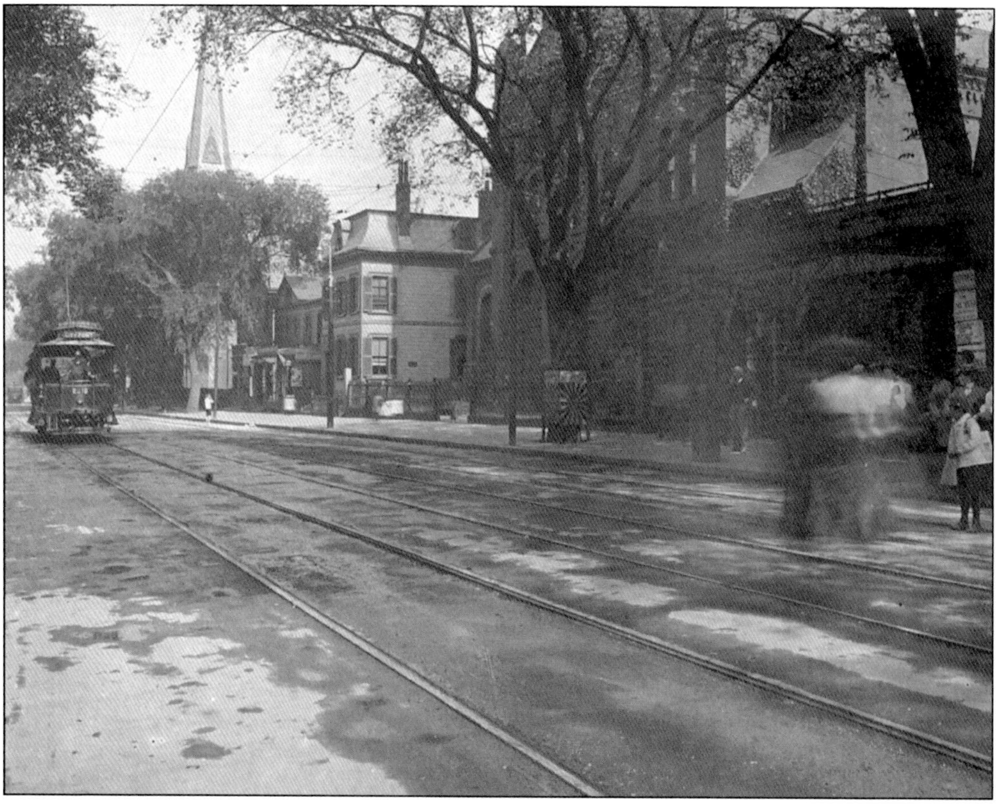

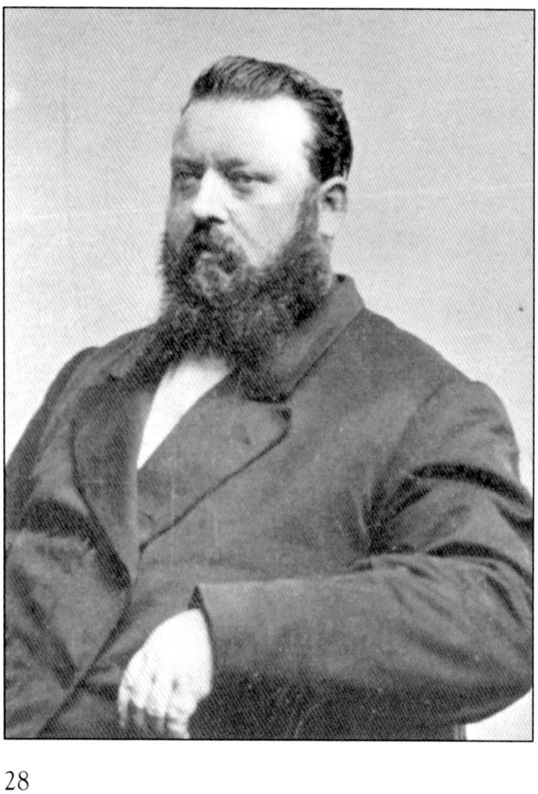

This view looking west on Broadway from Dorchester Street, *c.* 1910, shows a far different scene from what is there today. On the right is the Phillips Congregational Church, built in 1879; it is now the site of BankBoston and a large municipal parking lot to its left. The spire rising above the trees belongs to the Old South Baptist Church. The streetcar heads east on Broadway, bound for City Point. (Courtesy of Frank Cheney.)

James Milligan (1826–1889) was a "foreman of a large concern, and under his care not a few of the largest and best buildings in Boston were constructed. He purchased land on Ontario Street (often referred to as 'Cork Point') in South Boston in the late 1860's and 'erected a number of dwellings, and with a desire to advance the interests of the poor, he let these [houses] at a great disadvantage to his pecuniary prospects.'"

Flood Square at the junction of East Broadway, Emerson, and I Streets, was named for Thomas W. Flood (1857–1903). Once commissioner of wires and a member of the Boston Board of Aldermen, he was also principal of Flood & Mooney Real Estate at 457 Broadway.

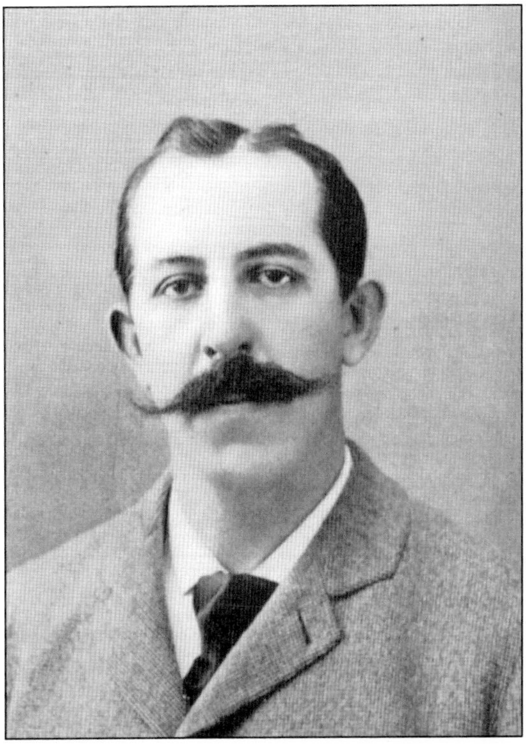

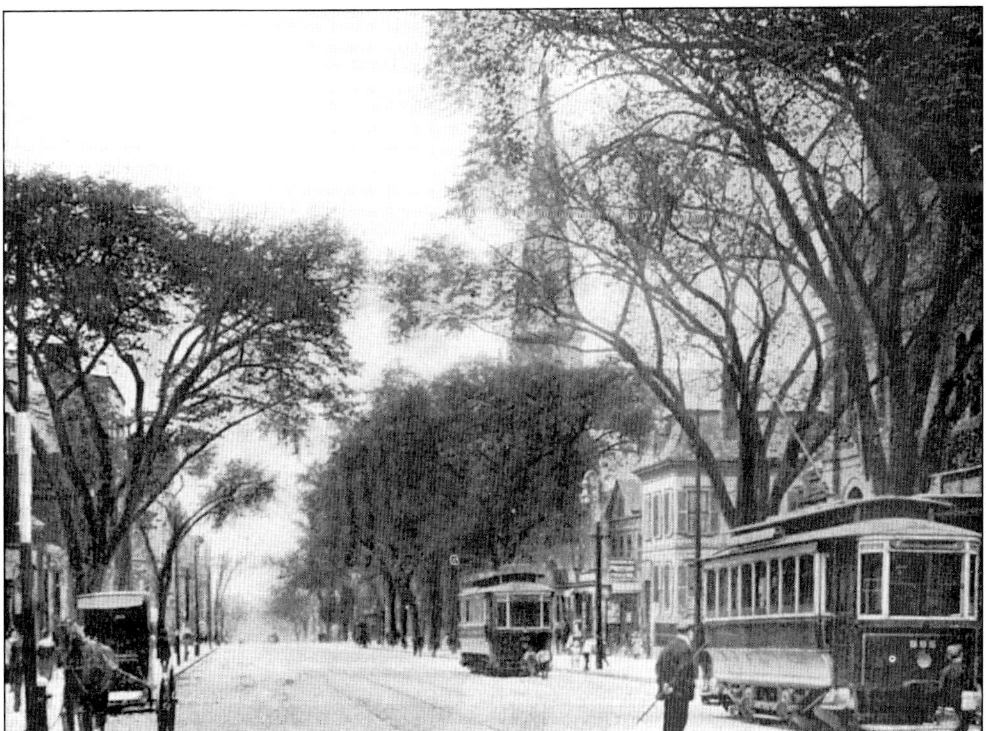

Looking west on Broadway *c.* 1915, a streetcar stops in front of the Phillips Congregational Church, now the site of BankBoston.

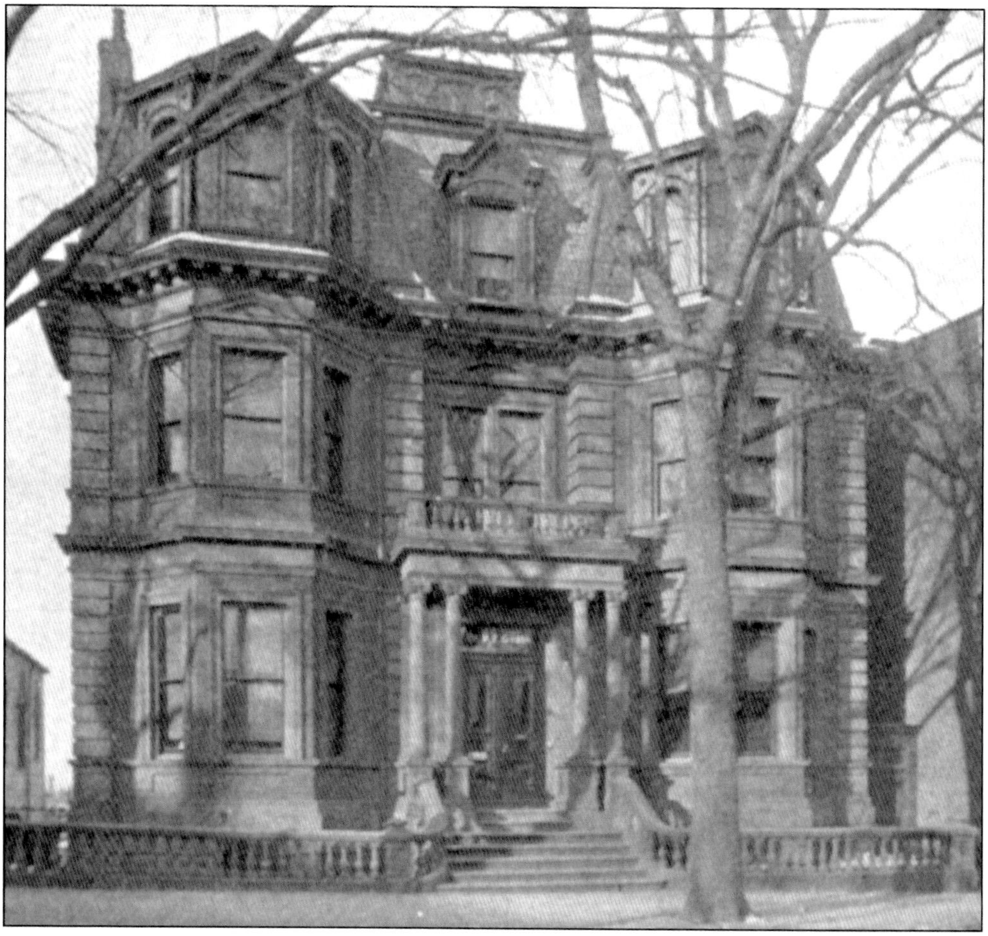

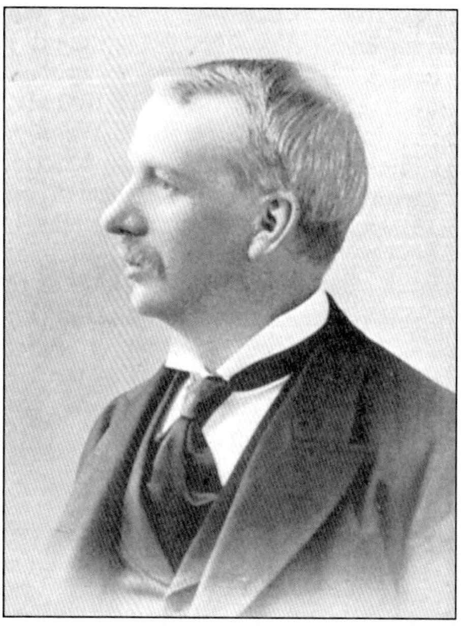

The impressive Gavin House, built in the Second French Empire style, is at 546 East Broadway. With its flanking bay windows on either side of an impressive columned entrance, mansard roof, and corner quoining, the red brick and brownstone house was among the most elegant built in South Boston in the mid-19th century. Today, this is the law office of John Day, Esq., and the offices of Coyne Real Estate.

Dr. Michael Freebern Gavin (1844–1915) was "one of the leading physicians and surgeons in this country. His high standard in his chosen profession is due to his general aptitude and thorough knowledge of the science of medicine." A founder of the Boston Emergency Hospital in 1891, he was also thought to be a political maverick. He "ran unsuccessfully in 1902 as the Socialist party candidate for mayor of Boston."

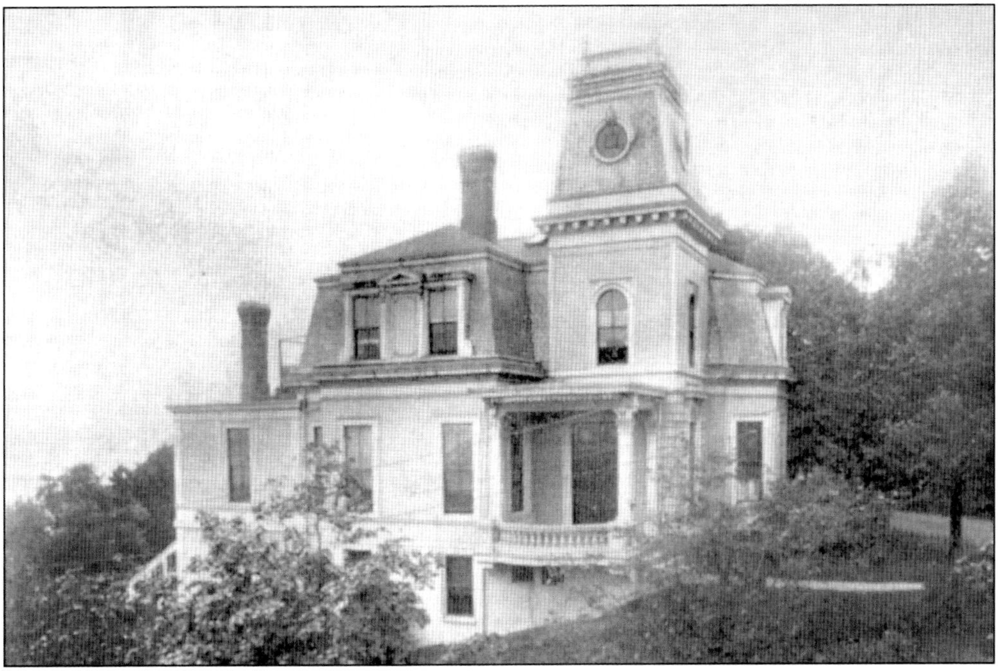

The Johnson House was built *c.* 1875 by Thomas Manning at 69 Thomas Park, where it had a "commanding view of the harbor and adjacent islands." The front of the garden has an interesting cast-iron fence, which that gives a picturesque quality to the house and its setting.

Samuel W. Johnson (1851–1925) was a builder who built "houses for investment and improvement, and has constructed nearly two hundred houses" in South Boston from 1884 to the beginning of the 20th century. It was said that he "confined his operations entirely to the district [of South Boston] and gives regular employment to a large number of men."

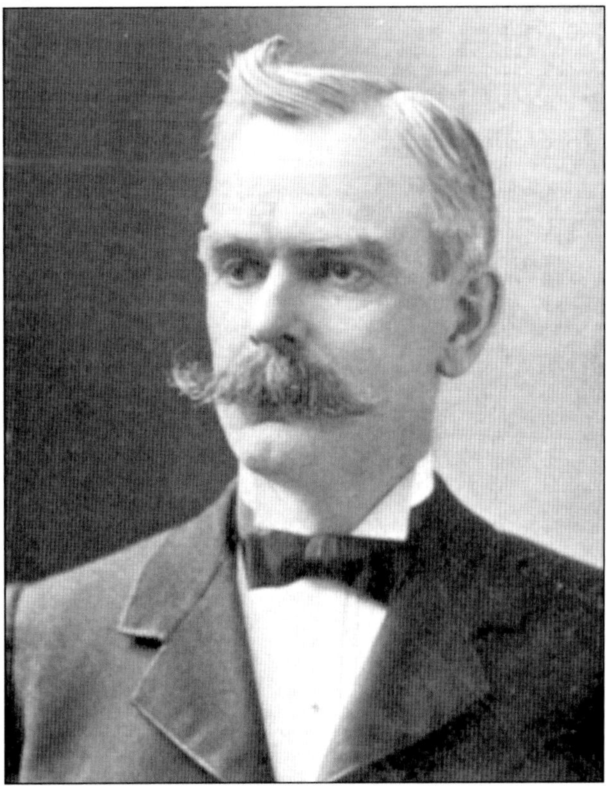

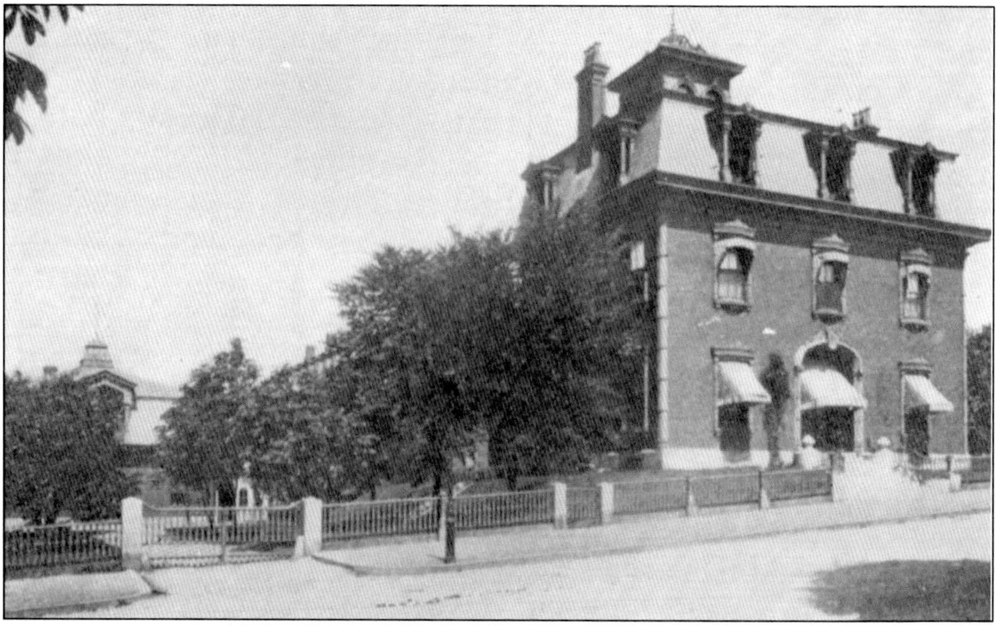

The impressive Dana House was built in the Second French Empire style at the corner of East Broadway and M Street. Built with huge slabs of granite as a foundation, this red brick and brownstone-trimmed house has a cast-iron balustrade fence along the sidewalk and an intact carriage house.

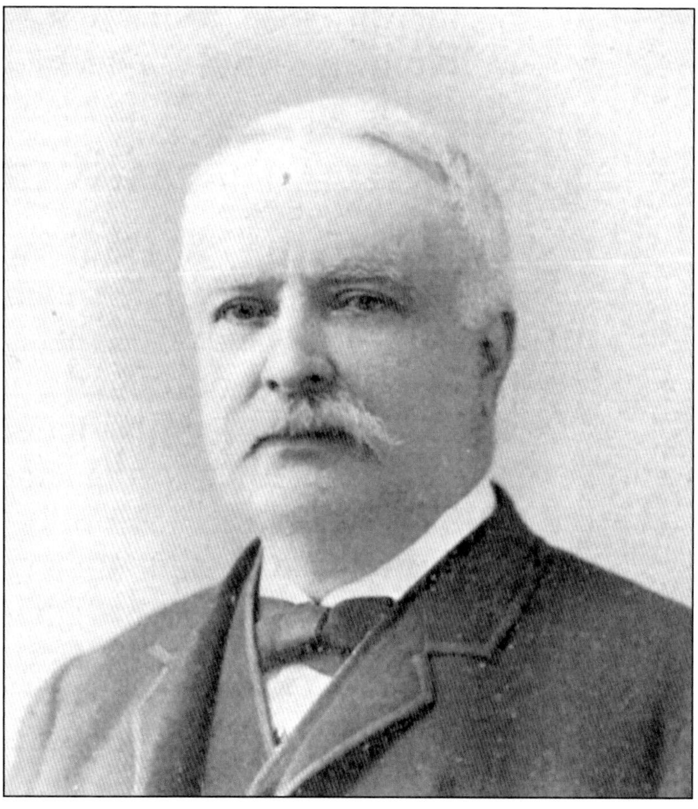

Otis D. Dana (1835–1893) was a hardware merchant with Eaton, Lovett, & Wellington. The business was known as the Dana Hardware Company after he became president in 1867. A developer in South Boston, he "built a large number of houses in this district, and improved property here to a noticeable extent."

Dr. Liberty L.D. Packard (1831–1895) was a beloved physician in South Boston, of whom it was said that his "sterling character, genial disposition and sympathetic interest in his friends and in his city, made him welcome in many homes, and in public gatherings." One of the familiar sights was the doctor with his favorite horse, Dolly, driving about the streets of South Boston on his daily round of calls.

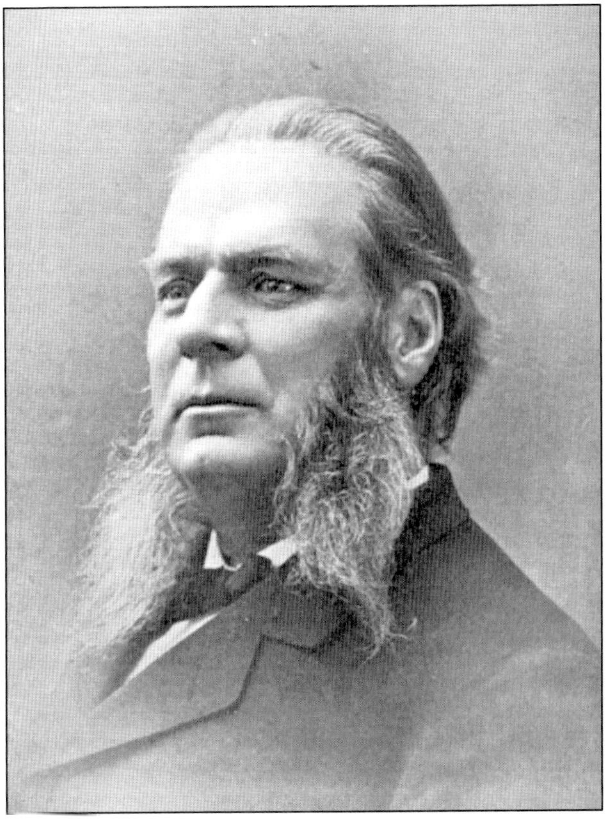

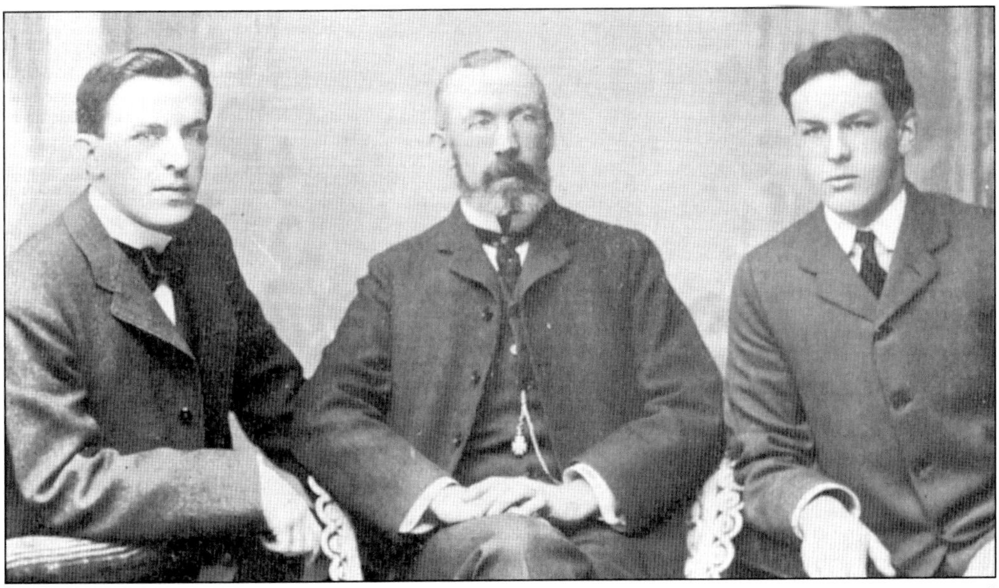

The Corbetts were "Boston's most active auctioneers, real estate and general insurance agents" at the beginning of the 20th century. Seen here, from left to right, are Nicholas D. Corbett, founder Peter B. Corbett, and Frederick A. Corbett. Their office was at 321 West Broadway, where they "handled and negotiated the sale of many hundred estates, amounting to several millions of dollars."

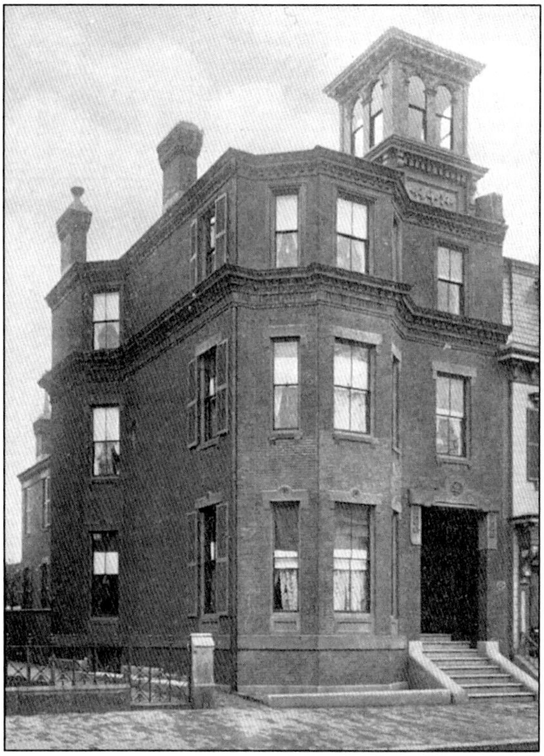

The elegant brick three-story Bowen House is located at 517 East Broadway, adjacent to the Albanian Orthodox Cathedral of St. George. The cathedral, built in 1872 at the crest of the hill on East Broadway, was formerly the Hawes Unitarian Church.

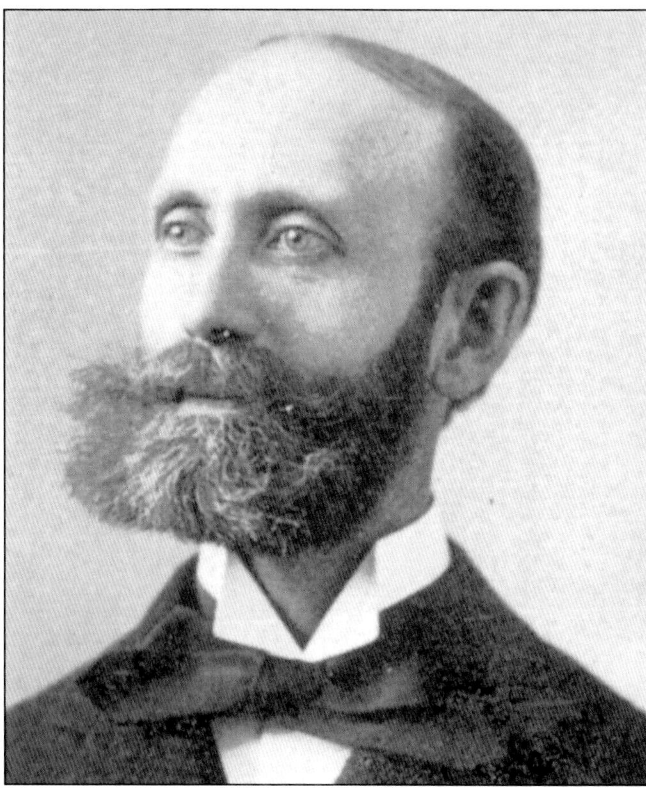

Henry J. Bowen was a real estate and insurance agent with an office at 469 East Broadway. As a member of the Real Estate Exchange and the Auction Board of Boston, he was a well-respected businessman and developer in South Boston, who was "a large land owner of real estate in [South Boston] and has charge of many properties for clients."

Mills D. Barber was the proprietor of Barber & Locke; he was considered a "successful grocer and provision dealer in South Boston." It was said of his very successful business that "five teams [of horses] are required to call for and deliver orders daily" in South Boston and Dorchester.

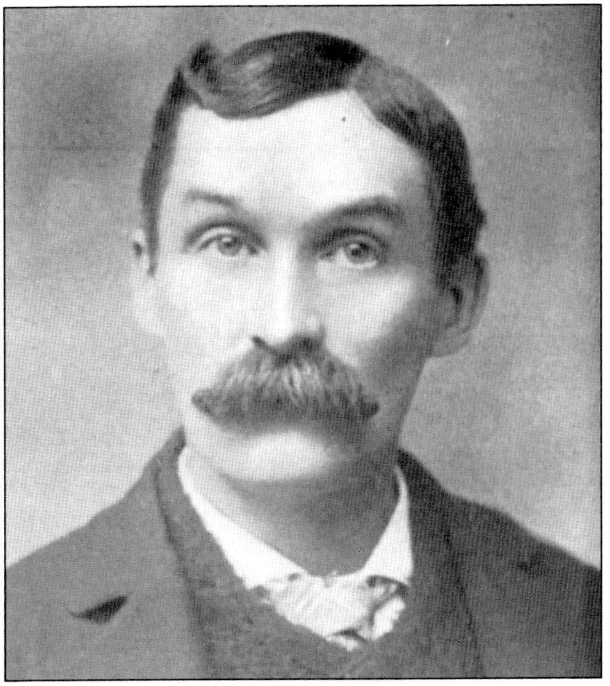

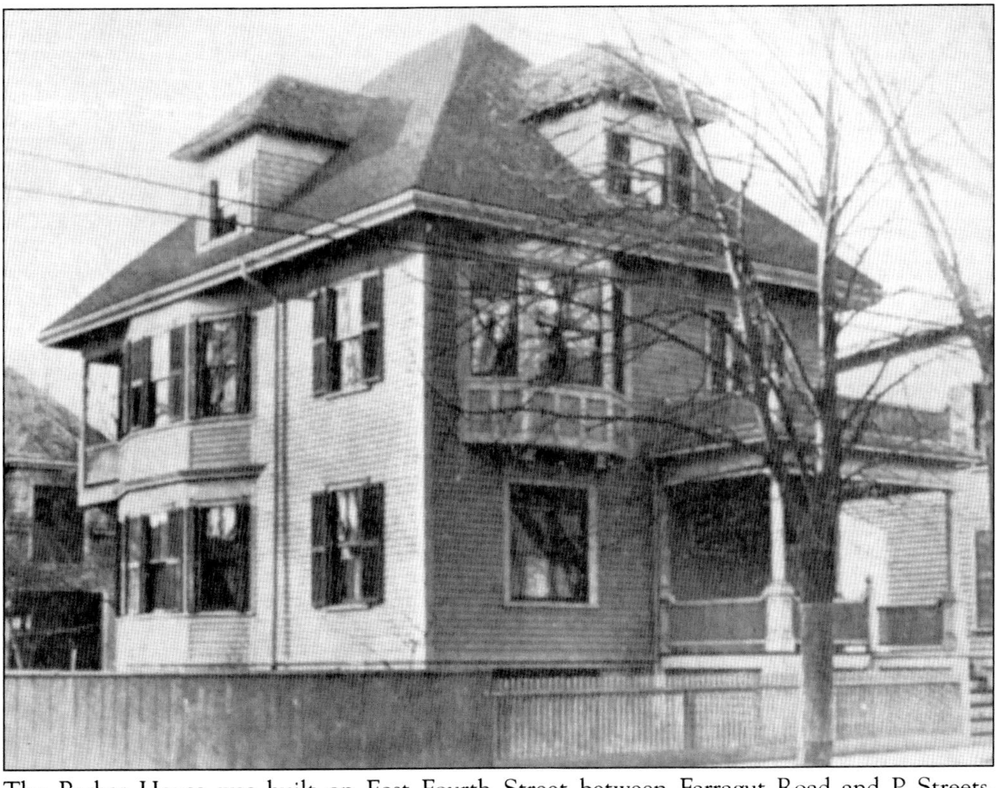

The Barber House was built on East Fourth Street between Farragut Road and P Streets, where the house commanded a full view of the harbor. An elegant Colonial Revival house, it differed in style from others in the neighborhood.

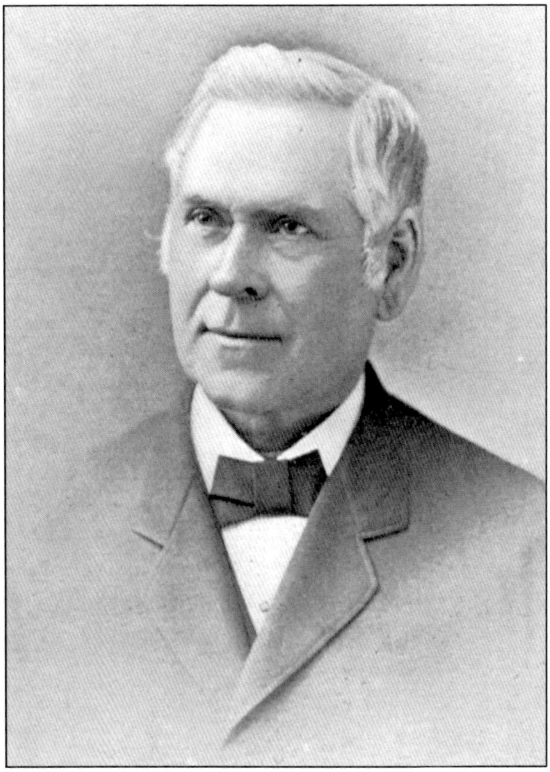

Patrick Lally (1825–1909) worked for John Souther for a short while before purchasing "the business of Green & Davis, general blacksmiths and wheelwrights, whose establishment was located at the corner of Dorchester Avenue and First Street." There, he constructed hose carriages and other wagons for the Boston Fire Department, coal wagons, and his own design of hoist and chute wagons. He also supplied the government with gun carriages and paddle arms for war vessels during the Civil War.

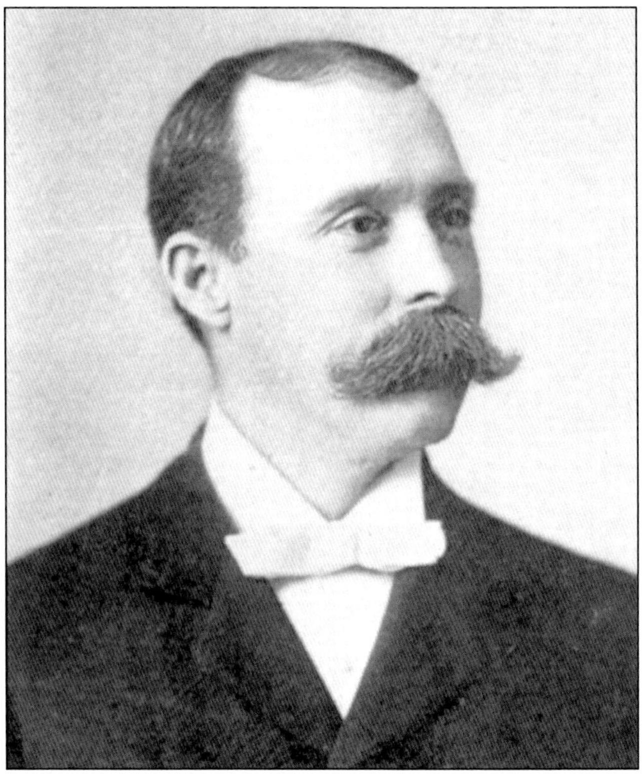

Charles S. Judkins was a real estate, insurance, and mortgage broker. He established an office at 599 Broadway in South Boston in 1872. A builder of a large number of houses in South Boston, he "handled and cut up the largest estates in South Boston, and is considered [in 1900] an expert and one of the best judges of real estate in Boston."

William H. Quirk was a leading wholesale and retail liquor merchant in Boston, whose "reputation is that of a merchant of strict integrity, whose goods comprise some of the finest brands of liquor in the world."

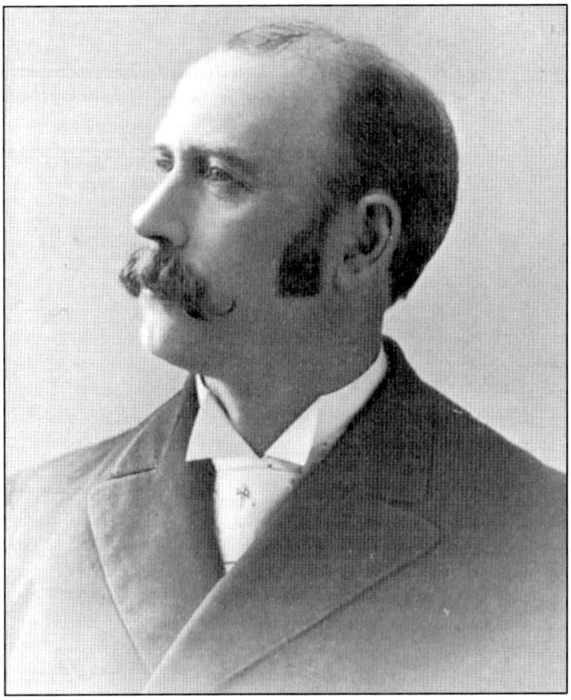

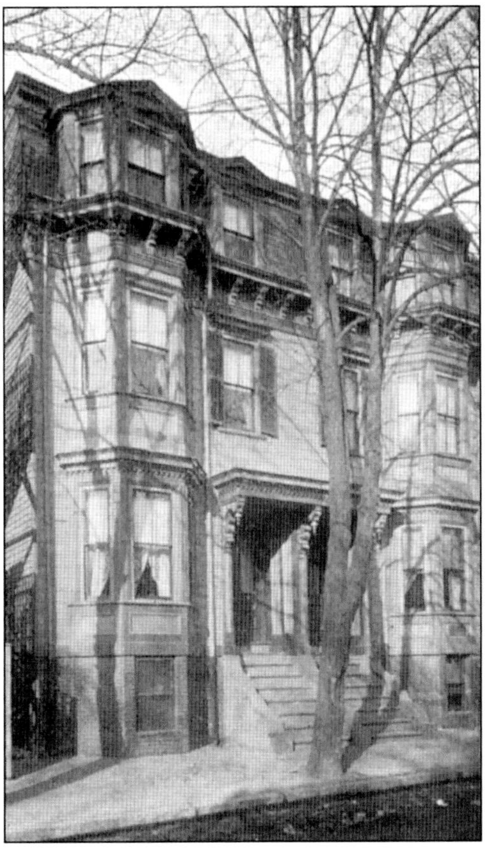

The Quirk House was a duplex house at 580 Seventh Street. William H. Quirk was "the owner of much real estate, and is [in 1895] one of the largest tax payers of South Boston."

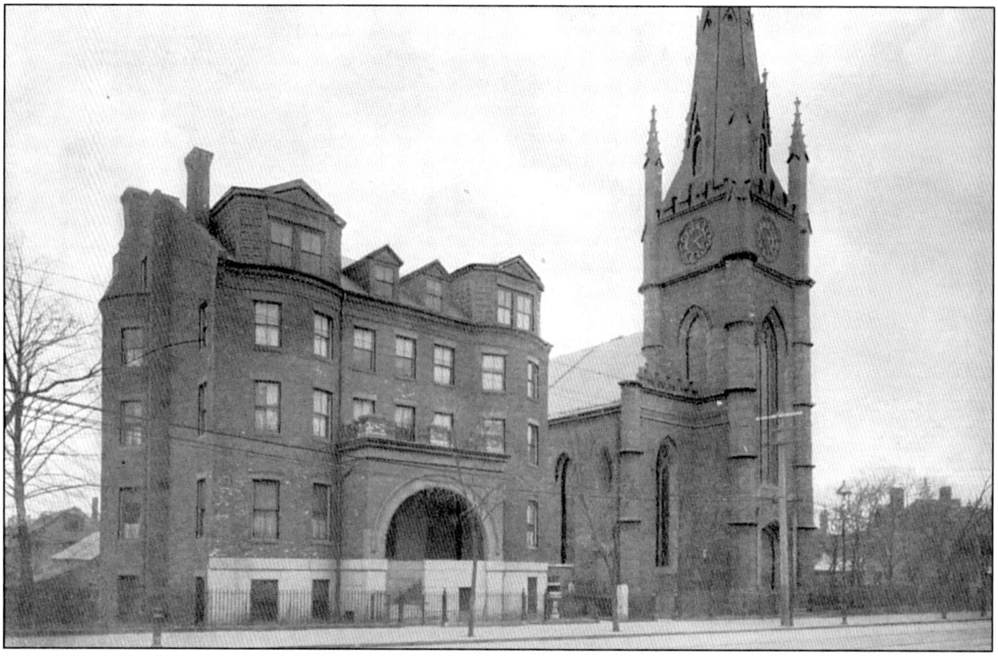

The Church of SS. Peter and Paul was built in 1844 and is the second oldest Roman Catholic church in Boston. It is an impressive edifice on West Broadway between Dorchester Avenue and A Street. Construction began in 1842 based on designs by Gridley J. Fox Bryant, and the building was consecrated by Bishop Fenwick. Gutted by fire in 1848, the granite church was rebuilt and was then reconsecrated in 1853. The structure on the left is the rectory, which was enlarged and remodeled in the 1880s.

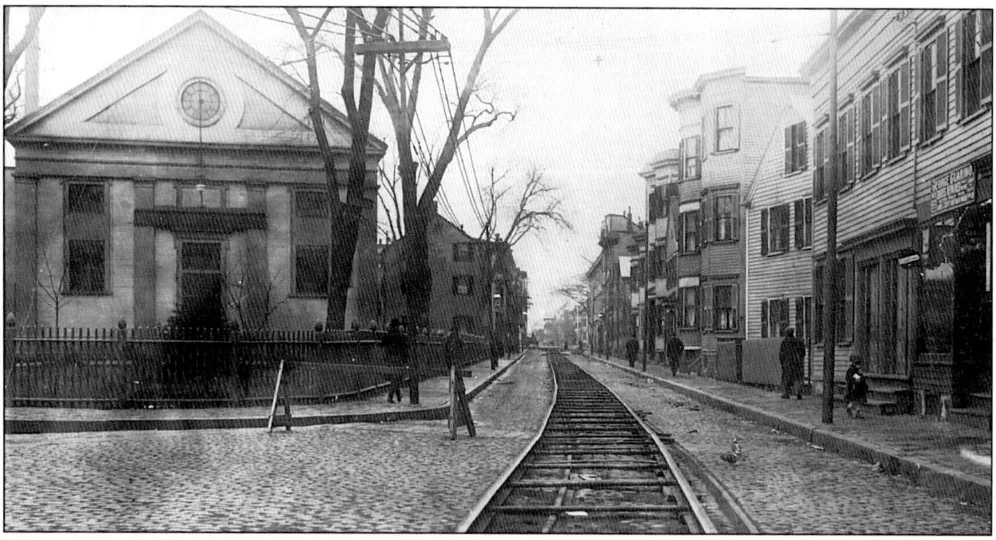

This view looks west on Emerson Street, which was named for Romanus Emerson (1780–1852). A portable track has been laid for streetcars going to City Point in 1919. On the left is the old Hawes Place Congregational Society, built in 1832 and named for John Hawes (1741–1829). The building, which later became the South Boston School of Art, is seen here minus its original cupola. The building was destroyed by fire on February 4, 1963. (Courtesy of Frank Cheney.)

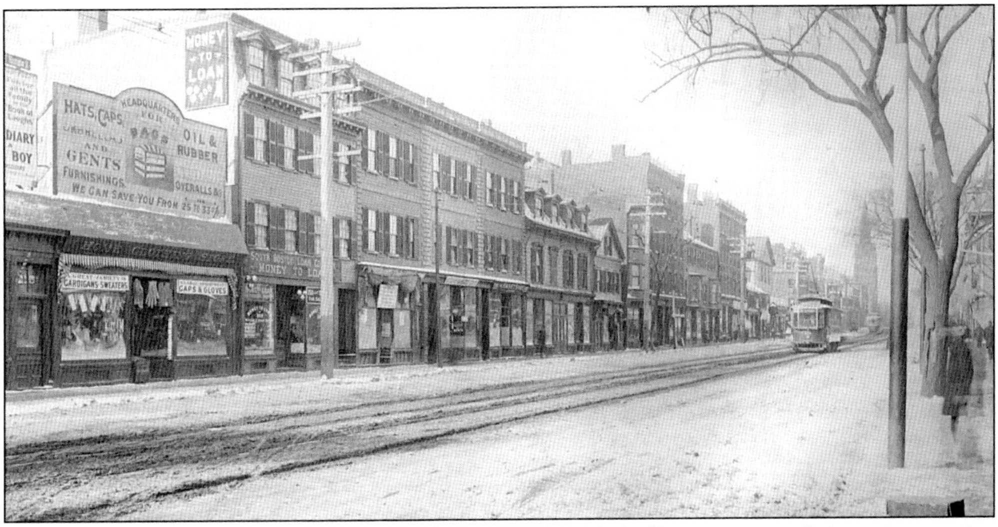


The view looking west on Broadway, between C and A Streets, provided an interesting streetscape at the start of the 20th century. These commercial buildings were demolished after World War II when the 27-acre D Street Housing Development of 27 buildings and 975 apartments was built on the site. The spire in the distance on West Broadway is that of the Church of SS. Peter and Paul. (Courtesy of Frank Cheney.)

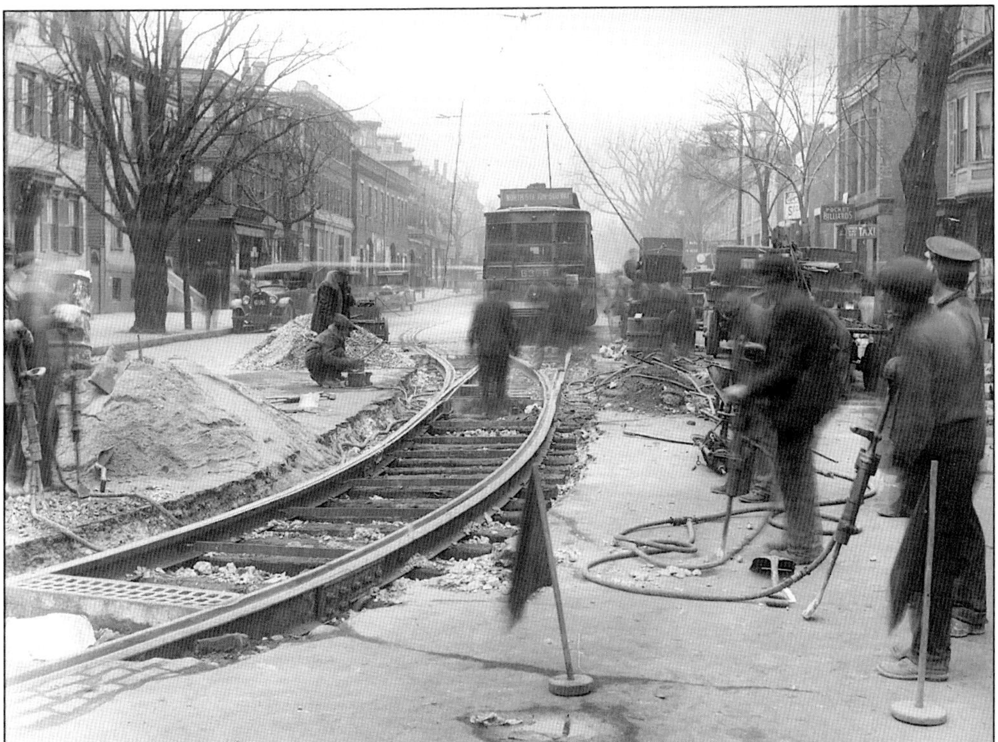


East Broadway near L Street had extensive roadwork done in the late 1920s. Built in 1890, Pilgrim Hall can be seen on the right; it is now the Boston Beer Garden. To the left of the streetcar is the First National Supermarket, at the site of today's Flanagan's Supermarket. (Courtesy of Frank Cheney.)

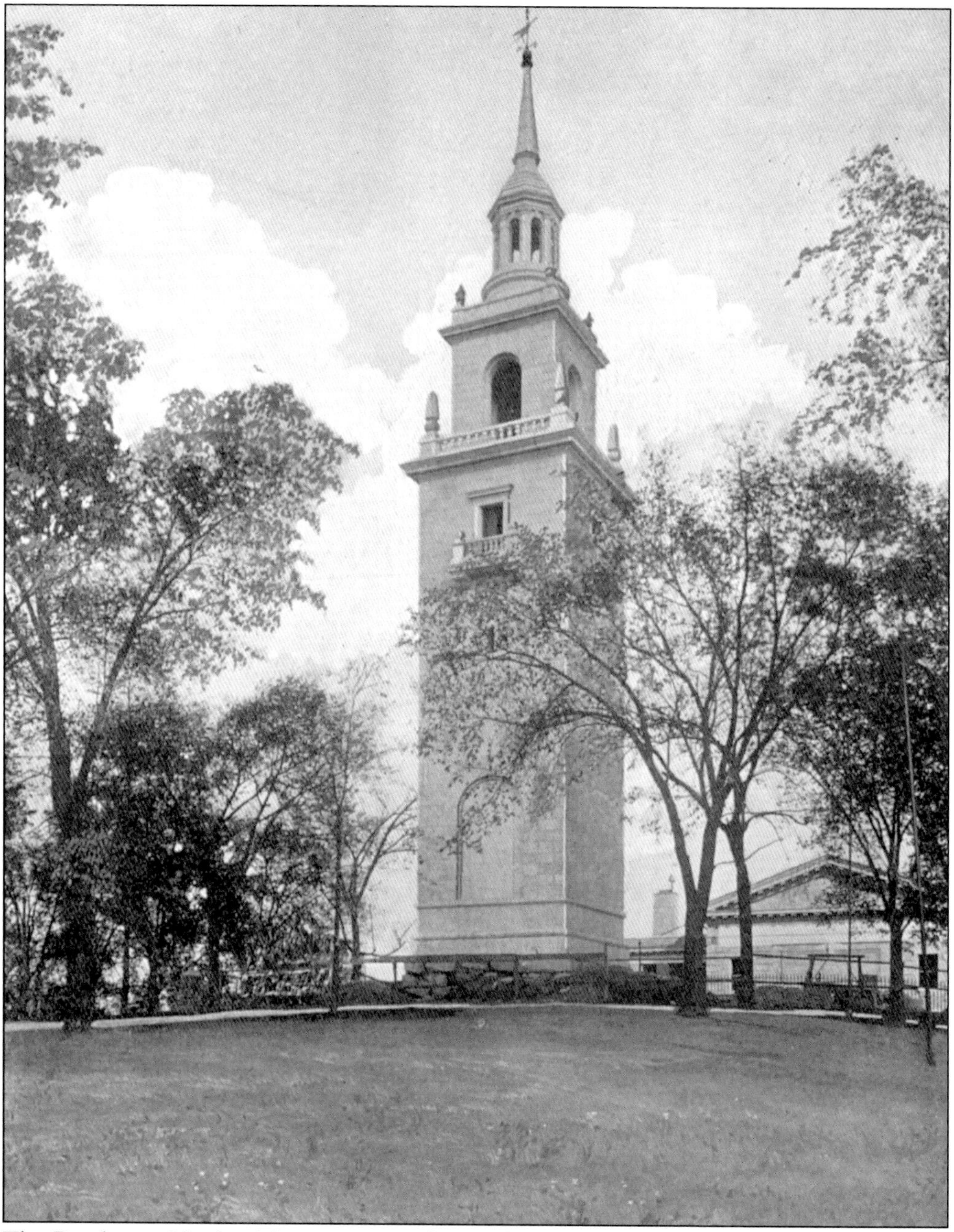

The Dorchester Heights Monument was designed by Peabody & Stearns and was dedicated on March 17, 1902. An impressive, classical, white marble monument 115 feet in height, it commemorated the evacuation of Boston by the British and the Loyalists on March 17, 1776. As Sen. Henry Cabot Lodge said at the dedication, "Here, on this spot we raise a monument which shall serve as a beacon light to guide future generations to one of the memorable scenes of our history." South Boston High School, built in 1901, can be seen on the right; notice its dentiled pediment.

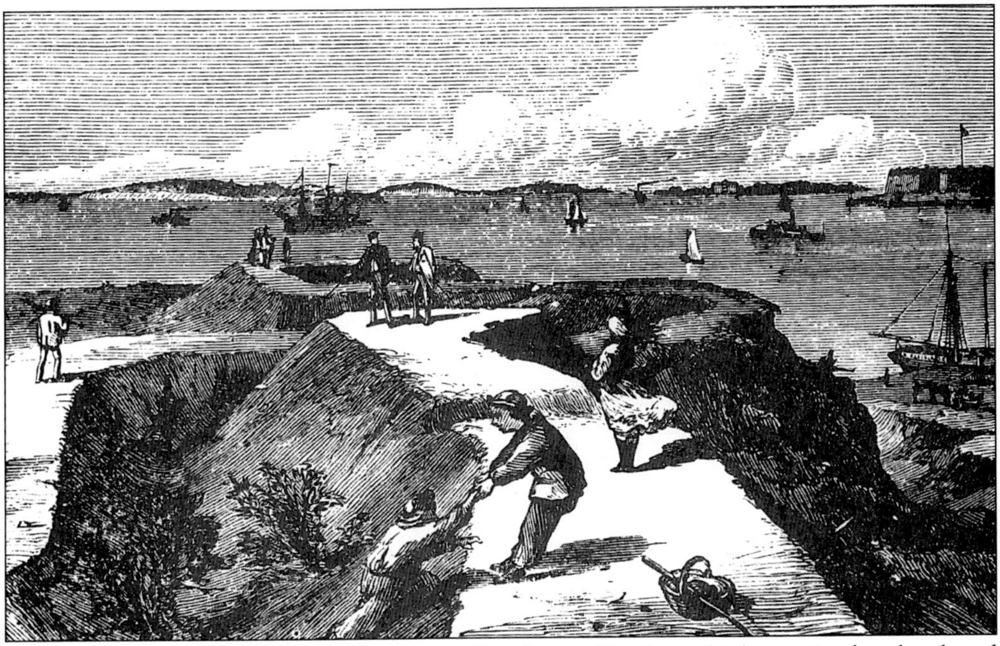

This *c.* 1880 woodcut shows the trenches on Dorchester Heights, which remained undeveloped until the late 19th century. Rev. Edward Everett Hale said that "Dorchester Heights witnessed 'more than victory' commemorated on the first medal of our minted history, with its proud motto, *Hostibus primo fugitas*: the first rout of the enemy." Notice Fort Independence on Castle Island to the right.

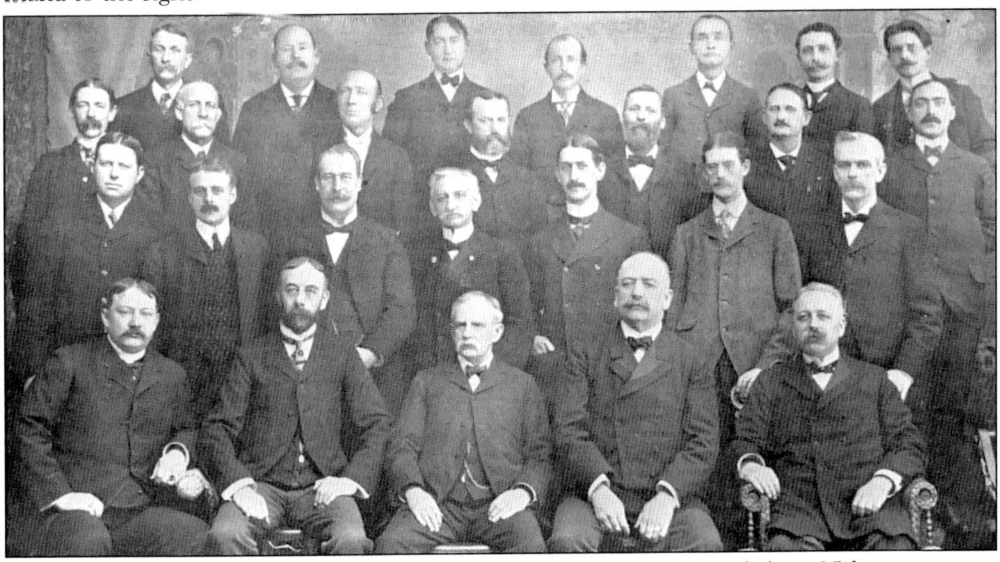

Members of the South Boston Citizens' Association Committee of the 125th anniversary celebration of Evacuation Day on March 18, 1901, from left to right, are as follows: (first row) E.J. Powers, David While, John Means, J.B. Martin, and Maj. George Murray; (second row) E.L. Hopkins, E.P. Barry, R. Kershaw, H.S. Treadwell, George Krey, W.L. Ford, and Samuel W. Johnson; (third row) C.P. Anderson, C.H. Carr, George Lawley, W.J. McDermott, James Lewis, M.J. Mahoney, and P.J. O'Brien; (fourth row) James Pray, M.J. Mullen, W.L. White, Alfred Smart, C.J. Desmond, J.P. Manning, and James H. Means Jr.

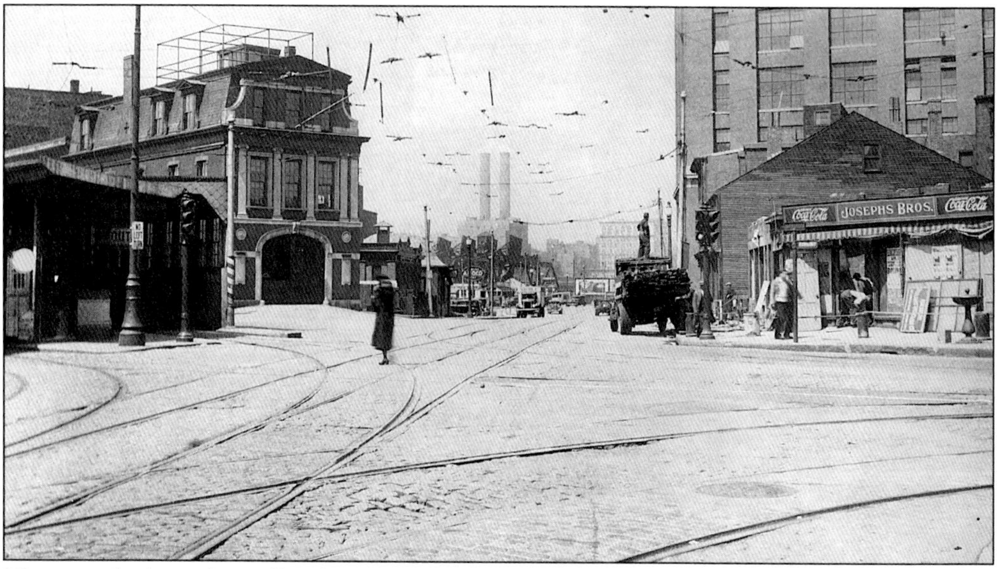


The view looking down Dorchester Avenue *c.* 1920 shows the Broadway Station area with Engine Company 15 on the left and Josephs Brothers Spa on the right. The façade of Engine Company 15 was remodeled in 1917. (Courtesy of Frank Cheney.)

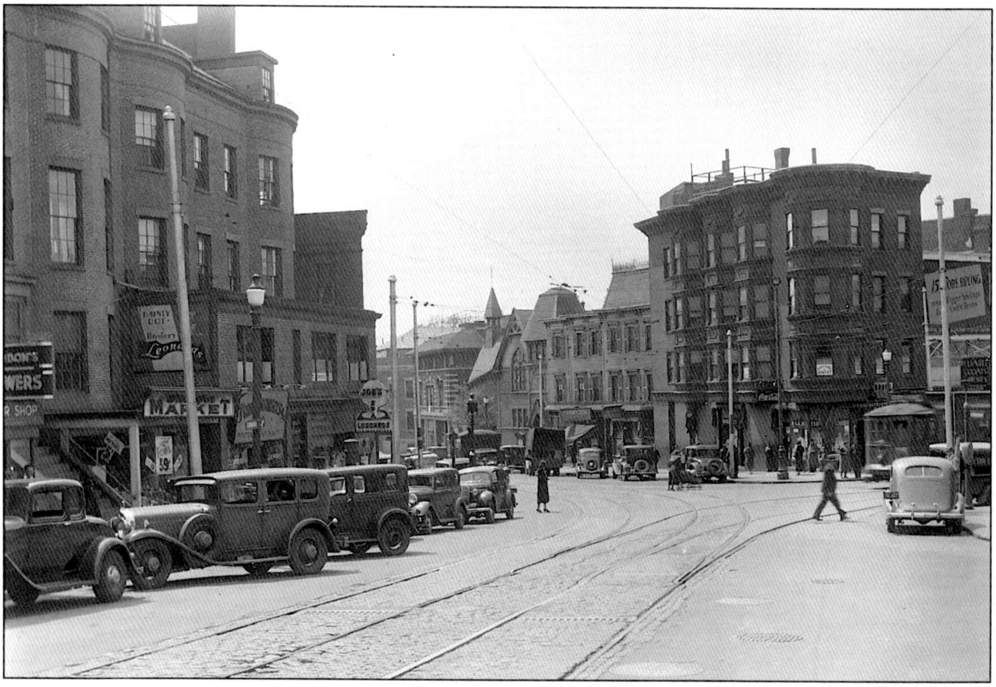


Perkins Square was named in memory of Michael J. Perkins (1892–1918) of Company D, 101st Infantry, who died at Belleau Wood during World War I. The square at the junction of Broadway and Dorchester Street was a bustling crossroads when it was photographed in 1936. The bowfront town houses have been converted into apartments with stores on the first floor; a four-story flatiron building is on the right. Engine Company 1 can be seen on Dorchester Street. Now demolished buildings to the right include the Fourth Presbyterian Church at the corner of Dorchester and Silver Streets. (Courtesy of Frank Cheney.)

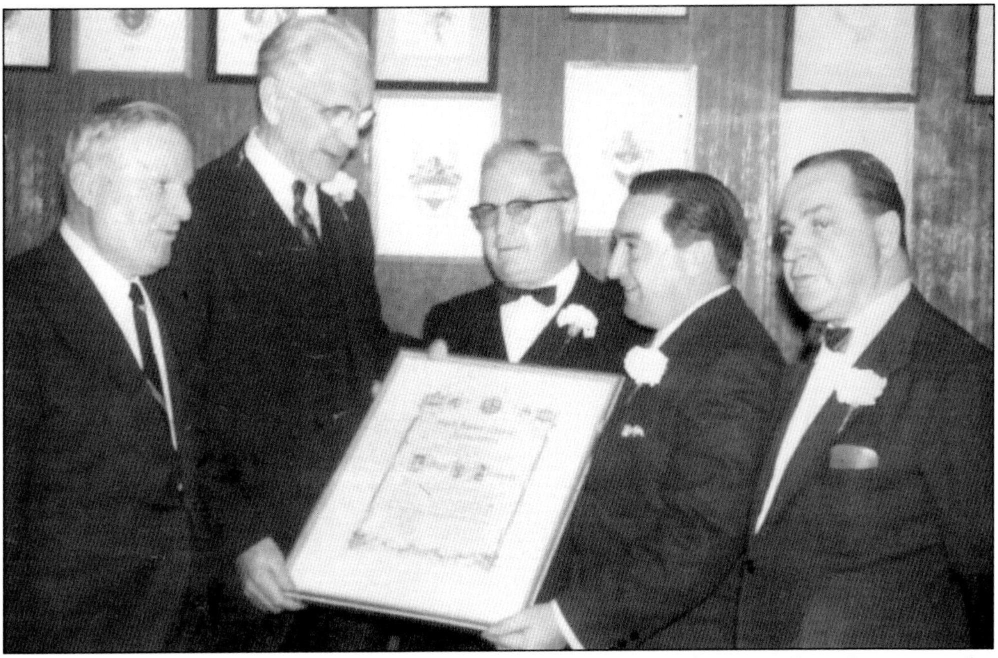

William H. Flanagan, center, proprietor of Bill Flanagan's Head House, later known as the Farragut House, receives a citation in 1958. The *Boston Globe* said he was the "private citizen who has done the most for South Boston in the past 25 years." With him, from left to right, are his uncle Thomas Dorgan, clerk of the superior court; John McCormack, speaker of the U.S. House of Representatives; state Sen. John Powers; and state Rep. Joseph Hines. (Courtesy of Anne Flanagan Thompson.)

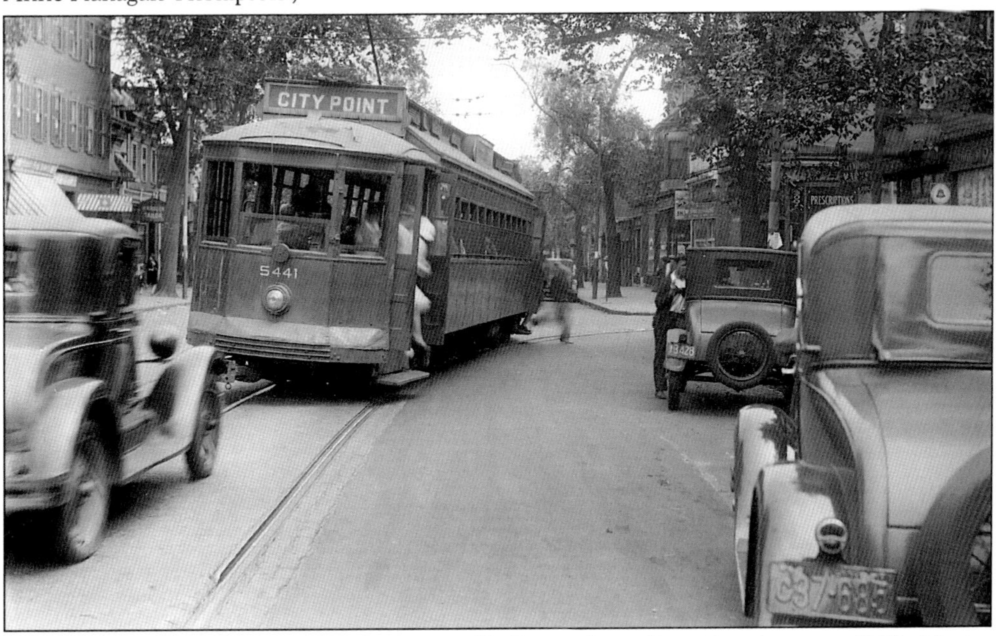


A City Point-bound streetcar turns onto K Street from East Broadway c. 1935. Notice the mature shade trees that line Broadway—a legacy of the Shade Tree Society. (Courtesy of Frank Cheney.)

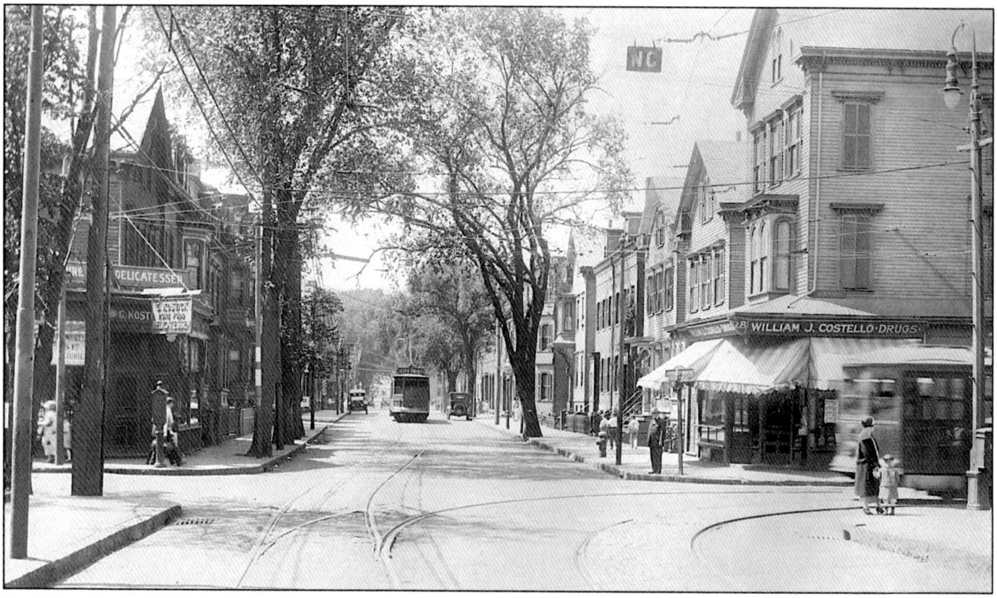


Looking west in 1925 at L and East Fourth Streets, two well-known stores are on either corner. On the left is Kostick's Delicatessen, a longtime area favorite, and on the right is William Costello's Drugstore. The streetcar heads east on East Fourth Street for City Point. Today, A&A Fisheries is on the left and the C&G Service Station is on the right. (Courtesy of Frank Cheney.)

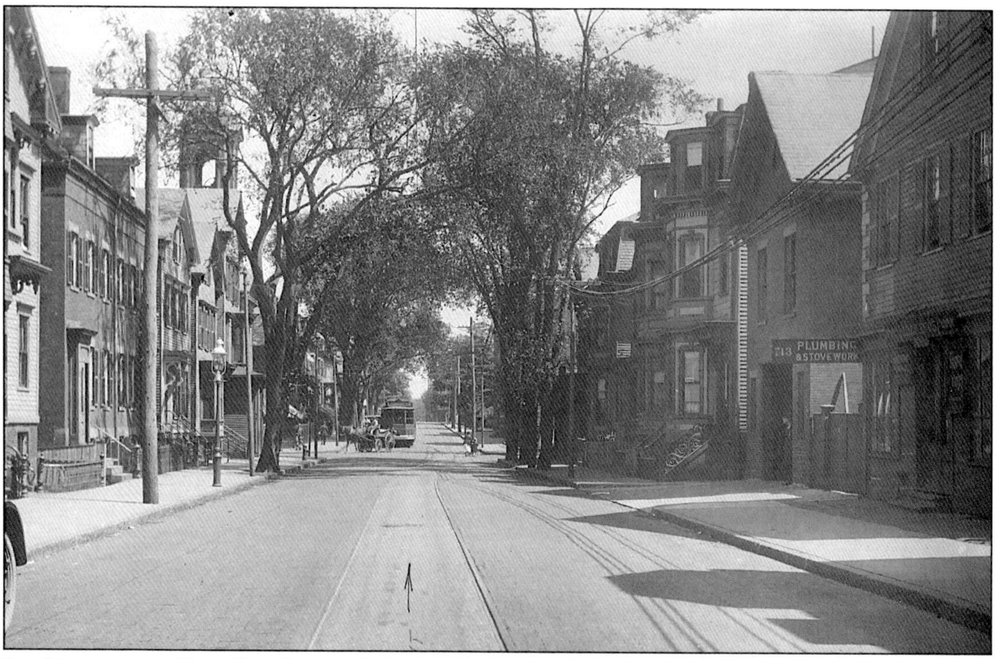


Looking east at East Fourth and L Streets c. 1925, brick and wood-frame houses can both be seen. On the right, Ladder Company 19 at 715 East Fourth Street is now the Thomas J. Fitzgerald Post 561 Veterans of Foreign Wars. The spire of the South Baptist Church can be seen on the left. The houses to the left of the firehouse are 717–721 East Fourth Street; on the left, the brick duplex is 720–722 East Fourth Street. (Courtesy of Frank Cheney.)

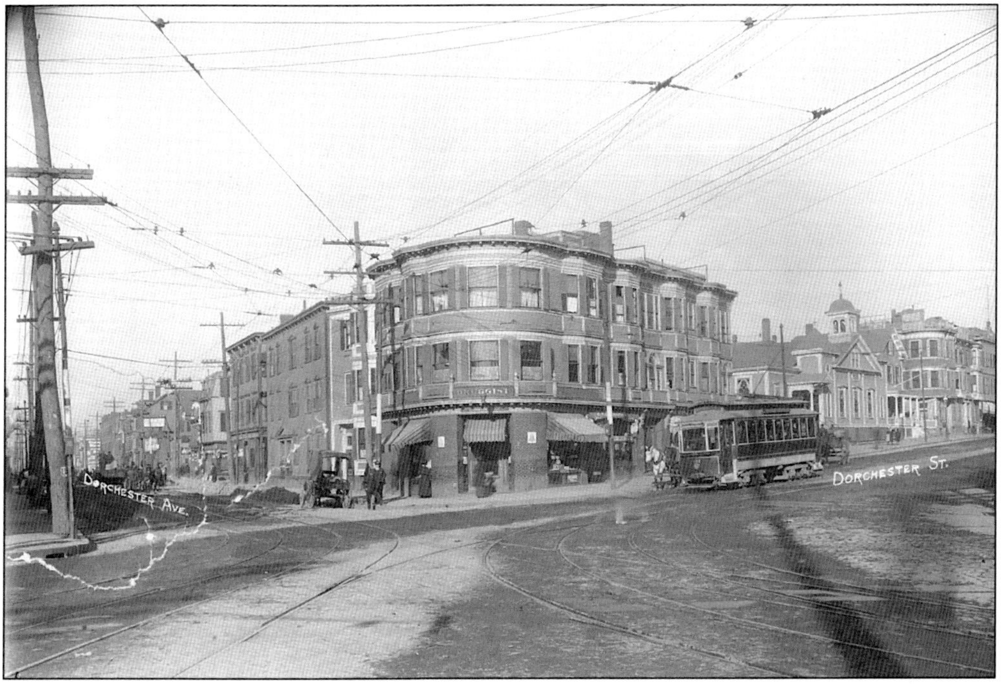


Andrew Square was originally called Washington Village in honor of Gen. George Washington (1732–1799). Washington oversaw the fortifications on Dorchester Heights, which routed the British and the Loyalists from Boston on March 17, 1776. The impressive Colonial Revival block at the corner of Dorchester Avenue and Dorchester Street commands the center of the square. On the right is the original St. Monica's Chapel, formerly the Unity Unitarian Chapel, which in 1987 was converted into apartments. (Courtesy of Frank Cheney.)

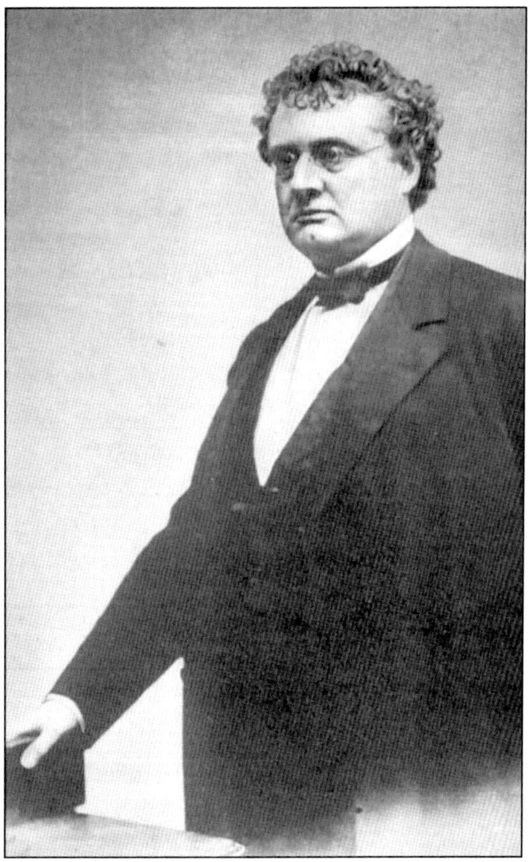

John Albion Andrew (1818–1867) is the man for whom Andrew Square was named. Known as the "War Governor," he served Massachusetts during the Civil War and was instrumental in raising the first African-American regiment to serve in the Union Army Company 54, led by Col. Robert Gould Shaw. The story was immortalized in the movie *Glory*. Andrew said that "I stand or fall as a man and a magistrate, with the rise and fall in the history of the 54th Massachusetts Regiment."

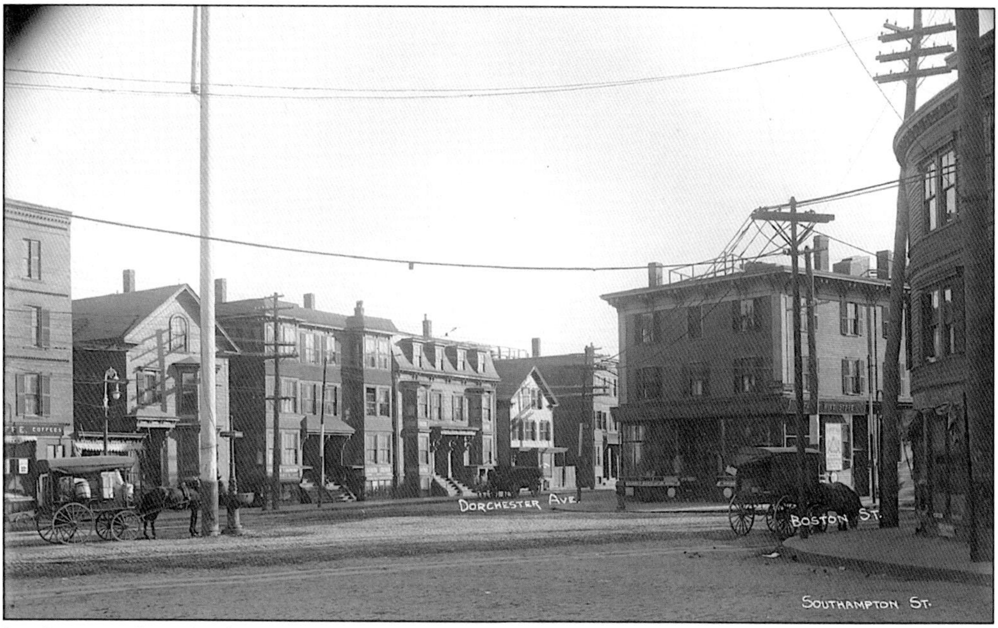


Looking south at Andrew Square in 1910, Dorchester Avenue and Boston Street can be seen in the center, with Southampton Street (formerly known as Swett Street) on the far right. Notice the horse drinking from the horse trough to the right of the flagpole at the junction of the streets. (Courtesy of Frank Cheney.)

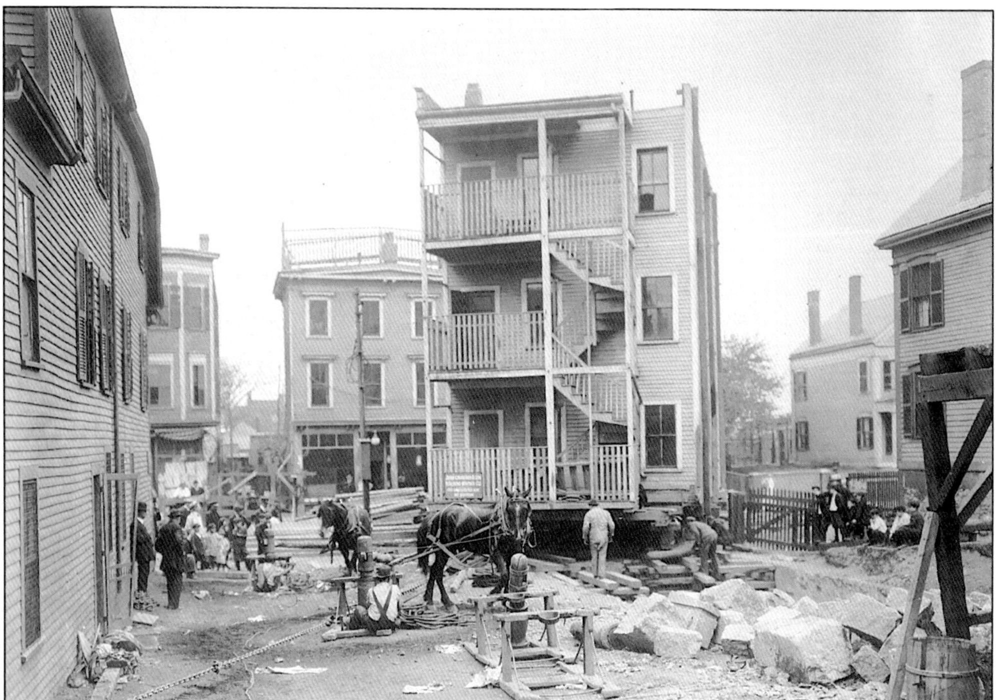

A three-decker is being moved onto a new foundation after having been removed from Dexter Place during the project extending the Dorchester Tunnel (the Red Line) to Andrew Square from Broadway. Horses pull the house on rollers to its new site. (Courtesy of Frank Cheney.)

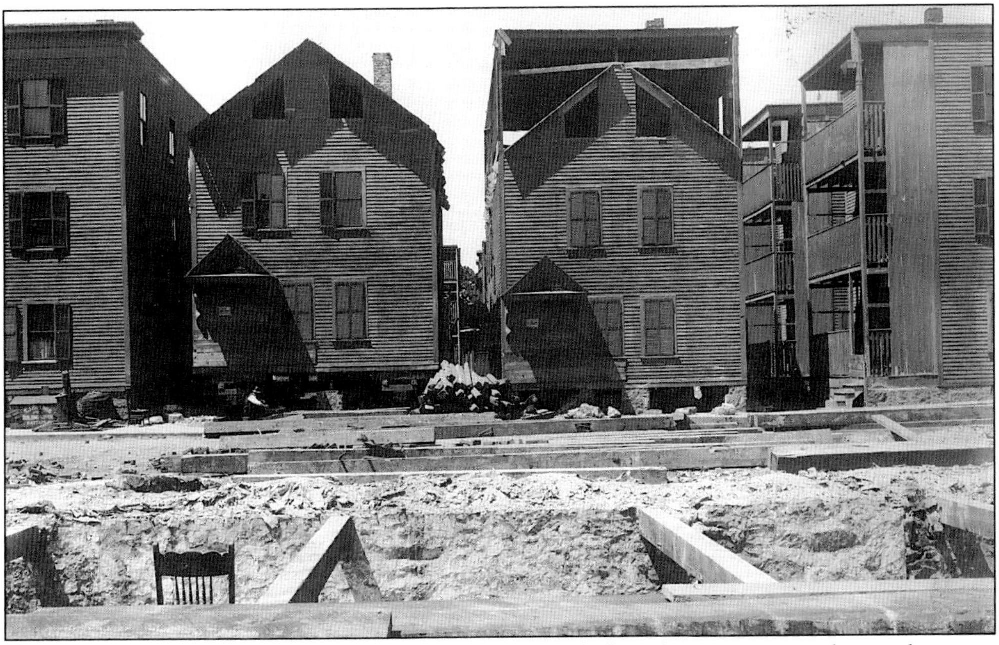

Three-deckers on Dexter Place were altered in 1916 before they were moved to make room for the new Andrew Square Station on the Dorchester Tunnel (the Red Line). The third floor of each three-decker was removed and a new gable was cut, creating a two-story house, which was then remodeled, moved, and sold to offset the overall cost of the project. (Courtesy of Frank Cheney.)

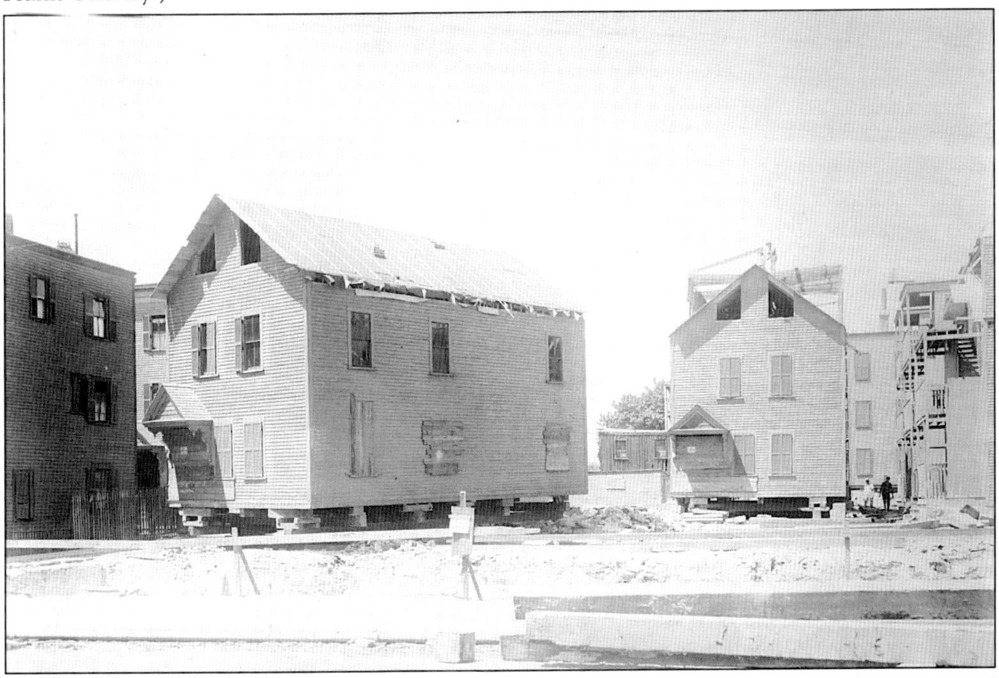

An altered three-decker is put on blocks before being moved in 1916. This "adaptive reuse" was prompted less by the architectural merit of the houses than by the control of project costs. (Courtesy of Frank Cheney.)

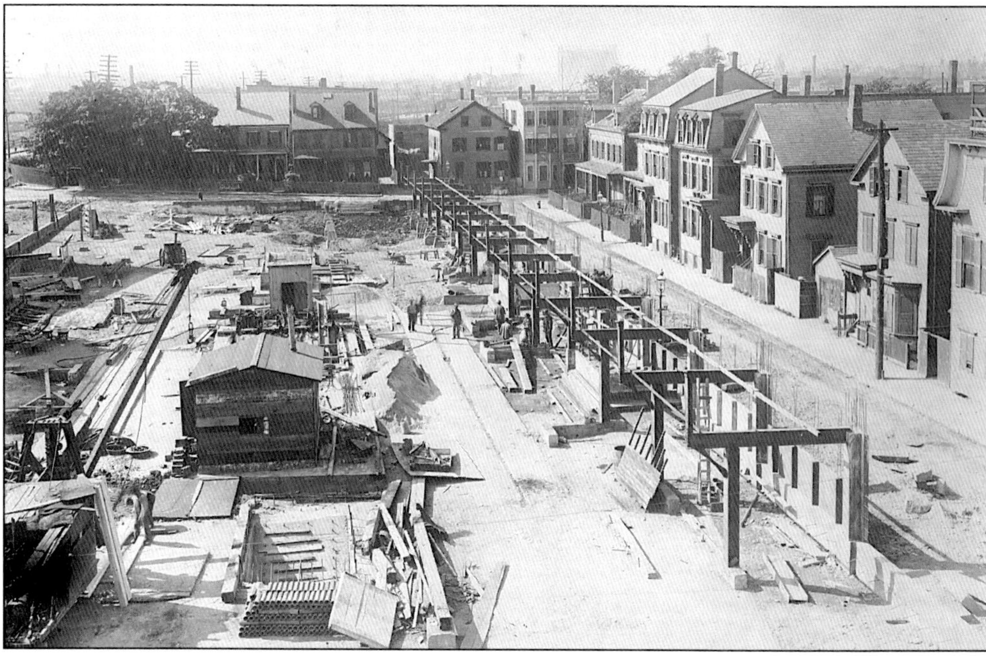

A bird's-eye view of the foundation of the new Andrew Square Station in this 1917 photograph shows the walls of the transfer station as they are being erected along Dexter Place, on the right. The houses on the right still survive and are significant examples of Greek Revival- and Italianate-style architecture. (Courtesy of Frank Cheney.)

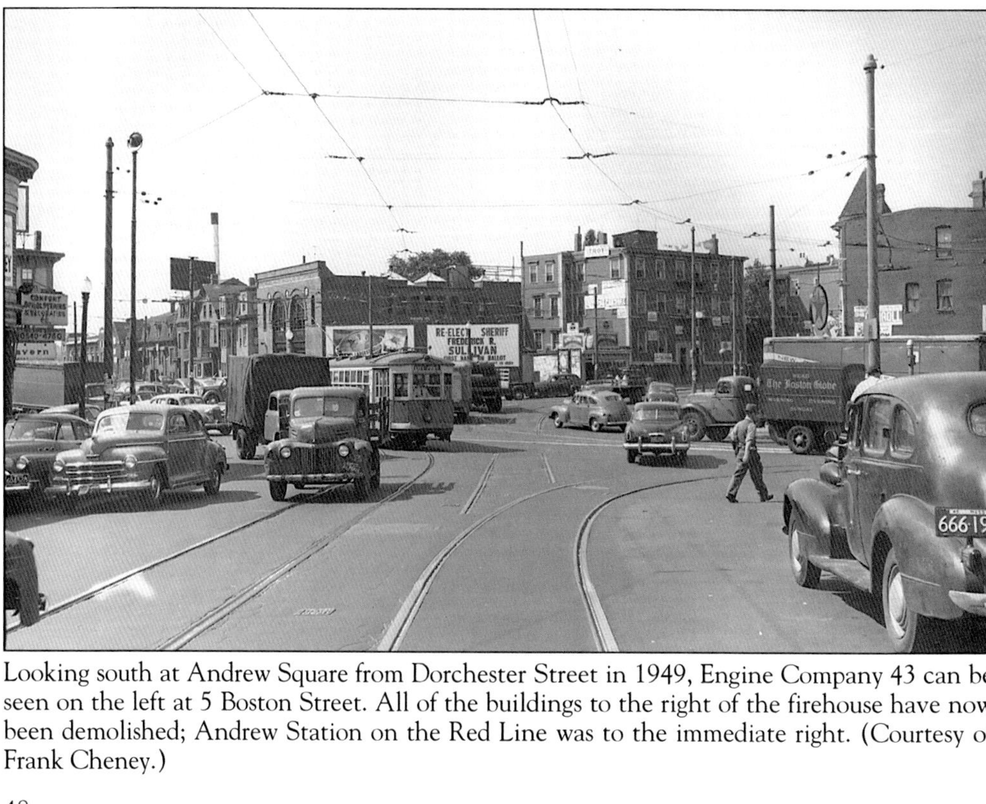


Looking south at Andrew Square from Dorchester Street in 1949, Engine Company 43 can be seen on the left at 5 Boston Street. All of the buildings to the right of the firehouse have now been demolished; Andrew Station on the Red Line was to the immediate right. (Courtesy of Frank Cheney.)

# *Three*

# All Modes of Transportation

In the early 1830s, an omnibus line known as the Warren Line connected Boston to City Point in South Boston via Broadway; the fare was 25¢. A competitive company known as the "White Line" (omnibuses were painted white) was begun and operated by Jonas Gipson and Horace Hammond. After 1842, they operated "twenty coaches, employ[ed] some forty men, and [kept] one hundred and five horses. Trips are run every five minutes" from Boston. By the mid-19th century, streetcar lines running along Dorchester Avenue and Broadway provided safe, fast, and inexpensive travel to and from town. By the late 19th century, the North Point Car House was built at City Point for the large number of streetcars in service. It was considered the "largest and finest horse-railroad stables in the country."

The South Boston Railway Company merged with the West End Railway Company in 1896. Electric streetcars ran along South Boston's streets and connected the neighborhood to Andrew Station, Broadway Station, Dudley Street Station in Roxbury, the North Station, and Harvard Square in Cambridge. By 1904, the streetcars were extended along Summer Street and connected South Station to South Boston. This maze of streetcar lines made South Boston not just a convenient place to live but also a popular destination on summer weekends, when multitudes of Bostonians departed for Marine Park, City Point, and Castle Island.

In 1917, the Dorchester Tunnel was extended from South Station to Broadway in South Boston, where a transfer station was built at the foot of the Broadway Bridge. A year later it was extended to Andrew Square, and passengers could travel to Harvard Square in Cambridge in a matter of minutes. The Dorchester Tunnel, now known as the Red Line of the Massachusetts Bay Transit Authority, is a busy and efficient way of traveling to the city and is supplemented by buses that connect all parts of South Boston. Today, South Boston's buses connect with downtown Boston and the Back Bay. The Red Line's stations at Andrew Square and Broadway provide ease of transportation to many parts of the city.

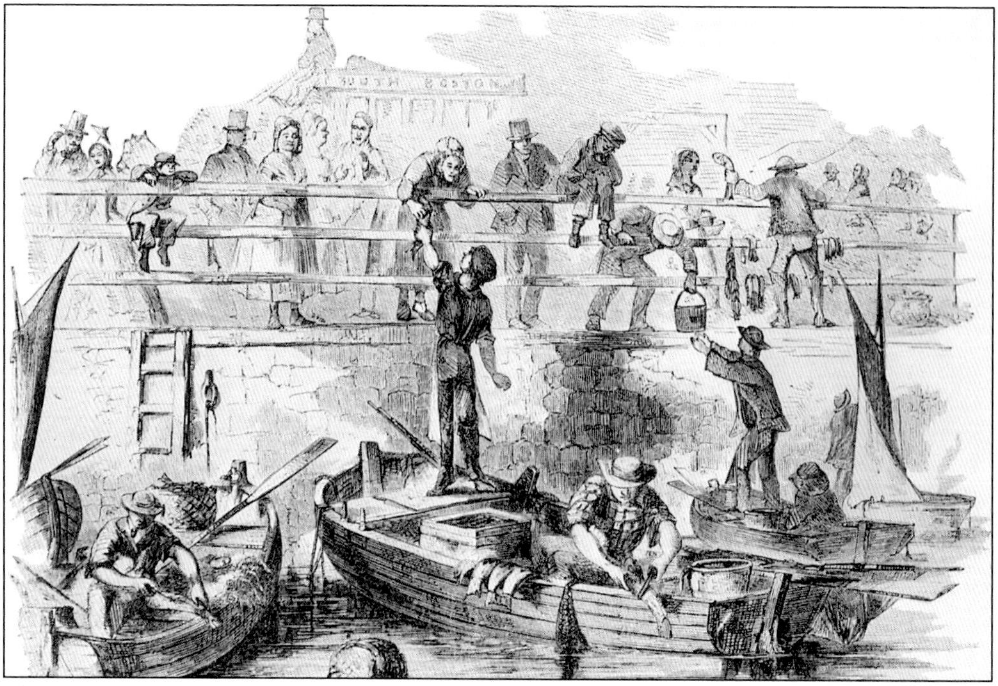

The South Boston omnibus crosses over the Dover Street Bridge in the 1830s, as people purchase fresh fish, which fishermen clean in their rowboats. This bridge was bustling since it was one of only two means of access to South Boston from town at the time.

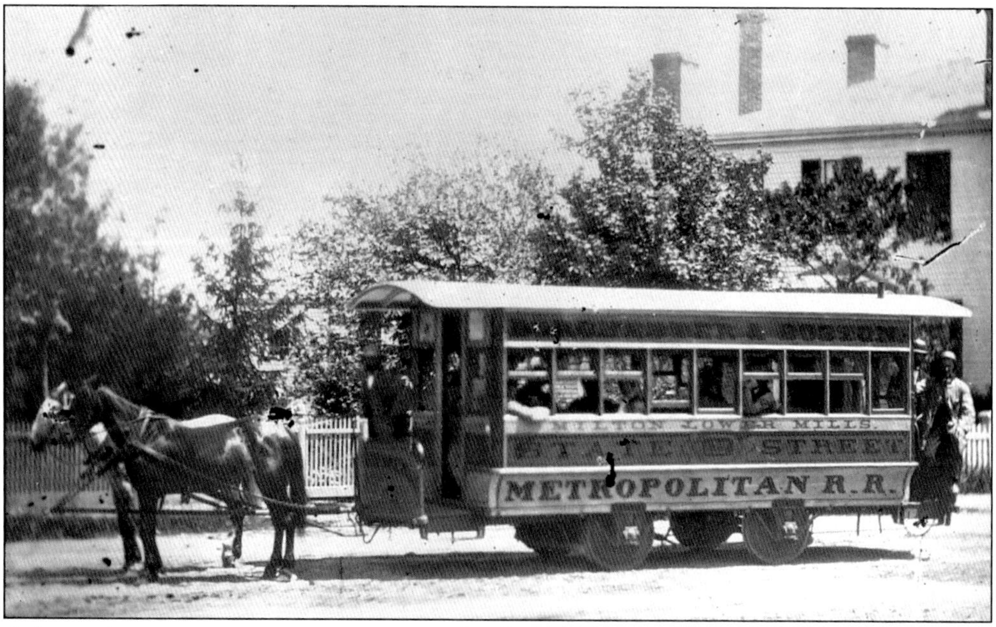


A horse-drawn streetcar pauses opposite the Field House at Field's Corner in Dorchester c. 1860 before going on to South Boston. The Metropolitan Railroad maintained the streetcar, which ran along Dorchester Avenue, connecting the Lower Mills in Dorchester with Boston. Dorchester Avenue was laid out in 1805 as the Dorchester and Milton Turnpike, and it was a toll road until 1854, when it became a public road. (Courtesy of Frank Cheney)

The South Boston Railroad maintained a horse-drawn streetcar along Broadway, as seen in this c. 1860 print. The streetcar passes the Church of SS. Peter and Paul on West Broadway between A Street and Dorchester Avenue. Designed by Gridley J. Fox Bryant, this granite structure was the first Roman Catholic church built in South Boston after St. Augustine's Chapel in 1819. The rectory on the left has been enlarged; a Romanesque porch was added in the late 19th century.

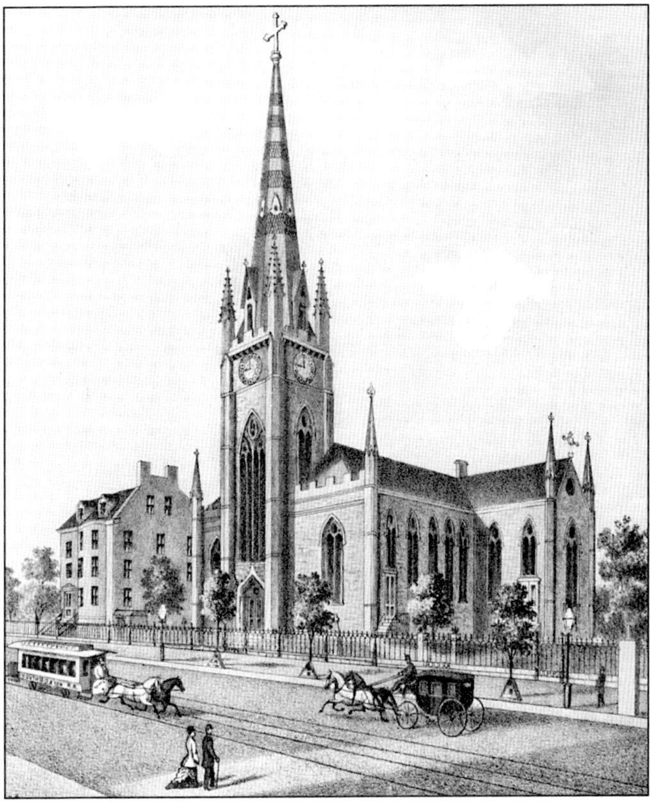

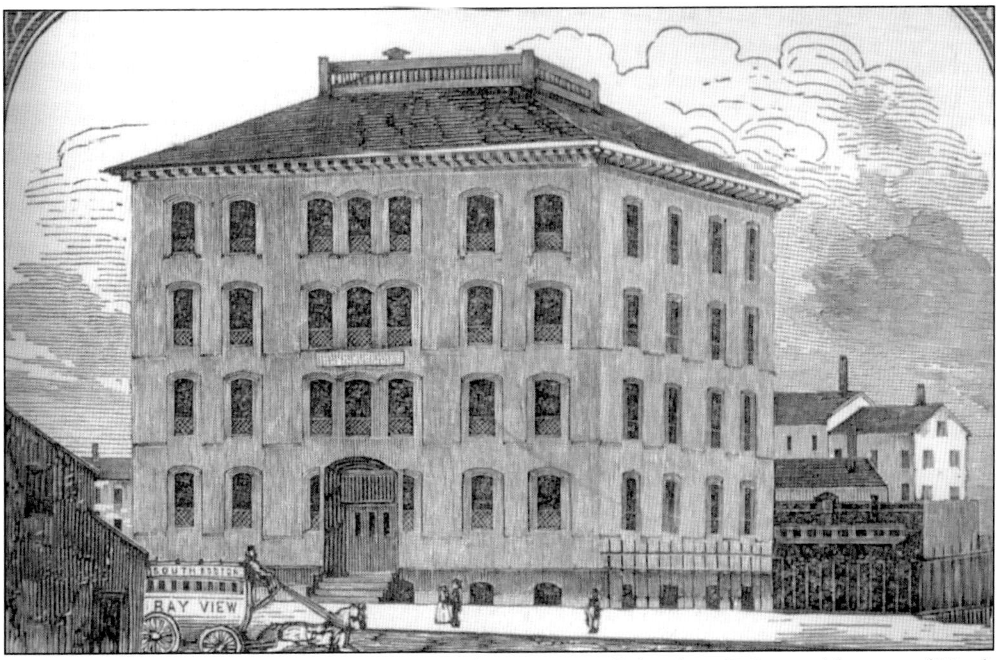


The Bay View horse-drawn omnibus passes the Lawrence School on B Street (the site of Nook Hill) c. 1857. The Bay View Line ran from Boston to B Street, down Broadway, and then down K Street to Bay View—the neighborhood between K and L Streets.

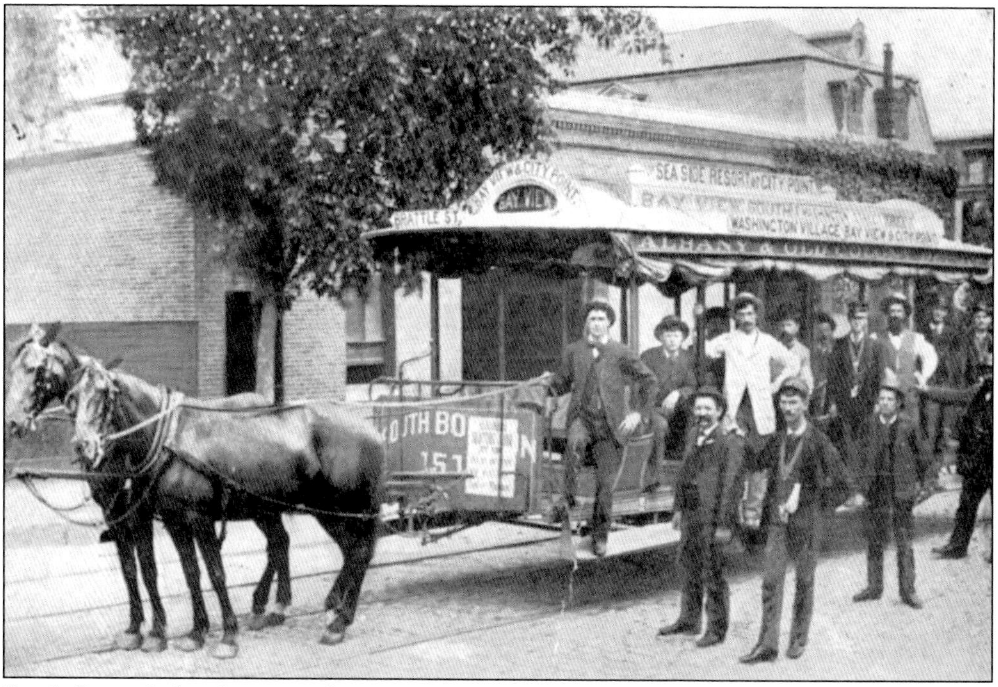


South Boston's first horsecars began operating along East and West Broadway to Boston in 1857, replacing an omnibus line which had been established in 1829. The Bay View Horse Car Line opened in 1874 and ran along East Sixth and East Eighth Streets. This photograph shows an open summer car on East Sixth Street, festooned with ads for the "Seaside Resort" at City Point, which had become a major attraction for Bostonians when this 1884 view was taken. (Courtesy of Frank Cheney.)

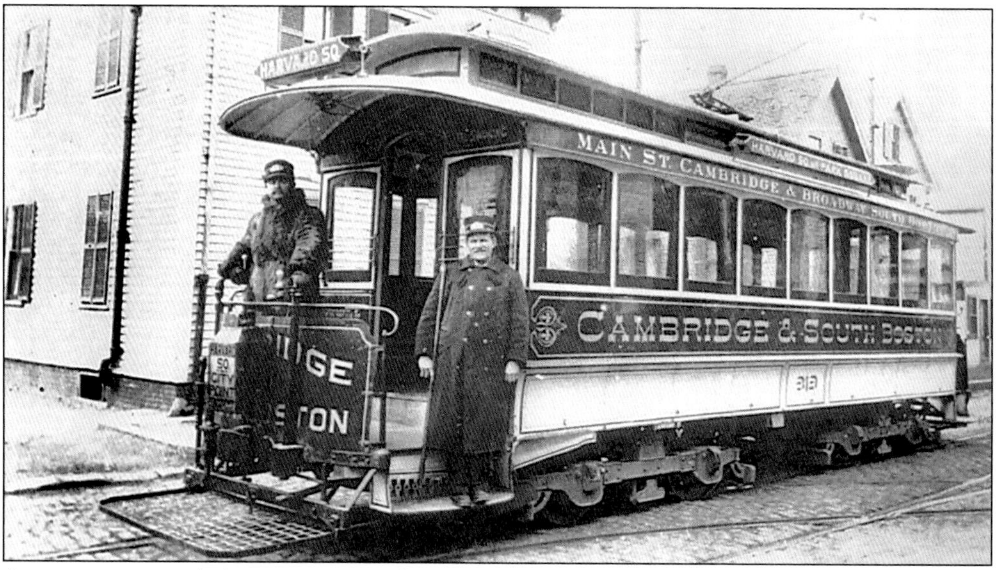


A raccoon coat-clad motorman and a starter pose for the photographer, *c*. 1900. The North Station streetcar ran from City Point, East Fourth Street to L Street, and then along Broadway in South Boston to Harvard Square in Cambridge via Main Street. (Courtesy of Frank Cheney.)

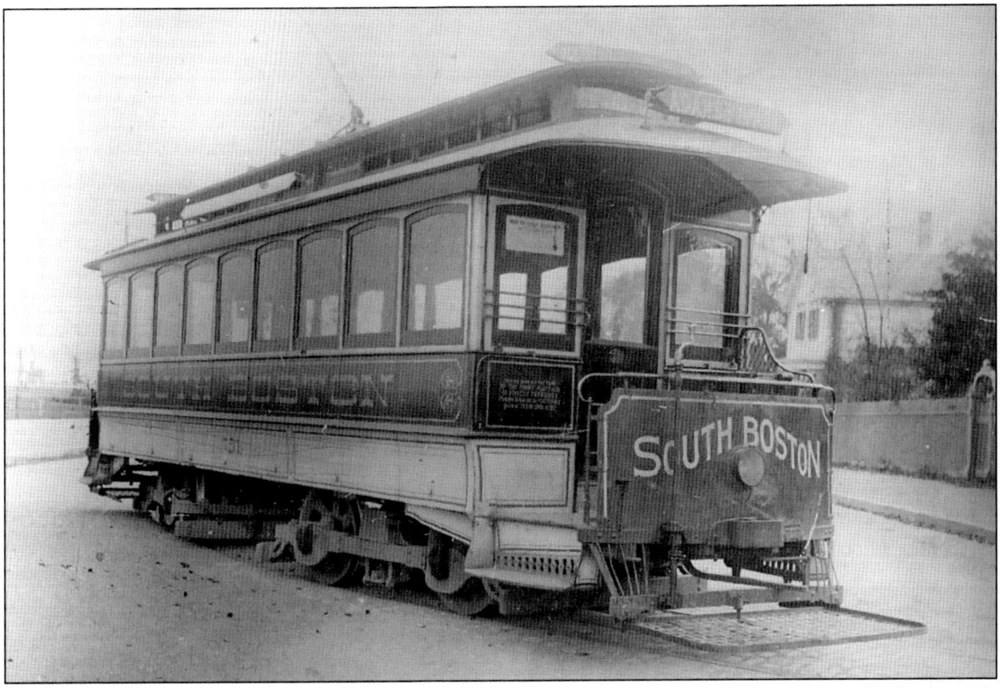


For 36 years, residents of South Boston were served by "standard box cars," originally built with open-end platforms and without interior heat. A car of this type, No. 781, built by the Pullman Car Works, is about to leave City Point for Adams Square in Boston via Farragut Road in this 1896 view. The house in the background is 109 Farragut Road, located near East Fifth Street. (Courtesy of Frank Cheney.)

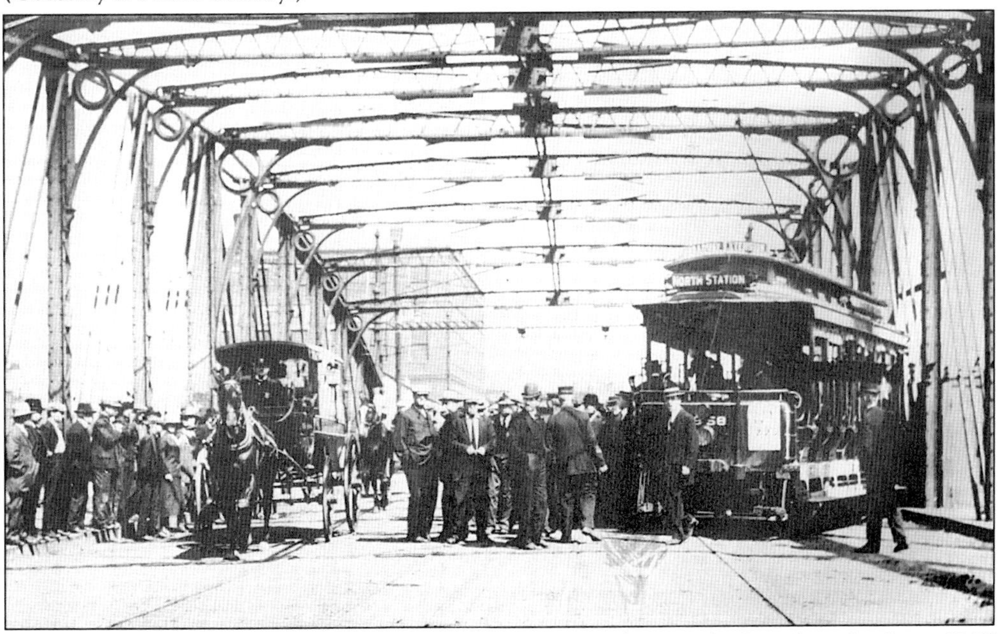


Not all streetcars always ran smoothly. This view of an accident on the Broadway Bridge c. 1905 shows a streetcar that ran off the rails and struck the side of the bridge. No matter when or where an accident occurred, a crowd always seemed to gather to view the damage.

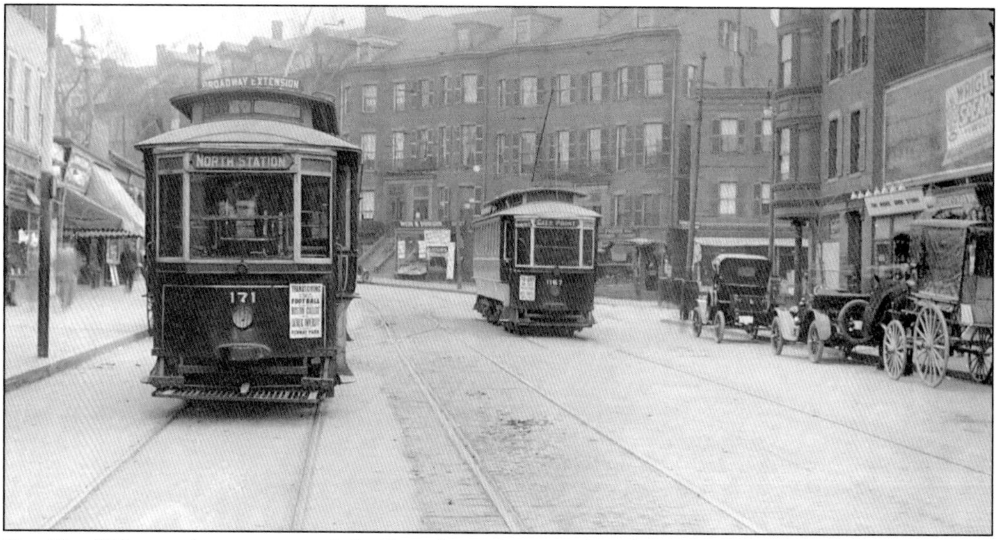


Car No. 171 travels west toward the Broadway Station, heading for the North Station in 1915. The impressive brick, bowfront town houses at the corner of East Broadway and Dorchester Street were built in the 1850s and are similar to houses in the South End of Boston. (Courtesy of Frank Cheney.)

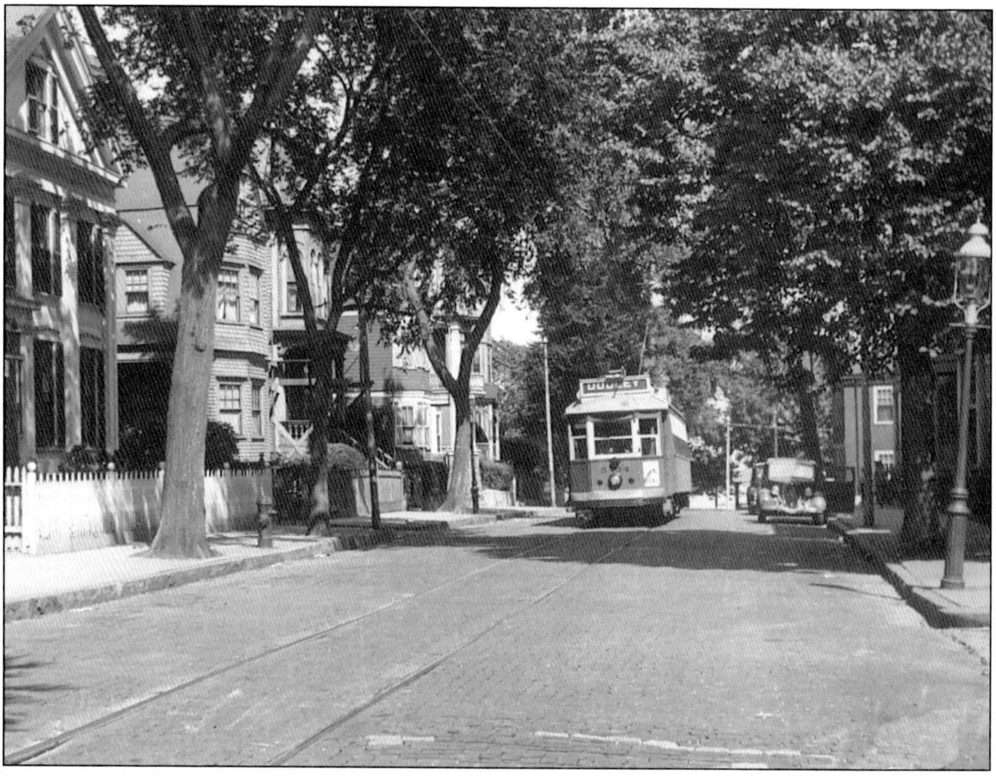


In August 1938, a streetcar heads west on East Fourth Street near Farragut Road for the Dudley Street Station in Roxbury. The impressive Greek Revival house on the left is 926 East Fourth Street at the corner of Dean Way; the houses to the right are 928 and 930 East Fourth Streets. (Courtesy of Frank Cheney.)

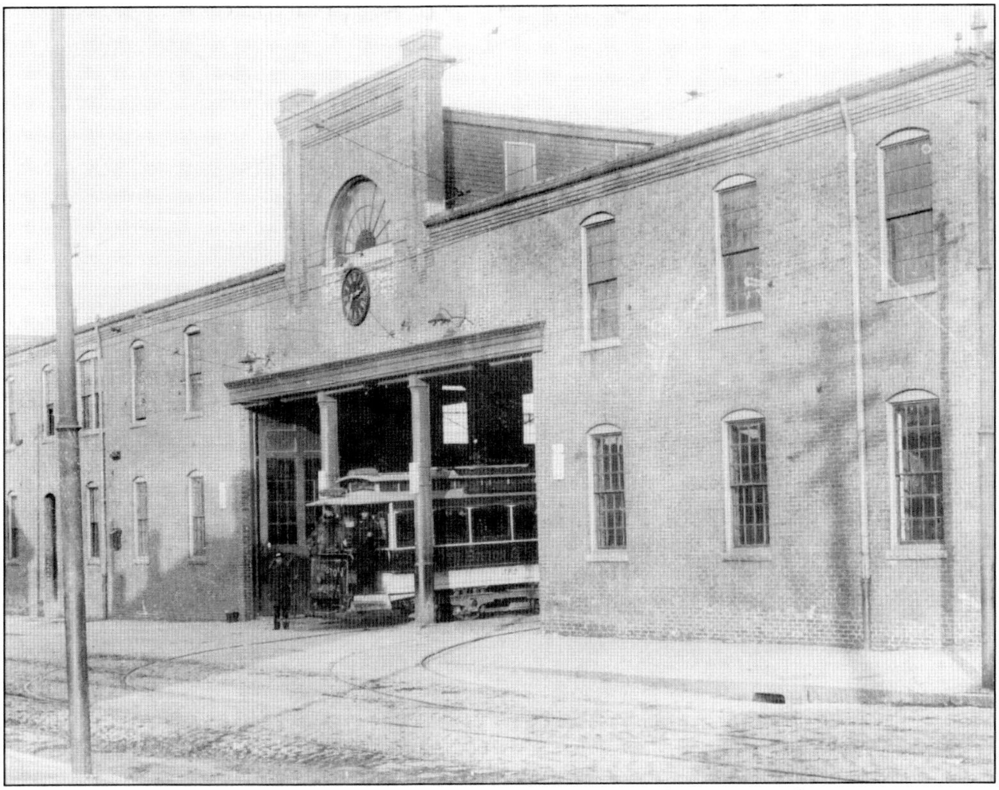

In this March 1892 view of the North Point Car House at P and East Second Streets, a streetcar emerges from the carhouse and heads for Harvard Square in Cambridge. The motorman piloting the streetcar wears a heavy raccoon coat to ward off the March winds. This part of the carhouse was torn down after being damaged in the September 1938 hurricane. (Courtesy of Frank Cheney.)

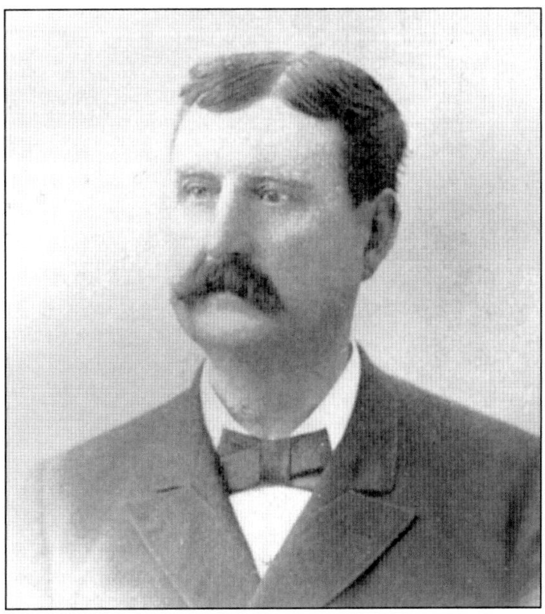

Walter Scott Sampson (1835–1908) was a partner in the building firm of Sampson, Clark, & Company, which "successfully completed some of the heaviest contracts known, contracting for every branch of the work of construction and finishing." The company built the North Point Car House at City Point, the "largest and finest horse-railroad stables in the country at South Boston" in 1892.

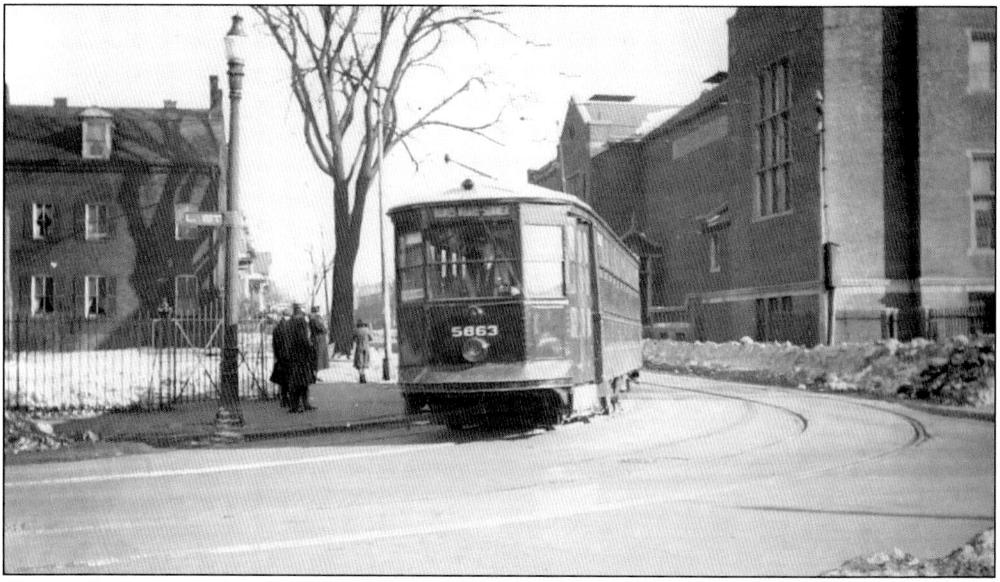


On a cold day in February 1936, a trolley rounds the corner from East Fourth Street onto L Street, en route to the South Station and Rowe's Wharf. Tuckerman School, on the right, was designed by Charles K. Cummings and was built in 1906. The school has now been converted to condominiums. The building to the left is 742 East Fourth Street, an interesting brick, gambrel-roofed house. (Courtesy of Frank Cheney.)

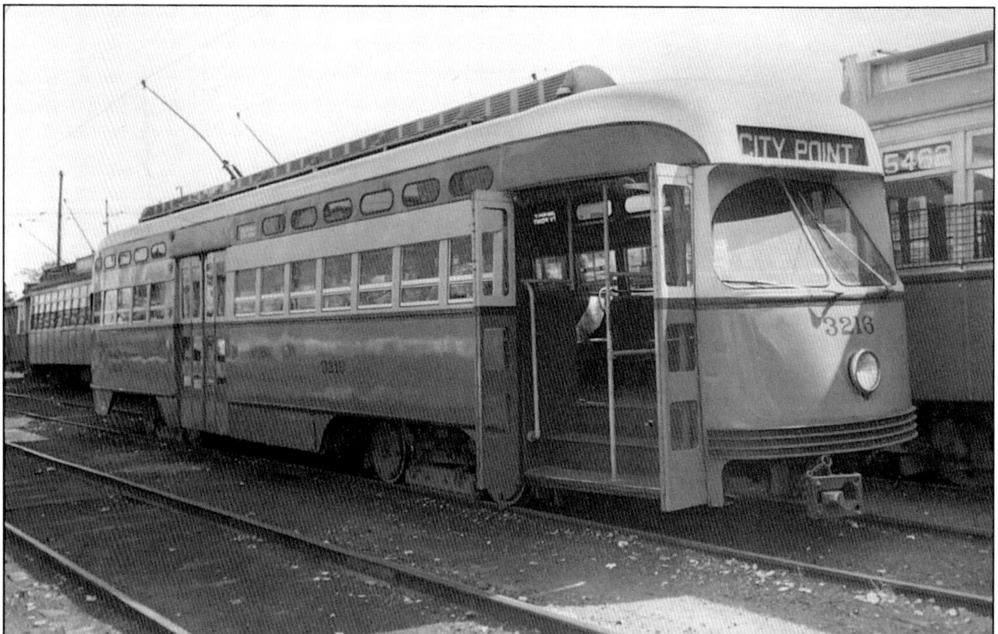


In April 1946, South Boston transit riders were delighted when a fleet of new PCC-type cars were placed in operation on the routes from City Point to the North Station and the Dudley Street Station. Built by the Pullman Company at its plant in Worcester, these popular cars were quiet, fast, and comfortable. They were assigned to Cambridge when buses took over in South Boston in 1953. (Courtesy of Frank Cheney.)

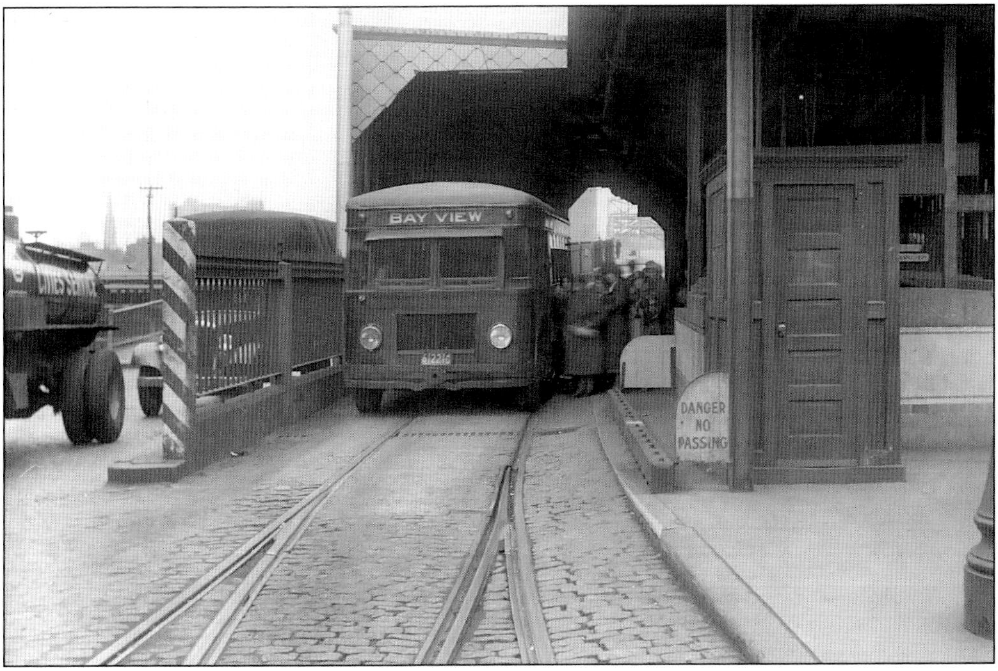


In December 1917, the Dorchester Tunnel (the Red Line) was extended to Broadway Station and a surface level transfer station opened at Broadway and Dorchester Avenue, above the Broadway Tunnel Station. This busy station offered free, sheltered transfer between the subway trains, the Broadway trolleys, and the Bay View buses. In this 1935 scene, a crowd boards a bus for Bay View. (Courtesy of Frank Cheney.)

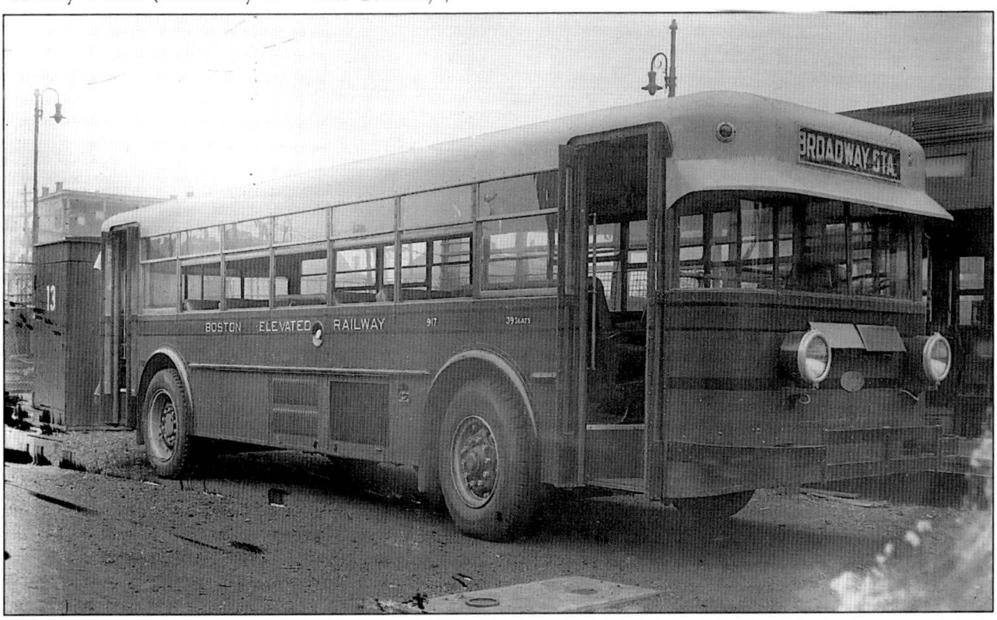


Motor buses first appeared in South Boston when they replaced trolley cars on the Bay View Line in January 1929. The buses were built by the Twin Coach Company of Kent, Ohio, and were powered by two four-cylinder engines mounted under seats in the center of the bus. This bus, No. 917, is bright orange with a gray roof. (Courtesy of Frank Cheney.)

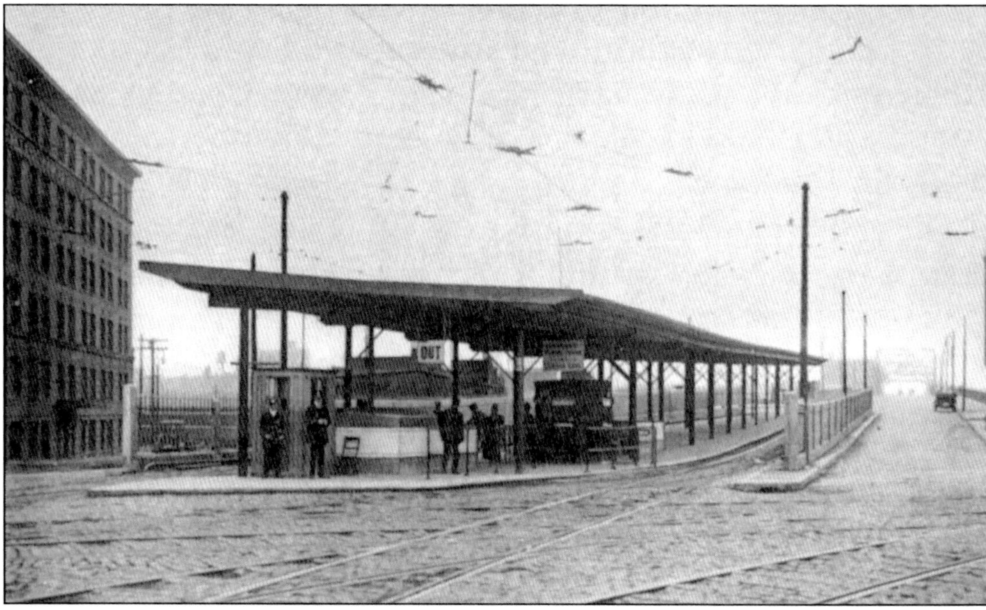


The original Broadway Station on the Dorchester Tunnel Line (the Red Line) was a large kiosk-type transfer station that provided shelter for riders transferring to buses bound for City Point, Bay View, or Downtown Boston. When it was built in 1918, the station was at the foot of the Broadway Bridge at Dorchester Avenue.

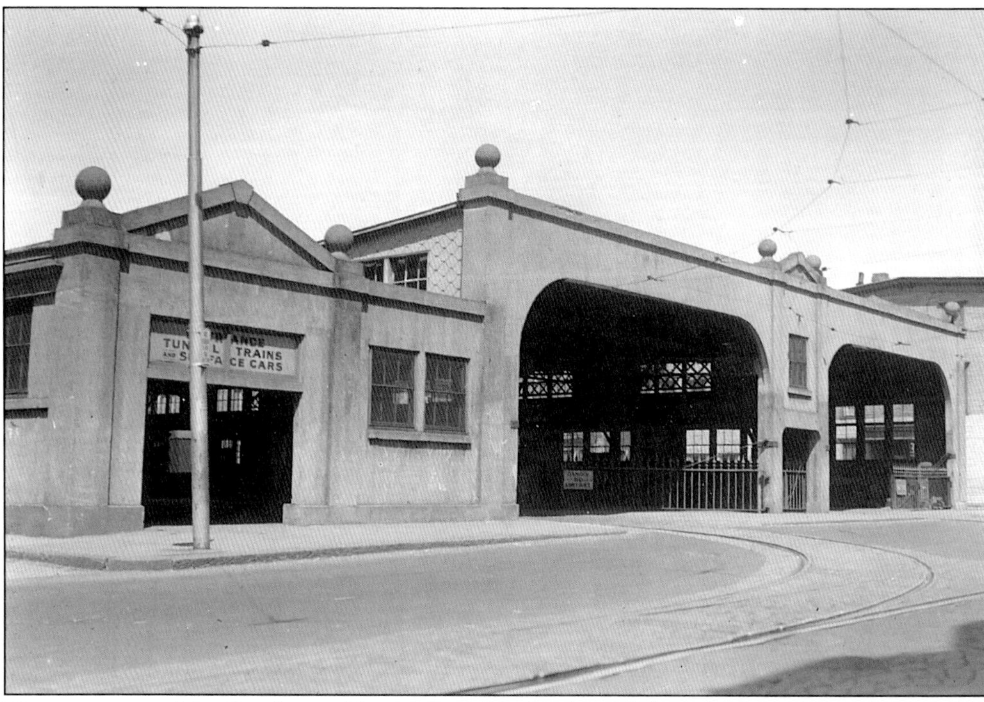


The extension of the Dorchester Tunnel Line (the Red Line) from the Broadway Station under Dorchester Avenue to Andrew Square was completed in June 1918. It included the attractive Andrew Square Station, where riders transferred to streetcars that took them to City Point and Dudley Street, as well as various points in Dorchester. (Courtesy of Frank Cheney.)

# *Four*

# Firefighting in South Boston

The first fire engine in South Boston was the Mezeppa 17, a Hunneman-built engine from Roxbury. It was placed in a firehouse on West Broadway next to the Hawes School, which is now the parking lot between the Mount Washington Savings Bank and BankBoston. Under the charge of Capt. Alpheus Stetson, the engine reputedly "did excellent service" for many years and was "manned by a gallant and courageous body of firemen, always ready for action." A new firehouse was built in 1829, and a new engine was provided. By the mid-19th century, South Boston had Perkins No. 16 on Dorchester Street; the S.R. Spinney, Steam Fire Engine No. 2 on East Fourth Street; the Walter E. Hawes, Steam Fire Engine No. 15 on Fourth Street; the Lawrence Hose Carriage No. 9 on B Street; the Bradlee Hose Carriage No. 10 on Dorchester Street; and the Hancock Hook and Ladder No. 5 on Fourth Street.

By the beginning of the 20th century, South Boston had numerous fire and hose houses, among them Combination Wagon 2 at 715 East Fourth Street, Chemical Company 8 at 116 B Street, Engine Company 15 at 109 Dorchester Avenue, Engine Company 2 at 863 East Fourth Street, Engine Company 38 and 39 at 344 Congress Street, Engine Company 1 at 119 Dorchester Street, Ladder Company 5 at 456 West Fourth Street, Engine Company 43 and Combination Ladder 3 at 5 Boston Street, and Ladder Company 18 at 9 Pittsburgh Street. Professional firemen staffed these firehouses; prior to 1872, the departments were supported by numerous volunteers, whose commitment echoed that of St. Florian, their patron saint. Today, South Boston is served by Engine Company 39 and Ladder Company 18, located in a modern firehouse built in 1977 at 272 D Street, and Engine Company 2 and Ladder Company 19 in a firehouse built in 1932 at 700 East Fourth Street.

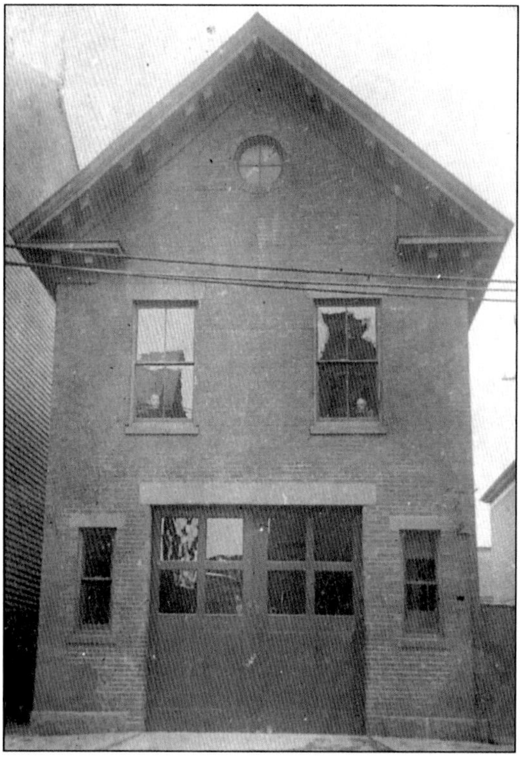

S.R. Spinney Hand Engine 14 was built in 1857 at 715 East Fourth Street. It was later occupied by Engine Company 2, Combination Wagon 2, and then by Ladder Company 19. This simple red brick firehouse was used until 1932. Notice the firemen sitting in both windows on the second floor. Today, the former firehouse is used as the Thomas J. Fitzgerald Post 561 Veterans of Foreign Wars. (Courtesy of William F. Noonan.)

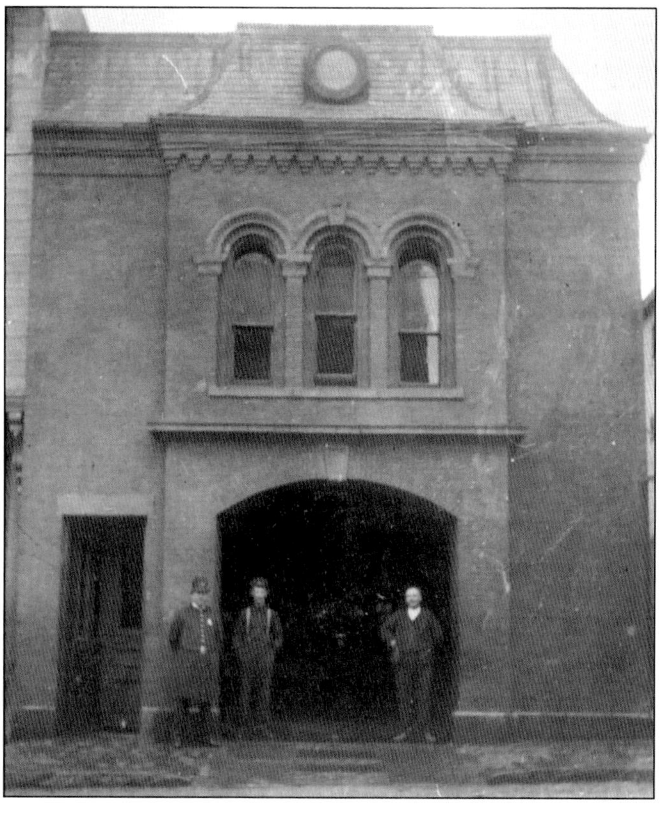

Lawrence Hose Company 9 and Chemical Company 8 was a Romanesque brick firehouse built in 1860 at 116 B Street on the corner of Athens Street. The hose house had a carriage built by Brigham, Mitchell, & Company that was used until 1917; the hose house is now Altec Plastics Inc. Standing outside are a policeman and two firemen (Courtesy of William F. Noonan.)

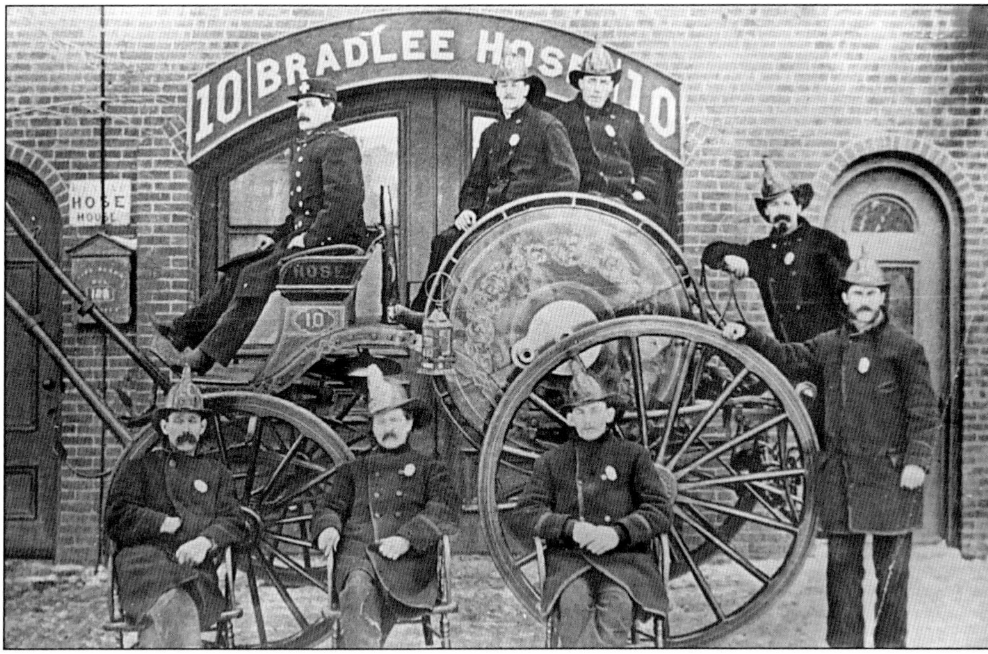


Members of Bradlee Hose 10 at 330 Dorchester Street pose around Hose 10 *c.* 1880. Built in 1861 just east of Washington Village (now known as Andrew Square), the hose house had a carriage built by the Amoskeag Manufacturing Company with 1,000 feet of 2.5-inch hose. The hose house was used until 1893. (Courtesy of William F. Noonan.)

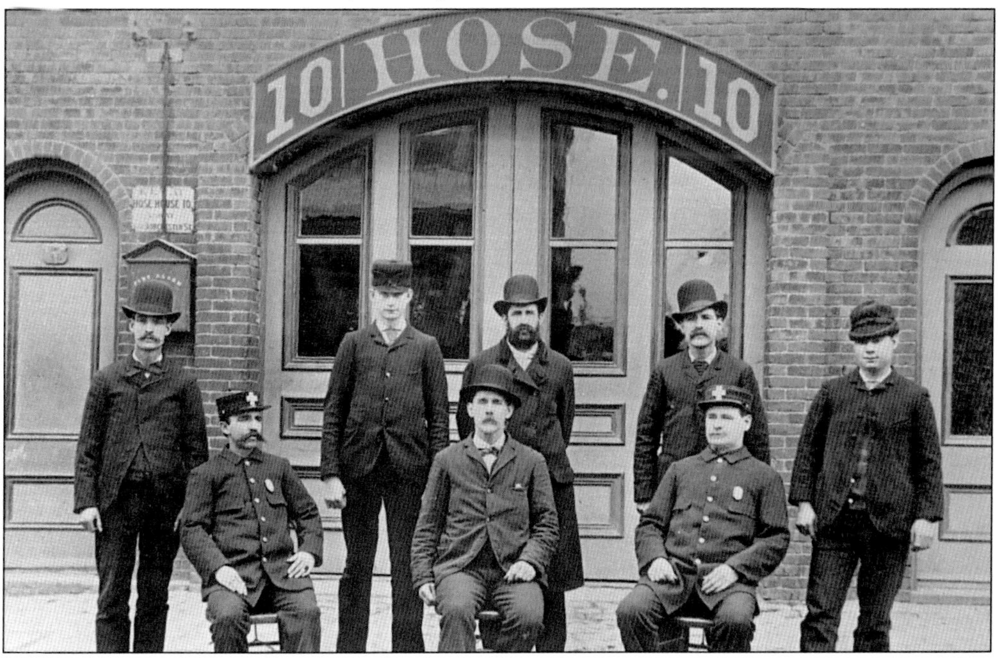


Members of Hose Company 10 pose in front of the fire doors, *c.* 1890. Hose wagons were first introduced in 1853; by the following year, they had demonstrated their superiority over hose carriages and a large number were added to the fire department. Today, the former hose house is the headquarters of Teamsters Local No. 82. (Courtesy of William F. Noonan.)

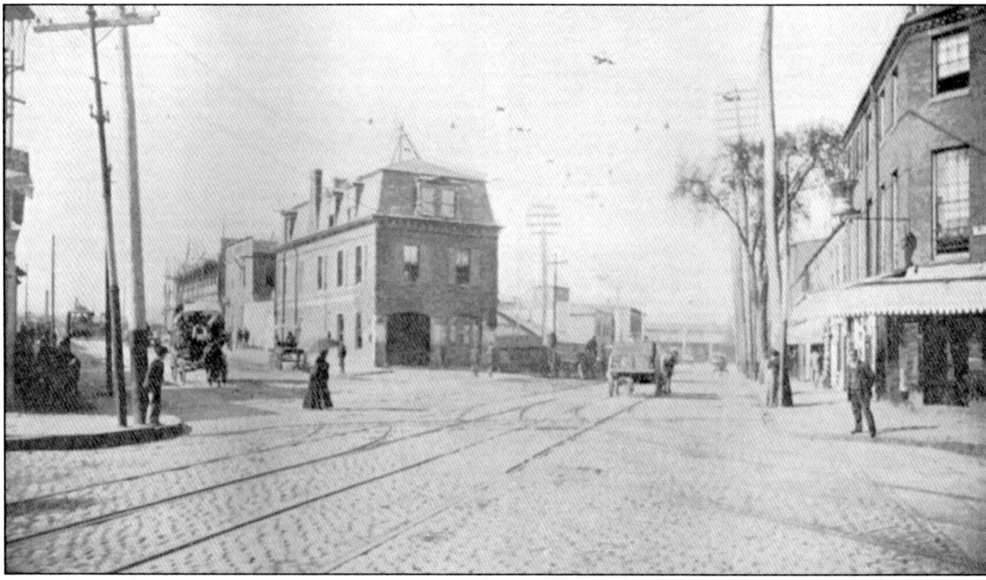

Engine Company 15 was built in 1872 at the junction of West Broadway, A Street, and the Broadway Bridge. On the right at the corner of West Broadway and A Street is a brick commercial block, with a superb gold-leaf mortar and pestle advertising an apothecary shop. On the left adjacent to the Broadway Bridge is a building under construction. Engine Company 15 was closed in 1954; the engine house was later demolished.

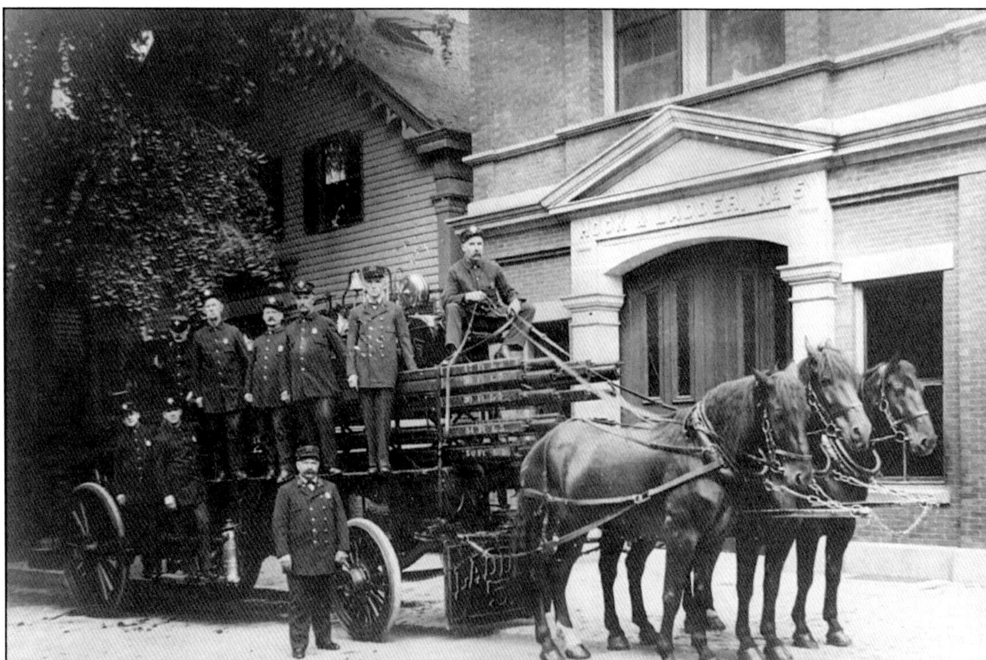

Members of Hook and Ladder Company 5 pose in front of the firehouse in 1910. The building was constructed in 1869 at 456 West Fourth Street, directly behind Engine Company 1, and was used as a firehouse until 1917. Today, it is the headquarters of the Dorchester Heights National Park Service. (Courtesy of William F. Noonan.)

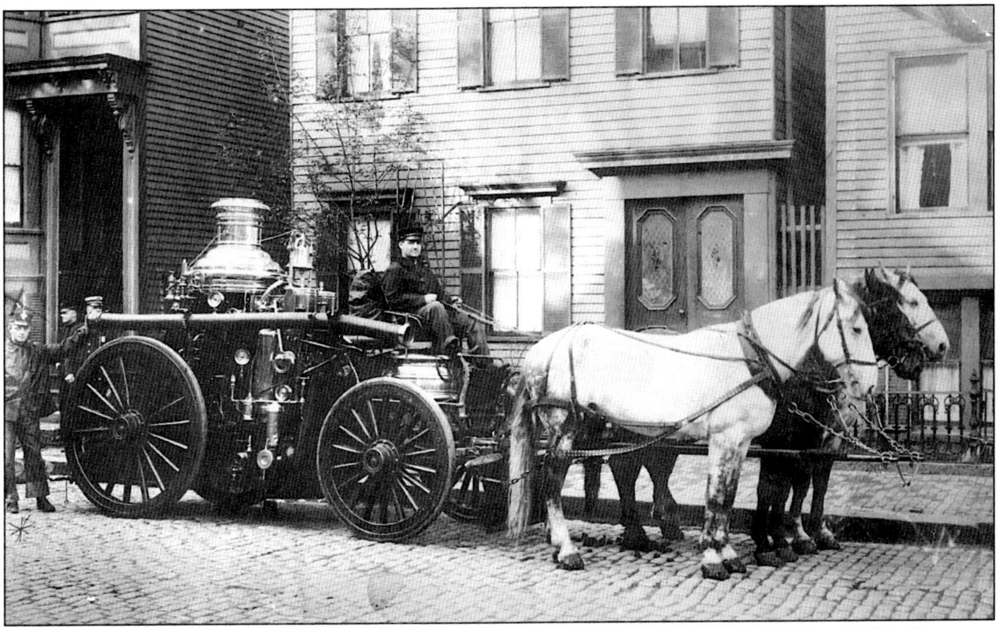

Firefighter Edward J. Twomey poses on Engine Company 2 with three horses in 1904. Twomey began as a Boston firefighter in 1902 and retired in 1944. (Courtesy of Paul A. Christian.)

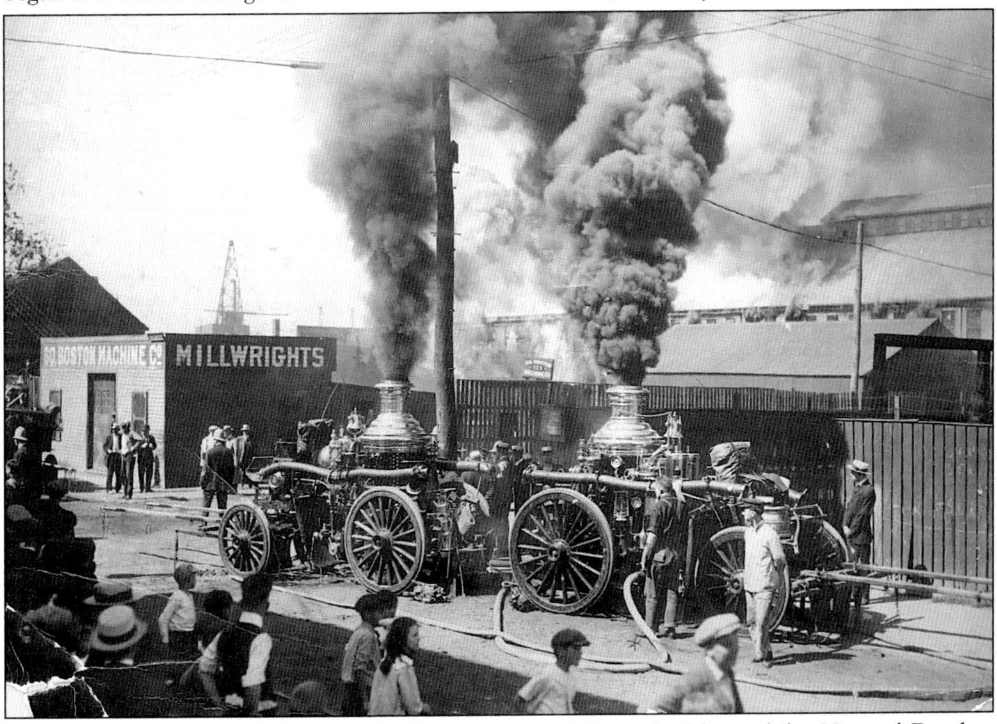


On June 12, 1913, fire destroyed the four-story wood-frame building of the Howard Dustless Duster Company at 566–588 East First Street. The fire was reported at 1:26 p.m. and four alarms were sounded. Fires always seem to attract people of all ages, who watch the spectacle intently, as the firefighters operate the steam engines that appear to belch as much smoke as the fire does. (Courtesy of Paul A. Christian.)

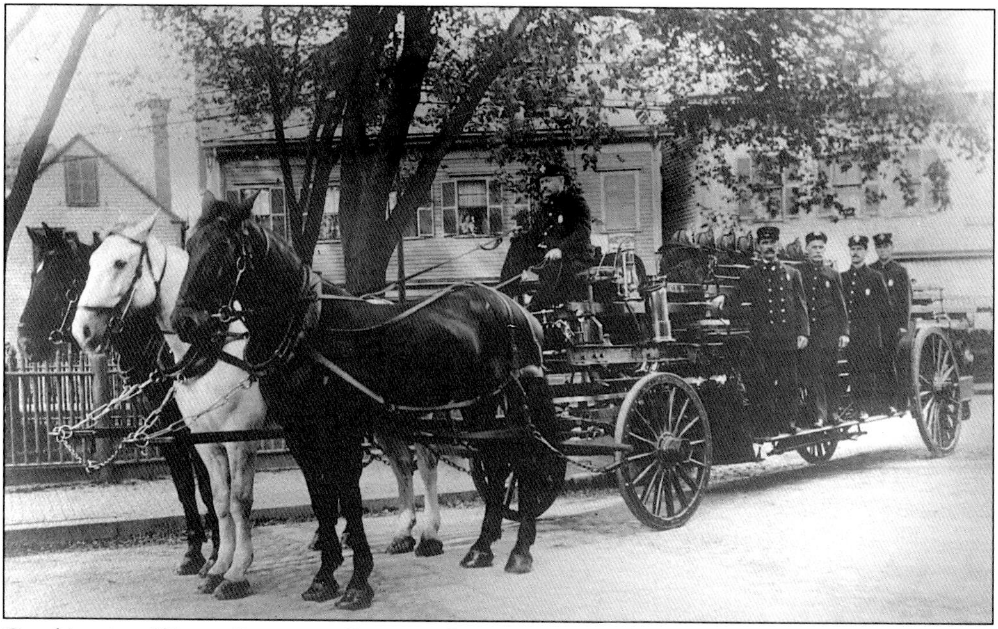

Combination Wagon 2 poses at Emerson Street, opposite the triangular green in front of the South Boston School of Art, bounded by Emerson and East Fourth Streets. The houses in the background are, from the left to right, 204, 206–208, and 212 (now Dudley's Tavern) Emerson Street. (Courtesy of William F. Noonan.)

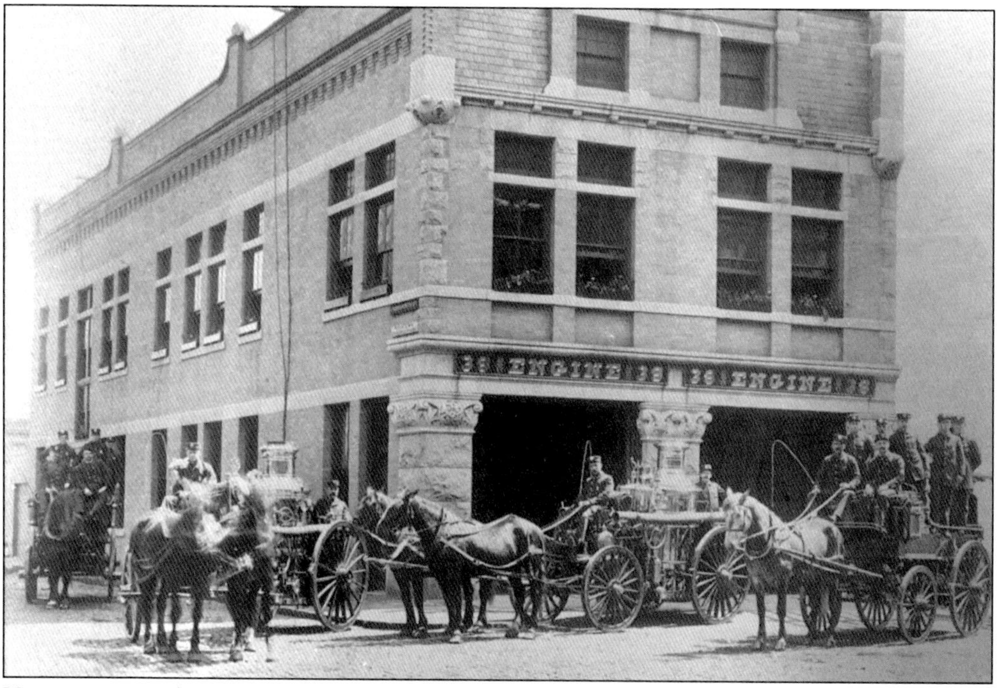


Hose wagons and steamers pose in front of Engine Companies 38 and 39 at 344 Congress Street c. 1905. Designed by city architect Edmund March Wheelwright and built in 1892, the firehouse later housed Ladder Company 18, until it was closed in 1977. Today, the building is used as the headquarters of the Boston Fire Museum. (Courtesy of William F. Noonan.)

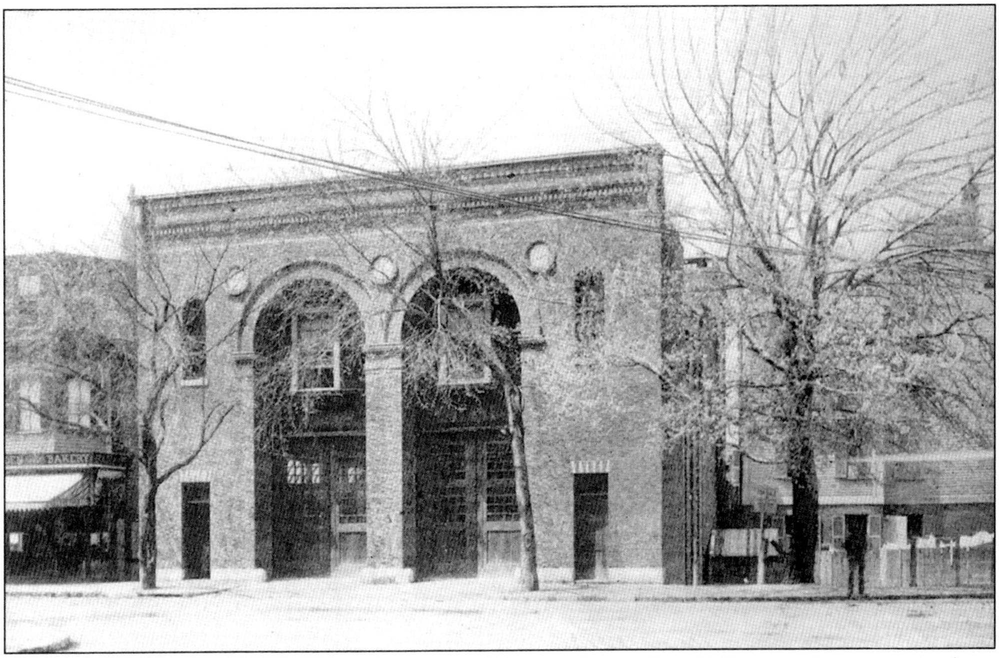


Engine Company 43 and Ladder Company 20 were located at 5 Boston Street in Andrew Square. Designed by city architect Edmund March Wheelwright and built in 1892, it had impressive Romanesque arches with fire doors on the first floor. This structure was the first engine house built for the city that had a system of artificial ventilation. Engine Company 43 was closed in 1961.

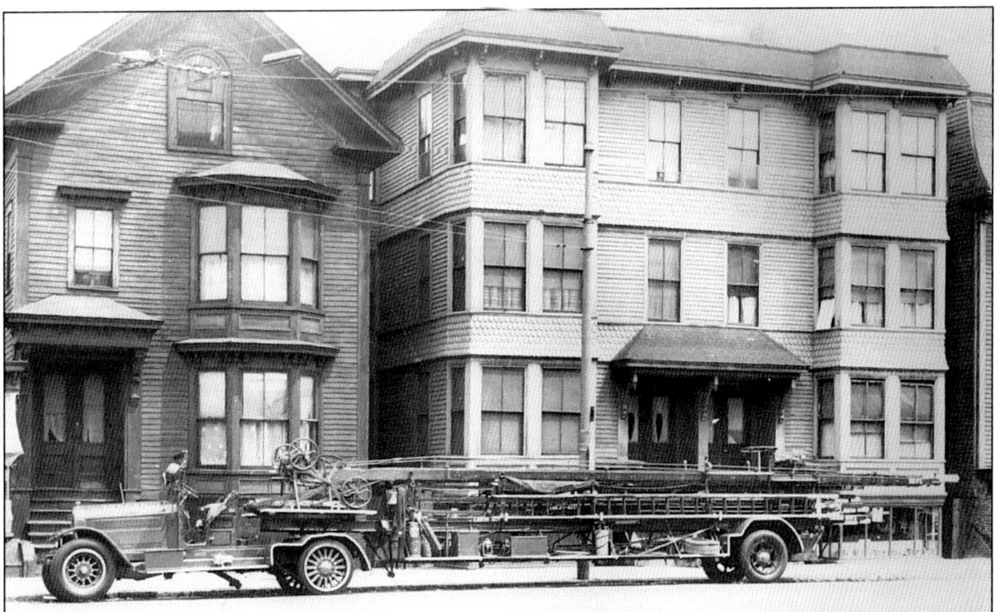

Ladder Company 20 is parked on Dorchester Avenue in Andrew Square c. 1945. The double three-decker on the right is at 602–604 Dorchester Avenue. The house on the left, now demolished, is currently the site of the W.T. Burke Building at the corner of Dorchester Avenue and Preble Street. (Courtesy of William F. Noonan.)

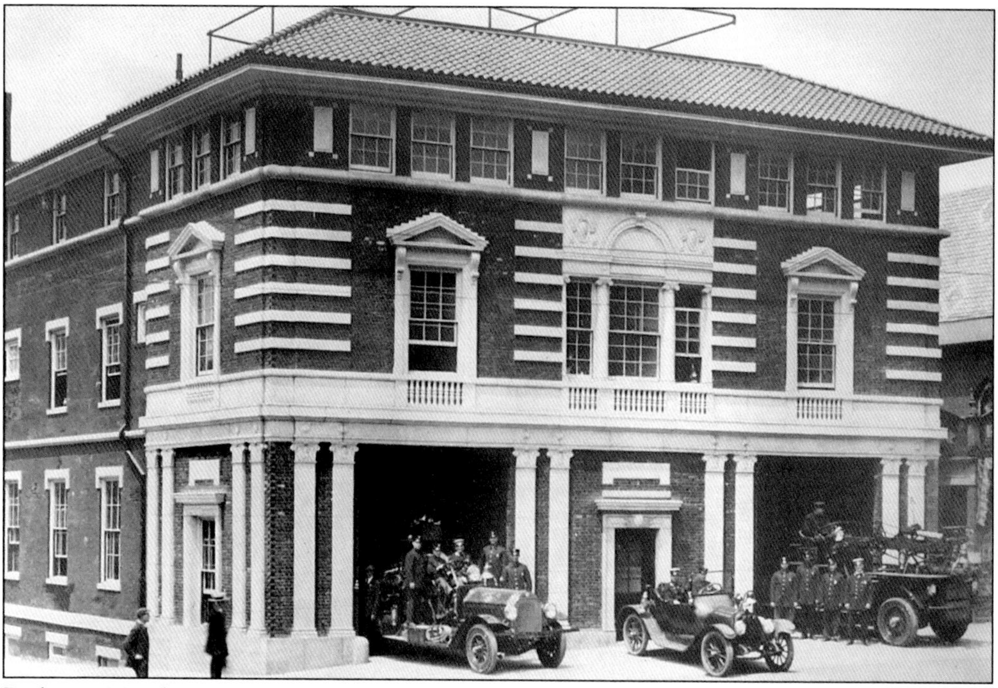

Built in 1868, the municipal courthouse building at 119 Dorchester Street was remodeled with new windows and a Spanish tile roof in 1917. At that time, fire doors were placed on either side of the entrance to Engine Company 1 and Ladder Company 5. Notice the district chief's car parked in the center, flanked by the engine and ladder truck. (Courtesy of the Boston Fire Department.)

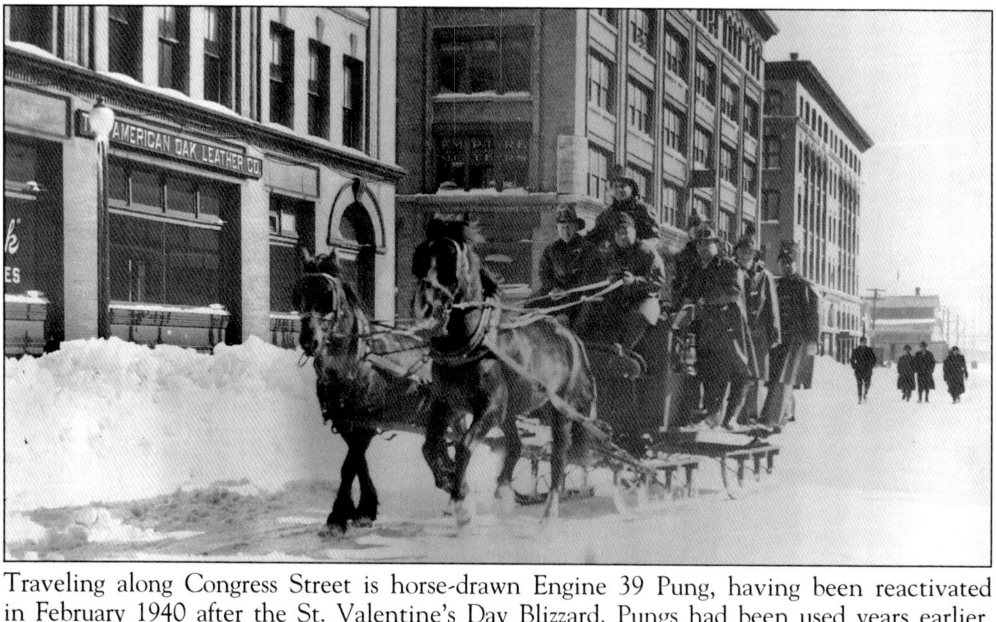


Traveling along Congress Street is horse-drawn Engine 39 Pung, having been reactivated in February 1940 after the St. Valentine's Day Blizzard. Pungs had been used years earlier, when the snow on Boston's streets was rolled rather than plowed. Notice the pedestrians walking in the center of Congress Street since the sidewalks are not shoveled. (Courtesy of the Boston Fire Department.)

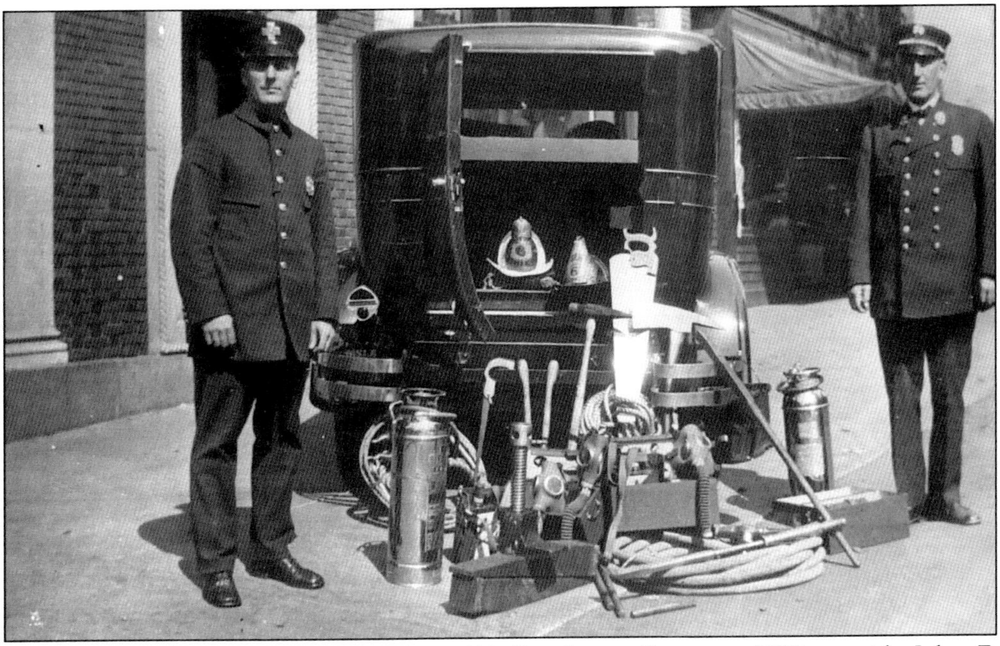

Standing outside Engine Company 1 at 119 Dorchester Street c. 1932 are aide John F. Howard, left, and Michael J. Teehan, chief of District 6. Between them are the chief's car its vast contents. On the right, the canvas awning shades O'Brien's Funeral Parlor, founded in 1910 by John and Chrisella O'Brien; it is now the site of a parking lot. (Courtesy of William F. Noonan.)

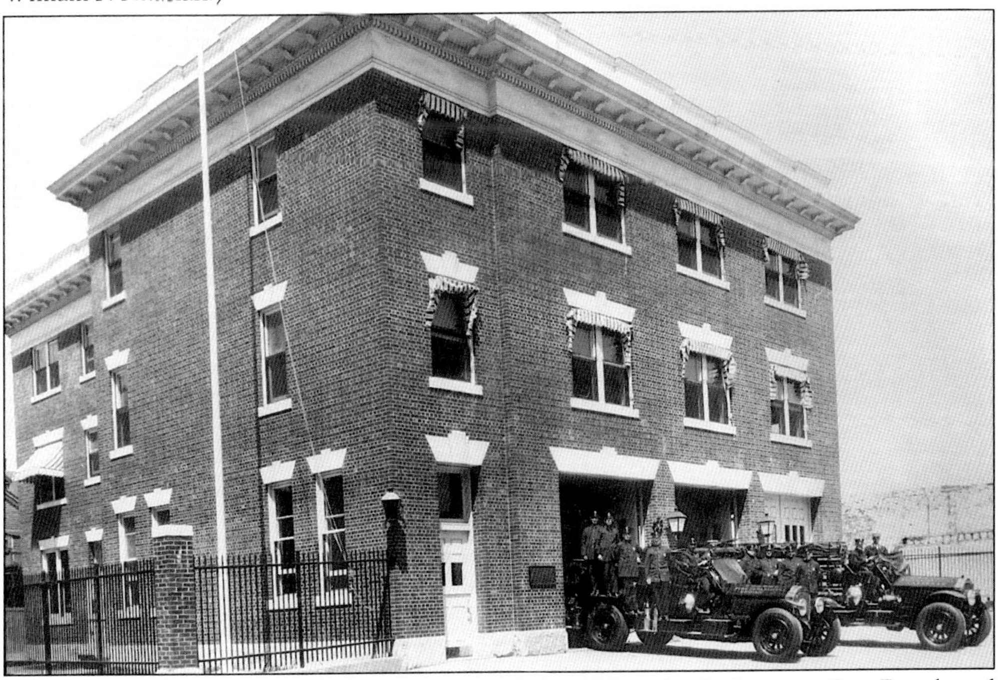

Firefighters pose on Engine 2 and Ladder 19 in July 1932 at the firehouse at East Fourth and K Streets. This impressive Neo-Georgian firehouse also has a four-story drill tower in the rear, where new recruits trained. (Courtesy of William F. Noonan.)

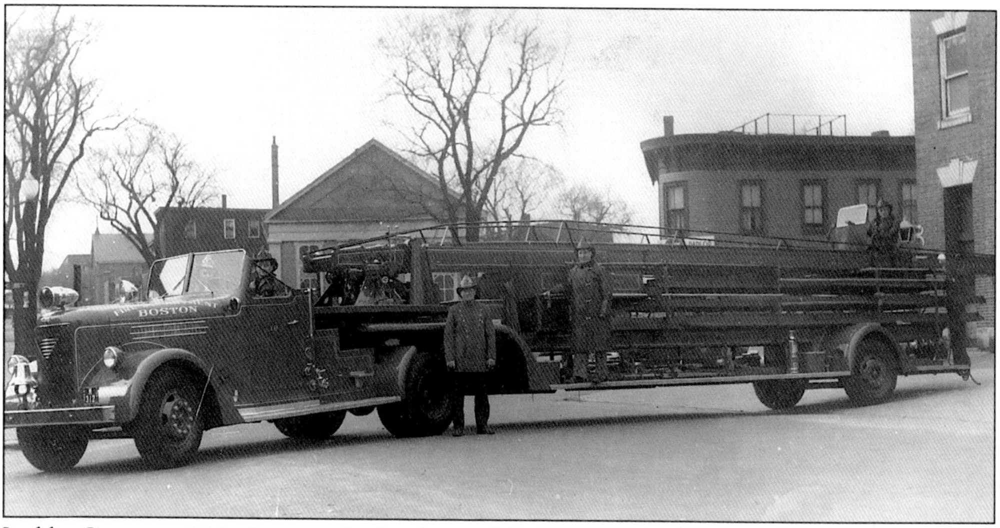


Ladder Company 19 is photographed in front of the firehouse at the corner of East Fourth and K Streets in 1950. Seen here, from left to right, are Lt. Peter Palmieri, Jim Shea, Lt. Jerry Coffey, Paul McCarthy, and George Wade. The pediment of the South Boston School of Art, formerly the Hawes Congregational Church—built in 1833 and named in memory of Mr. John Hawes (1741–1829)—can be seen at the triangle of East Fourth and Emerson Streets. (Courtesy of William F. Noonan.)

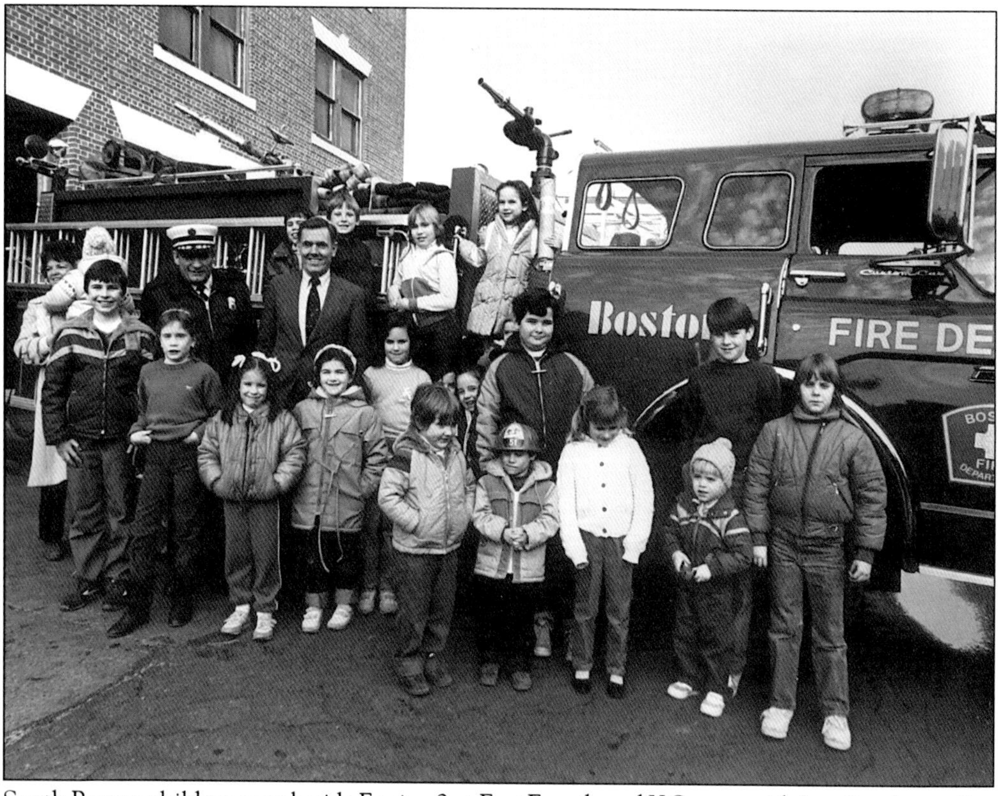


South Boston children pose beside Engine 2 at East Fourth and K Streets with Leo Stapleton, fire commissioner, and Raymond L. Flynn, mayor of Boston. (Courtesy of William F. Noonan.)

*Five*

# The South Boston Library

When the South Boston Branch Library was established in 1872 under the direction of librarian Justin Winsor (1831–1897), it became the second branch library in the United States. The branch was originally located in the South Boston Savings Bank Building at 372 West Broadway on the corner of E Street. There, it maintained a reading room with a few thousand books, many of them from the former Mattapan Literary Association, a young men's organization that was founded in South Boston in 1848 "for mutual improvement of its members in literary accomplishments." The circulating library proved itself "very successful from the start and had an annual circulation in excess of 100,000 volumes per year." The success of the branch library was obvious for within three decades, another branch was opened at Andrew Square in 1901, followed by a third branch at 615 East Broadway near I Street in 1906.

The branch library, which "has played a vital role in the intellectual, cultural and social life of the community since it first opened in 1872" remained at West Broadway and E Streets until 1950, when it was relocated to 386–388 West Broadway; a fire caused its closing in 1957. The city had begun a new modern library on the site of the Frederick W. Lincoln School on East Broadway, which was designed by the noted architectural firm of Shepley, Bulfinch, Abbot, and Richardson. This new library, the first in South Boston expressly designed to be library, "won an award for its unique design and idea planning for the physically handicapped." In this modern library, perennially favorite activities, such as children's storytelling, movies, lectures, and the popular Artist of the Month are held.

South Boston Branch librarians (with the year of their appointment) include Anna Keen (1872), Alice Bragdon (1875), N. Josephine Bullard (1883), Alice Robinson (1902), Mary Minton (1911), M. Florence Cufflin (1917), Mary Harris (1937), Mary Hackett (1943), Irene Tuttle (1948), Marjorie Gibbons (1965), Gaynell Mathson (1975), Toby Paff (1978), Helen Maniadis (1980), and Mary Linn (1997).

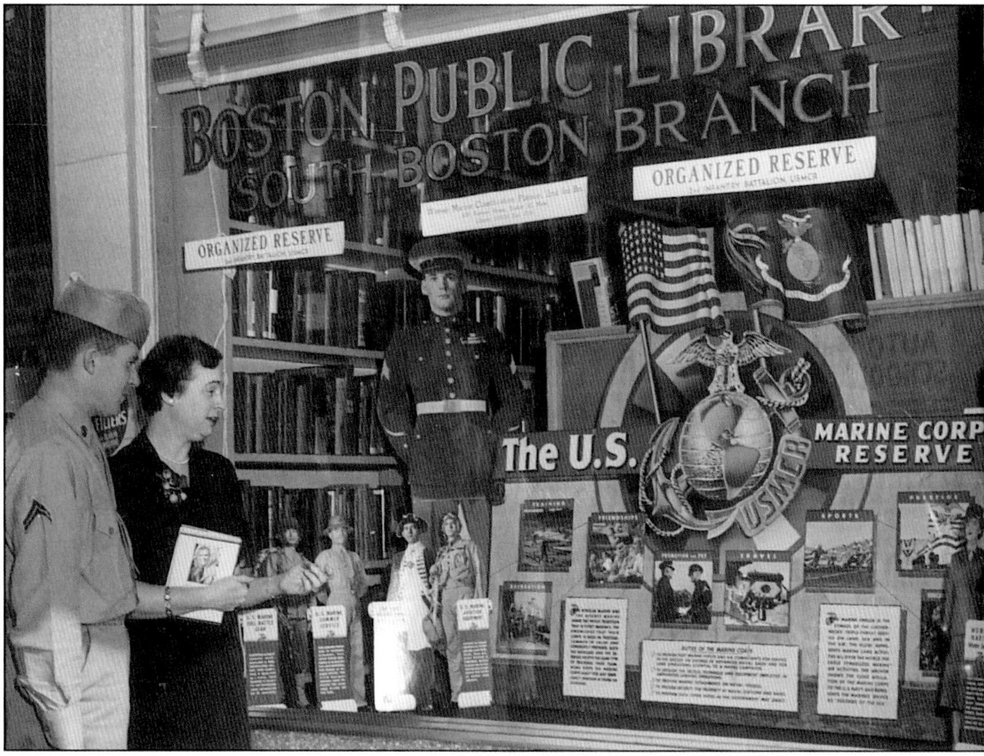


At the South Boston Branch Library in 1952, Irene Tuttle, branch librarian from 1948 to 1965, proudly shows a reservist soldier the window exhibit on the U.S. Marine Corp Reserve. (Courtesy of the Boston Public Library.)

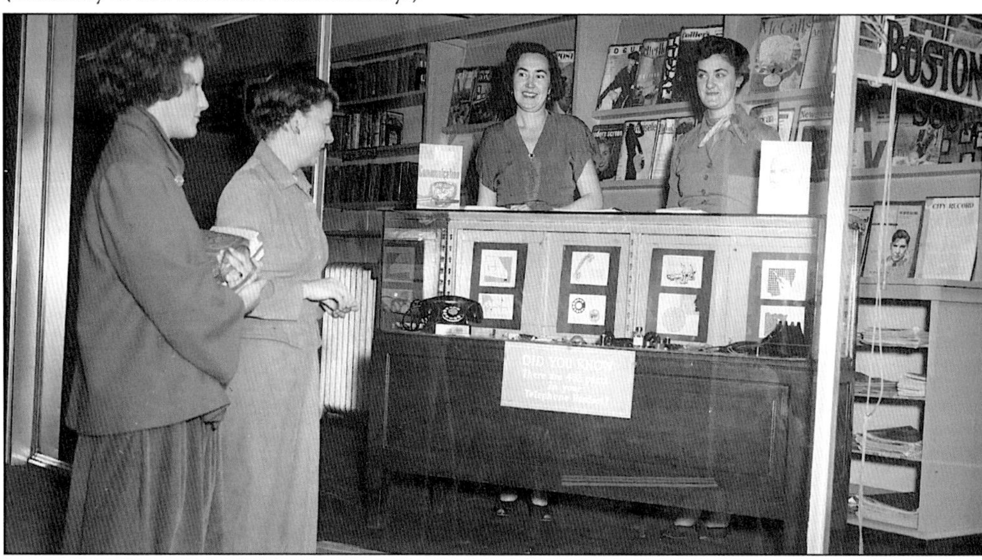


At the South Boston Branch Library in 1953, Lillian Gallagher, center, and Veronica Yotts smile at library patrons admiring a window exhibit on the workings of the telephone. As the sign says, "Did you know there are 433 parts in your telephone headset?" Notice on the right of the shelf the sketch of telephone inventor Alexander Graham Bell (1847–1922), an advocate for education of the deaf. (Courtesy of the Boston Public Library.)

Storytelling has always been an important part of the children's activities at the library. Mr. Conway, a noted storyteller, reads to a young patron *c.* 1950. (Courtesy of the Boston Public Library.)

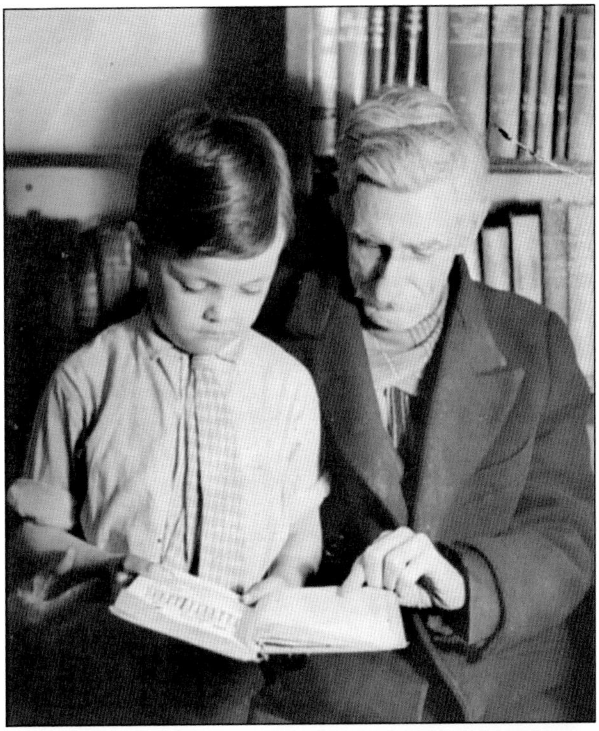

Extremely well-dressed members of the Imagination Club pose at the South Boston Branch Library in 1960. Seen here, from left to right, are Edward Sloane, Donna Garvey, Martin Canavan, and Linda Munsie. (Courtesy of the Boston Public Library.)

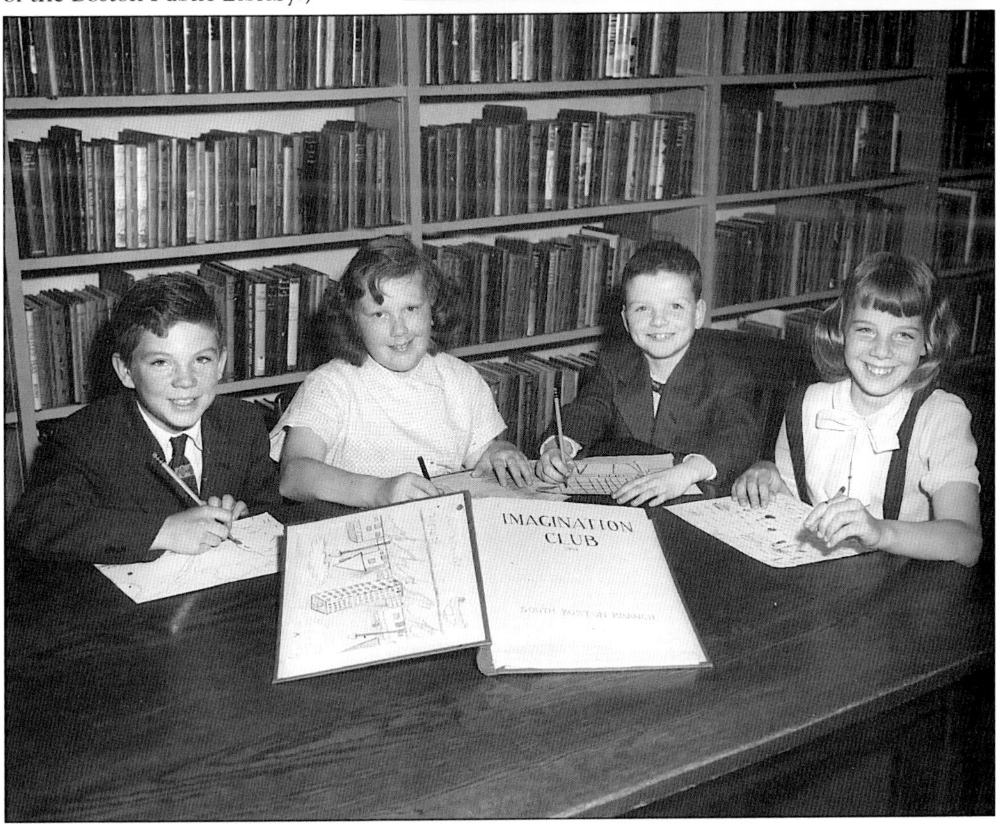

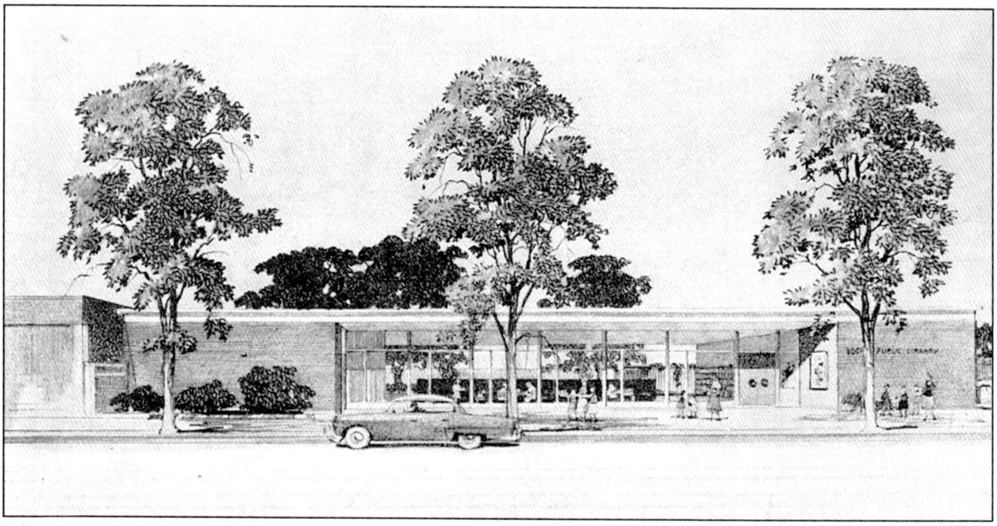

The present South Boston Branch Library, with its award-winning design by the Boston architectural firm of Shepley, Bulfinch, Richardson, and Abbot, was dedicated on October 31, 1957 by John B. Hynes, mayor of Boston; Edwin Carnham, president of the library's Board of Trustees; and Milton Lord, director of the library. The modern library was built of "cinder blocks, brick, steel and acoustic plastic" by the Columbia Construction Company. (Courtesy of the Boston Public Library.)

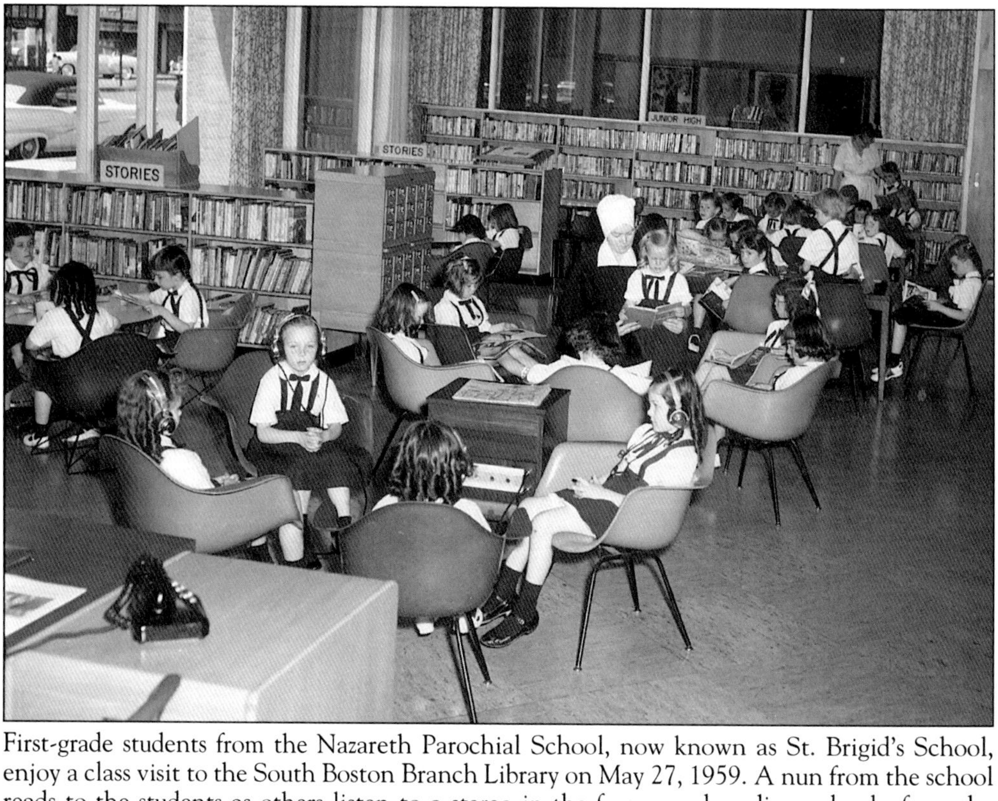


First-grade students from the Nazareth Parochial School, now known as St. Brigid's School, enjoy a class visit to the South Boston Branch Library on May 27, 1959. A nun from the school reads to the students as others listen to a stereo in the foreground or discuss books from the library collection. (Courtesy of the Boston Public Library.)

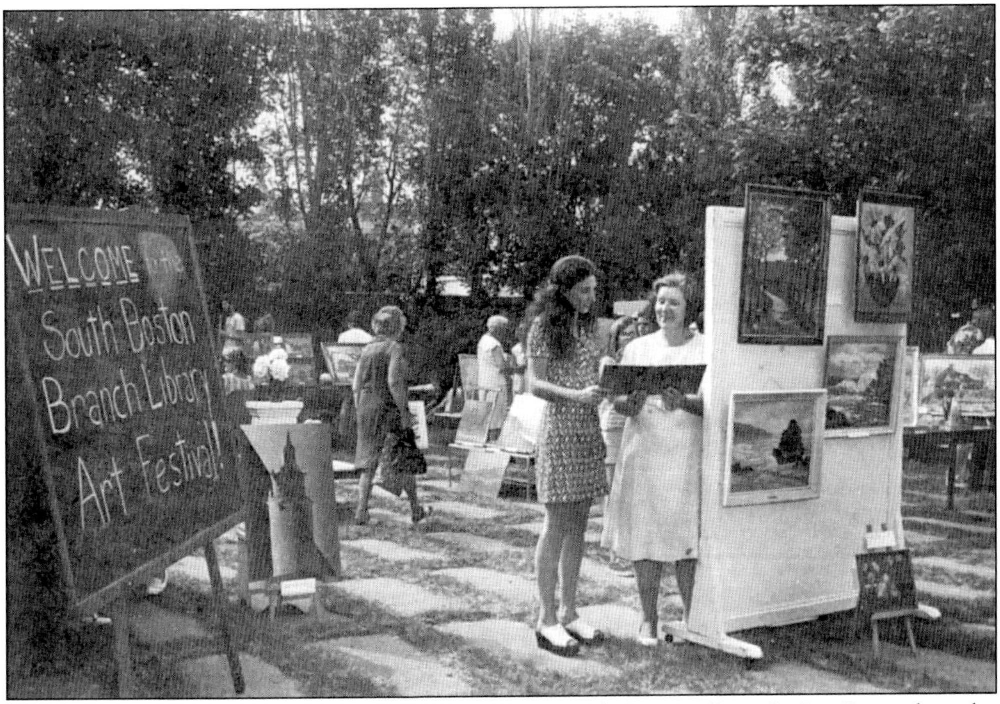


Admiring a painting by a local artist at the 1972 South Boston Branch Art Festival in the library's garden are Jayne Friedman, young adults' librarian, and Marjorie M. Gibbons, South Boston Branch librarian from 1965 to 1975. (Courtesy of the Boston Public Library.)

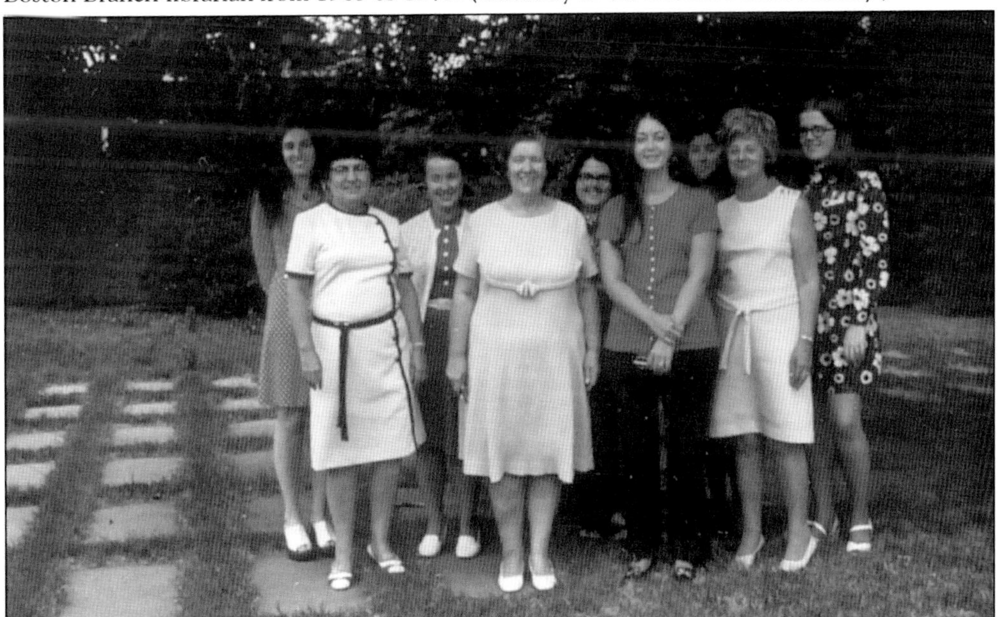

Members of the staff of the South Boston Branch Library pose in the garden in 1972. Seen here, from left to right, are Jayne Friedman, Mary Gifford, Paula Fleming, branch librarian Marjorie Gibbons, Pauline Morgan, Kris Bramer Briggs, Barbara Wicker, Jennie Kielczewski, and Dorothy Barnett Keller. (Courtesy of the Boston Public Library.)

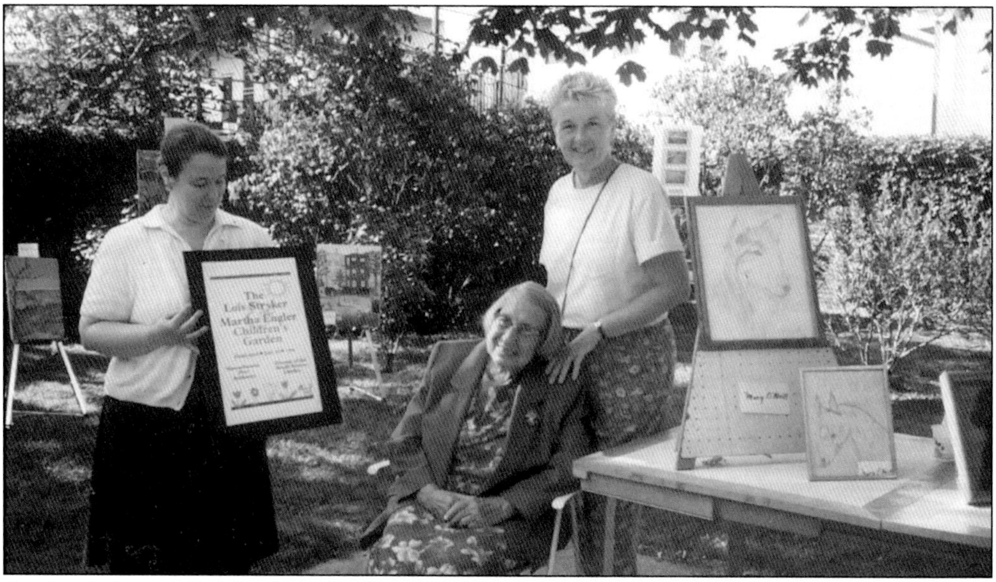


At the dedication of the Lois Stryker-Martha Engler Children's Garden in August 1998 are, from left to right, Paula Fleming, holding a citation, Martha Engler, and Eleanor Engle, a former library aide. The Children's Garden was dedicated to Martha Engler, a retired children's librarian at the Boston Public Library, and the late Lois Stryker, a member of the Citywide Friends of the Library and a former president of the Friends of the South Boston Branch Library. (Courtesy of the Boston Public Library.)

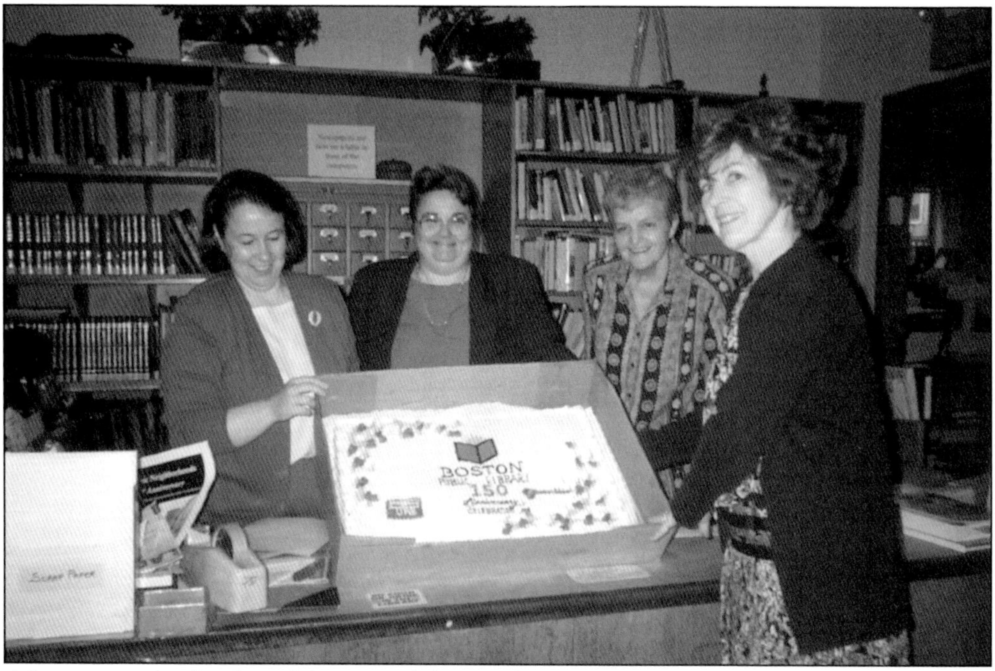


Admiring a cake for the celebration of the 150th anniversary of the founding of the Boston Public Library in May 1999 are, from left to right, Paula Fleming, children's librarian; Elaine Sullivan; Katherine Roche; and Mary Linn, branch librarian since 1997 at the South Boston Branch Library. (Courtesy of the Boston Public Library.)

## *Six*

# The Perkins School for the Blind

The Perkins Institution and Massachusetts Asylum for the Blind, initially known as the New England Asylum for the Blind, was established in 1829 to educate the blind, following the proposal of Dr. John D. Fisher, who succeeded in interesting others in his plans. That year, Dr. Samuel Gridley Howe traveled to Europe, where for three years he gathered information on schools for the blind. He returned in 1832, accompanied by Mr. Trencheri, a blind teacher, and John Pringle, a blind mechanic—both of whom were to educate the students in various aspects of the school where "books with raised letters were printed for their use, and in six months they were able to read correctly with their fingers the volumes that had been prepared." Exhibitions ensued and brought in much needed revenue to expand the school, which eventually was supported by Massachusetts, Connecticut, New Hampshire, and Vermont through state appropriations.

Howe, later assisted by his son-in-law Michael Anagnos, played a vitally important role in supporting the Perkins School: through the solicitation of the two men, the school was endowed by Thomas H. Perkins, the wealthy Boston merchant for whom the institution was named. Upon the death of Howe in 1874, the school lost a true supporter. In the late 19th century, the school developed a safe and nurturing environment, which enabled the blind to learn and to acquire the skills necessary to become financially self-sufficient. It was said in 1889 that "if as much were done in the next half century as in the last, blindness will almost cease to be a calamity."

In 1912, the school moved to a larger campus in Watertown, where it still offers a day and residential school, as well as workshops for the blind. The traditions of excellence established by Howe and Fisher are still maintained today and can be traced to the crest of East Broadway in South Boston, where it all began in 1839.

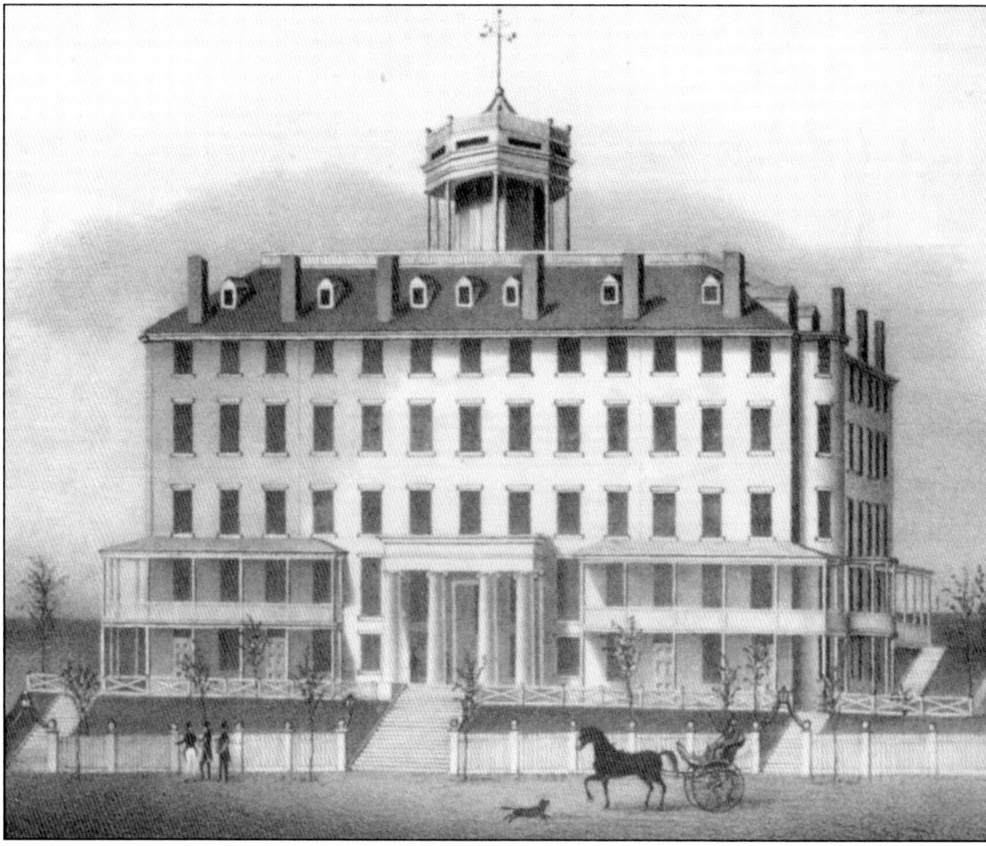

The Perkins School for the Blind relocated from Pearl Street to the former Mount Washington House in 1839. An impressive building with every room having an ocean view, the new location was high on a slope overlooking East Broadway between H and G Streets. The site currently houses the South Boston Municipal Court. The school relocated to Watertown in 1912.

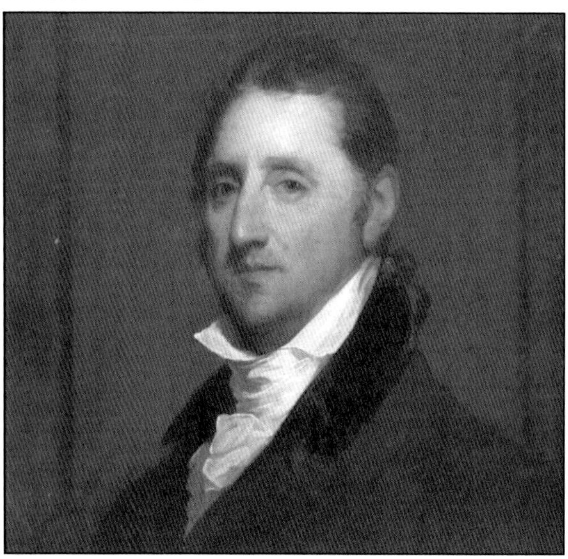

Col. Thomas Handasyd Perkins (1754–1854) was a wealthy China trade merchant in the firm of J. & T.H. Perkins and Company, who gave his mansion on Pearl Street in Boston to be the first site of the Perkins School for the Blind in 1833. His generosity allowed the school to begin its mission in educating the blind, and as a token of esteem, the trustees of the school named it in his honor. (Courtesy of the Boston Athenaeum.)

Dr. Samuel Gridley Howe (1801–1876), with his associate Dr. John Fisher, was a pioneer in the education of the blind. Howe was well known to Bostonians for his efforts on behalf of the independence of Greece and his subsequent European adventures. With Fisher and Edward Brooks, Howe was sent abroad by the trustees of the school in 1829 to study the work of teaching the blind.

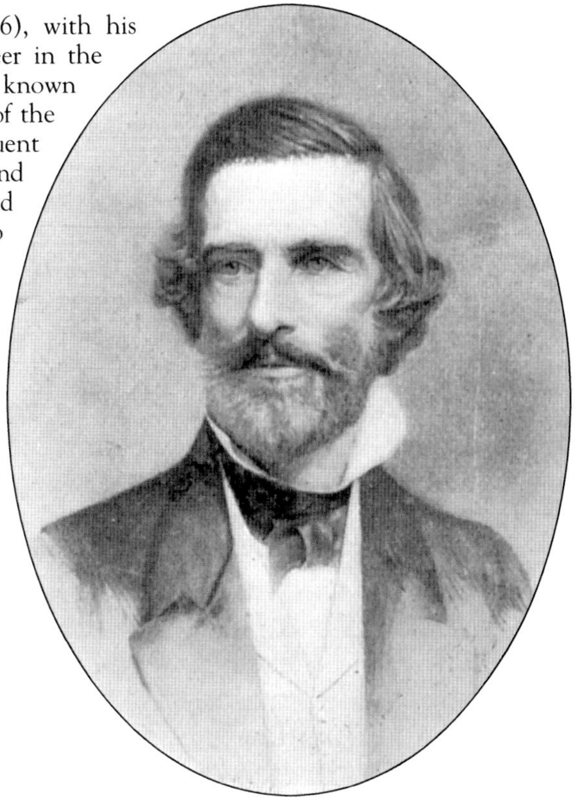

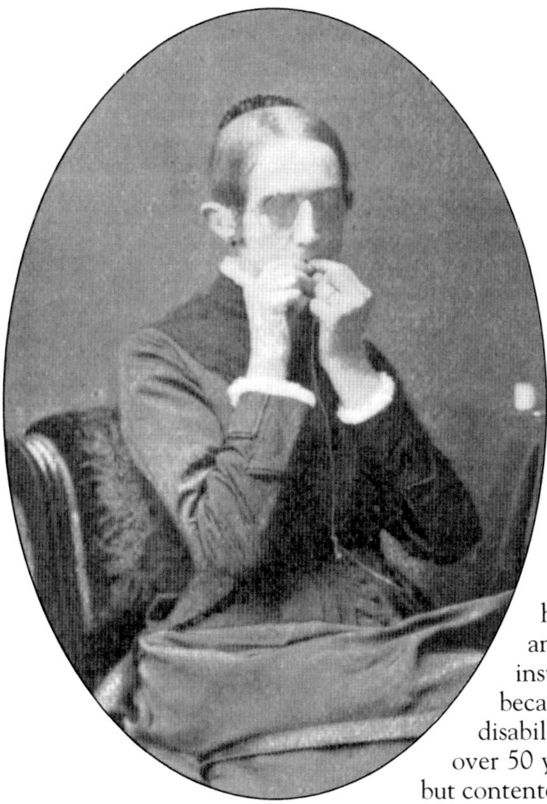

Laura Dewey Bridgeman (1829–1889), who was blind, deaf, and mute, was brought to the Perkins School from Hanover, New Hampshire, by Dr. Samuel Gridley Howe in 1837. Hers was a success story in that "her intellectual development has encouraged multitudes of teachers, and favored the foundation of twenty-seven institutions for the blind in this country." She became a skillful teacher of others with the same disabilities as her own and lived at the school for over 50 years, where she was "not only unrepining, but contented and happy."

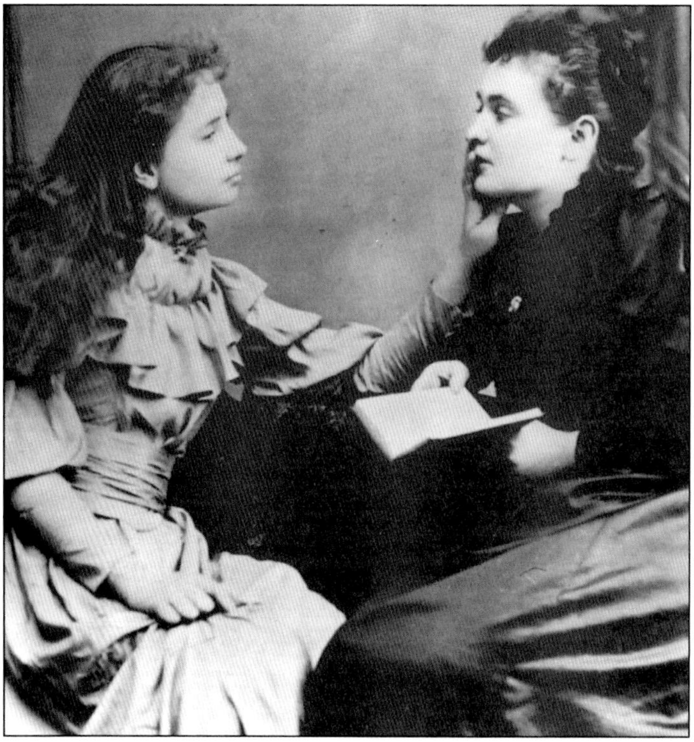

The story of Helen Adams Keller (1880–1968), left, and her teacher Anne Mansfield Sullivan (1866–1936) made the Perkins School for the Blind even more famous when the movie *The Miracle Worker* was released, starring Patty Duke as Helen Keller. In 1887, Anne Sullivan, a graduate of the Perkins School, taught Helen Keller the manual alphabet, which later led to her cum laude graduation from Radcliffe College in 1904. Helen Keller went on to be a lecturer and crusader for the handicapped and wrote *The Story of My Life* in 1902.

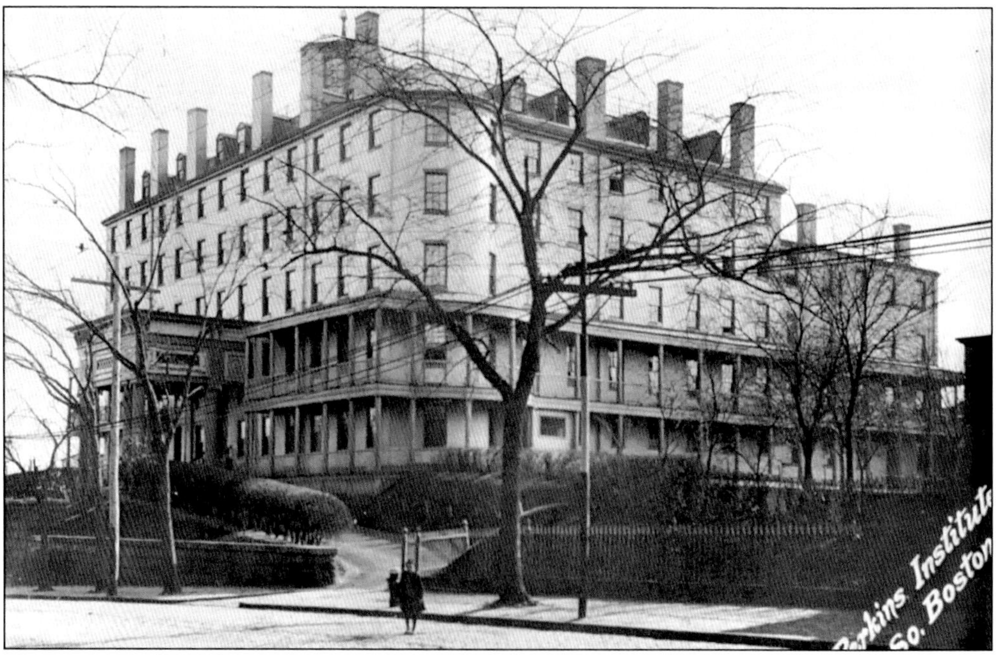


Seen in an early-20th-century postcard, the Perkins School for the Blind served children and adults as both a place of residence and a school. The school was a success and "everything which could be done to render the establishment useful as a place of instruction for those deprived of the blessing of sight, has been accomplished." By 1880, there were 137 pupils at the school and 19 adults in the workshops.

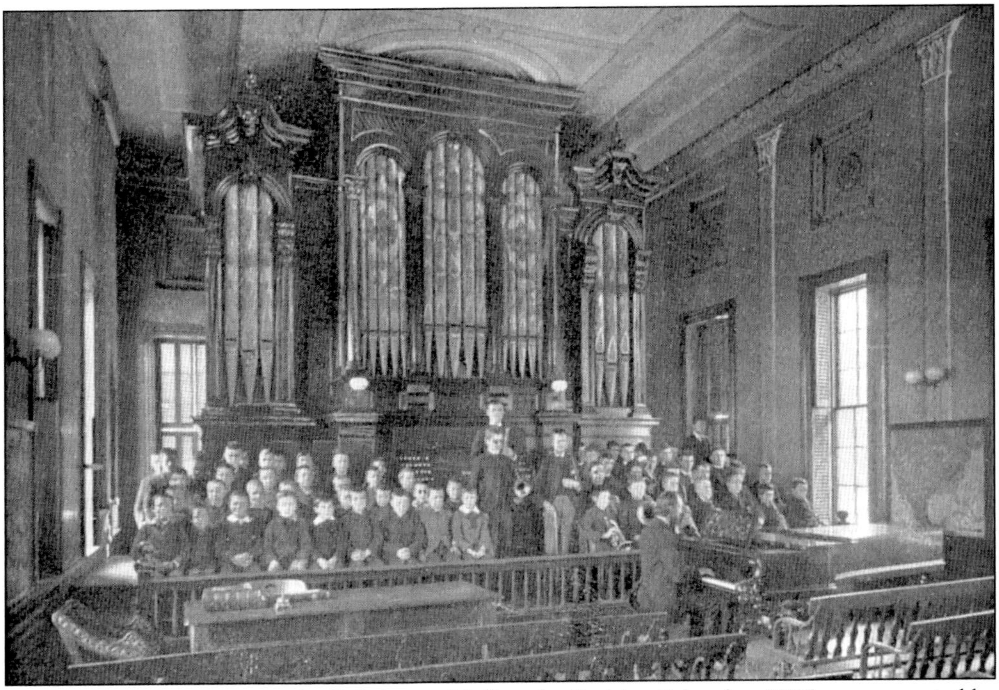

A choir of students sing in the Exhibition Hall at the Perkins School *c.* 1895, accompanied by a pianist. The organ, valued at $3,000 in 1840, was the gift of George Lee of Boston. As early as 1834, there was a band formed at the school, with students playing the clarinet, flute, horn, violin, violoncello, and bass viol in "a manner that would do credit to any orchestra." Lowell Mason "had been engaged to instruct the pupils in the art of using the voice in singing, and also the pianoforte and organ."

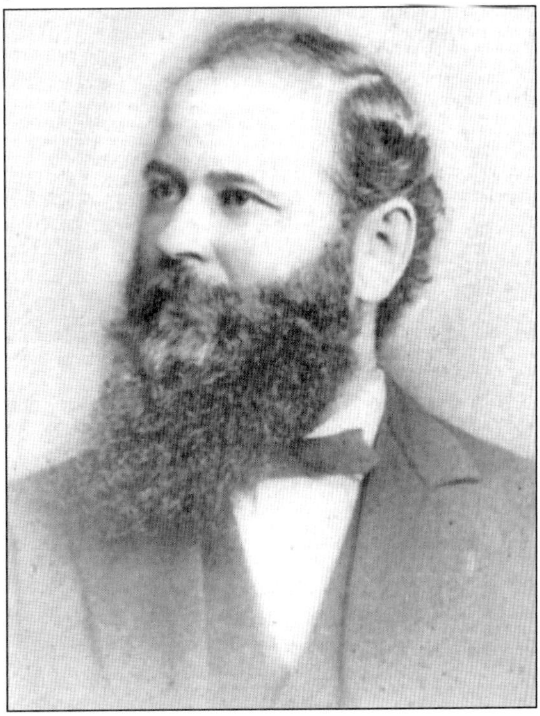

Prof. Michael Anagnos (1837–1906) was a native of Greece and successor to Dr. Samuel Gridley Howe at the Perkins School for the Blind. Anagnos was married to Julia Romana Howe, daughter of Dr. and Julia Howe, and was considered the "counterpart [of Dr. Howe] in his interest in the blind." Anagnos established a kindergarten for the blind, known as the Day School, which later relocated to Jamaica Plain. It was said of him that he was "a deep thinker, a wise counselor, a profit of good" and that he "taught to Helen Keller and Edith Thomas all that Dr. Howe taught to Laura Bridgeman, and in addition has given them the power of speech."

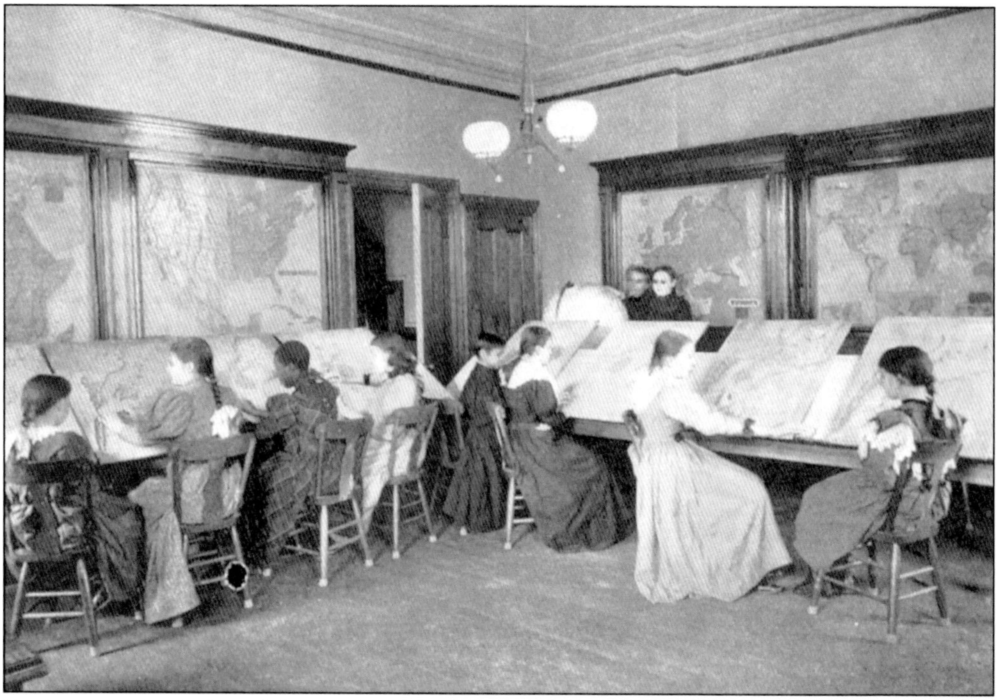

Students at the Perkins School often made three dimensional maps of the world that allowed them to feel the country's shape and correlate it to its continent. In the Geography Room, students match dissected maps of countries to larger maps mounted on boards.

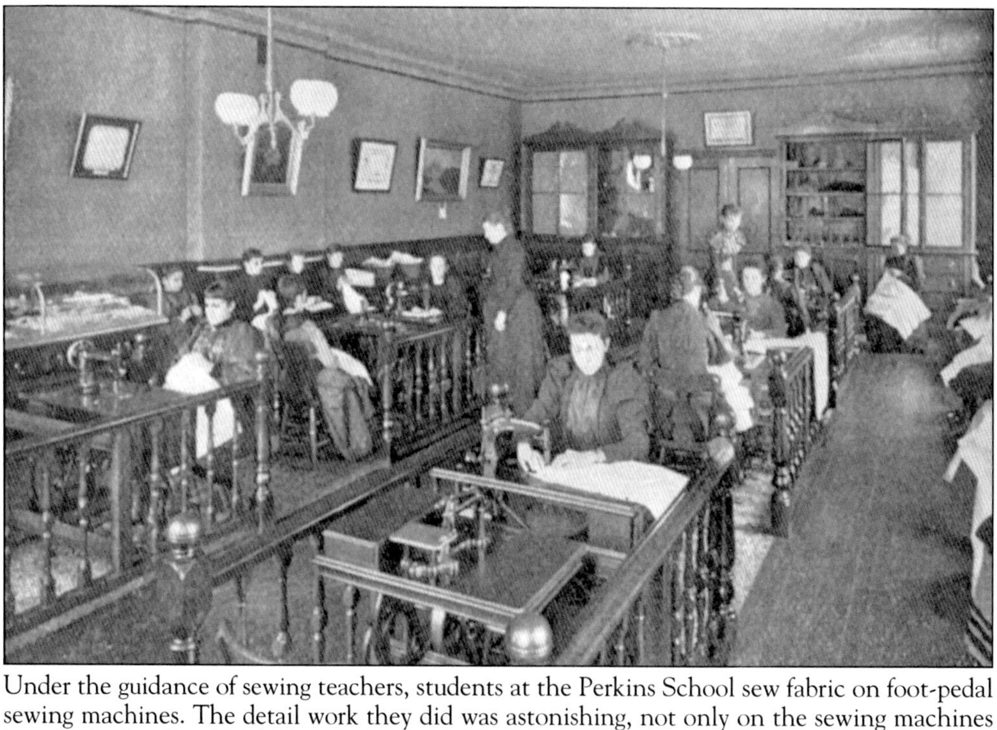

Under the guidance of sewing teachers, students at the Perkins School sew fabric on foot-pedal sewing machines. The detail work they did was astonishing, not only on the sewing machines but also by hand embroidery.

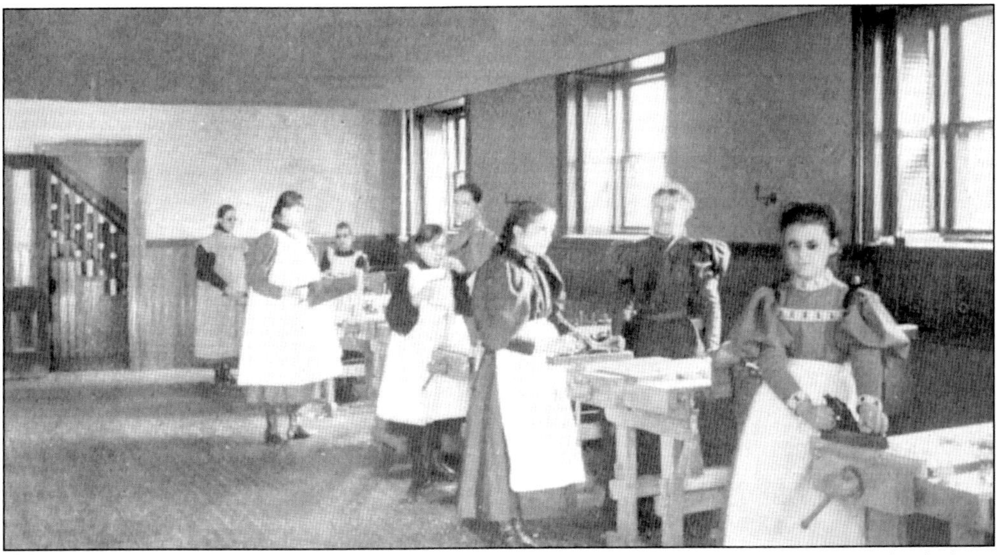

Sloyd, which was a Swedish version of skilled mechanical work, was offered to both boys and girls. In this class they worked with wood, using planes, saws, and auger bits to make small crafts. In addition, students and adult residents worked on the printing of books with raised letters, the manufacturing of mattresses and pew cushions and cane-seated chairs, and the upholstering of furniture—all of which allowed them to earn a living and to be a productive member of society.

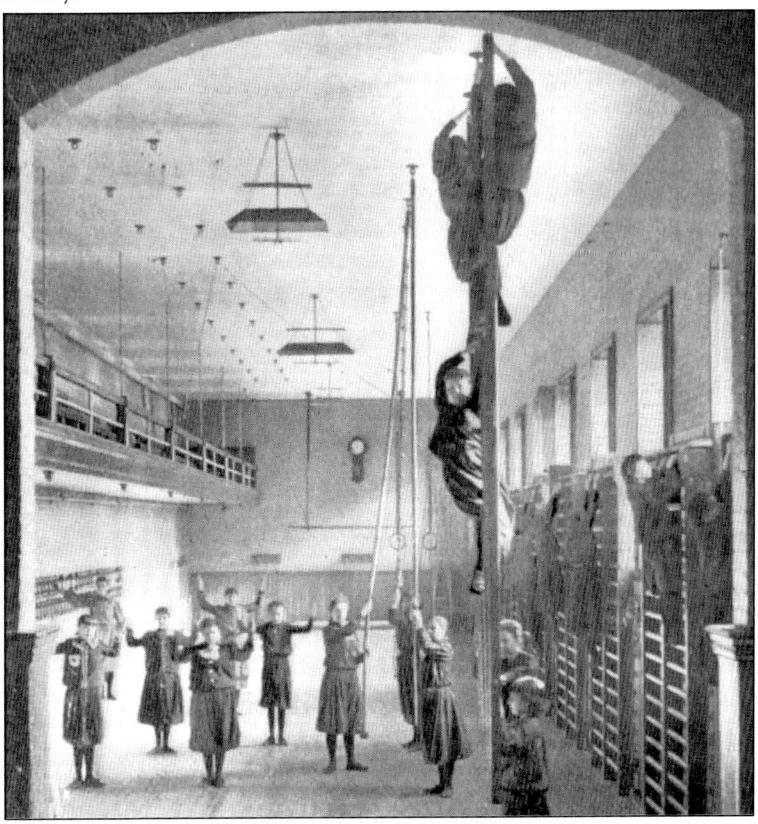

Students at the Perkins School do calisthenics in the gymnasium at the start of the 20th century. With great agility these blind students exercised by climbing the straps hanging from the ceiling in the foreground and the wall ladders on the right. Exercise of both the body and mind is an important aspect of remaining fit.

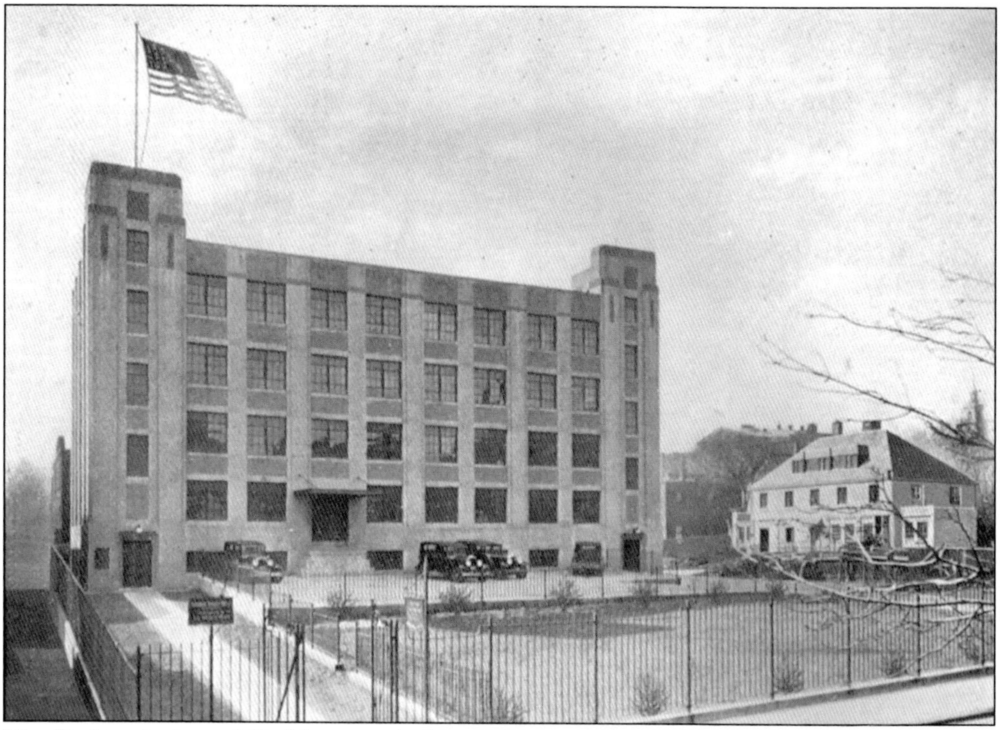

The Perkins Industrial Building was built in 1930 on East Fourth Street behind the school. In this building the blind performed work that enabled them each to be not only somewhat independent but also a contributing member of society. The house on the right is that of the caretaker; the spire of the Evacuation Monument can be seen on the far right. Today, the former industrial building has been converted into condominiums.

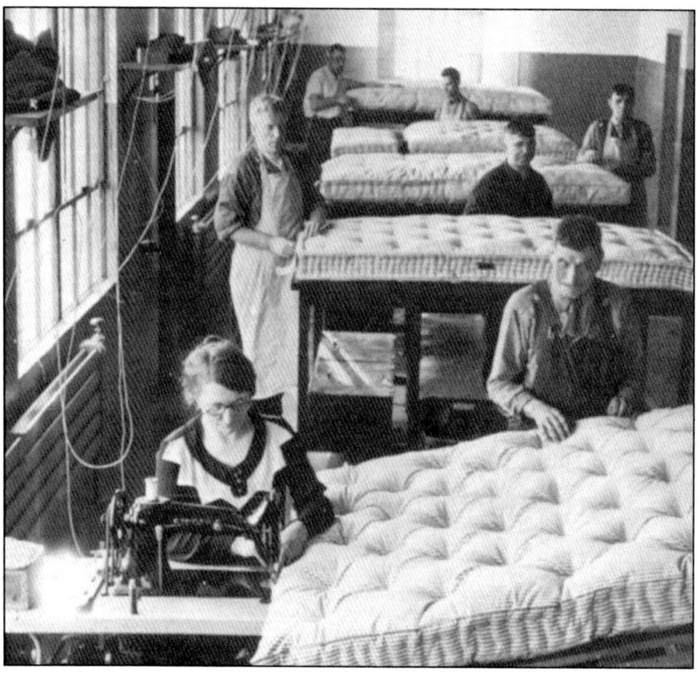

Blind men and women work in a mattress workshop, preparing the filling and sewing the edges before the mattress is tufted. Other workshops included a printing press, a basketry, and fibre mat making, where blind men and women could develop remunerative skills. The Perkins Industrial Building continued until 1952, after which the building was disused. Today, the building has been converted into condominiums.

# *Seven*

# The Carney Hospital

The Carney Hospital was founded in South Boston in 1863 with a donation from Andrew Carney (1794–1864), a retired partner in the clothing firm of Carney and Sleeper, to provide "a hospital where the sick without distinction of creed, color or nation shall be received and cared for, and that no patient within its walls be deprived of his or her minister." Opening in the former Howe Estate on Old Harbor Street on Telegraph Hill, the hospital began with 53 patients, most of whom were unable to receive medical care elsewhere. For over 90 years, the Sisters of Charity of St. Vincent de Paul ministered to the poor, the ill, and the forgotten. Sr. Ann Alexis Shorb (1805–1875) began as administrator of the Carney Hospital at the request of Andrew Carney in 1863 and continued for seven years. Formerly supervisor of St. Vincent's Orphan Asylum on Camden Street in Boston, she was known as the "Servant of the Poor" and had been persuaded to come to the first Catholic hospital in New England, where she began to organize it with "the benefit of her good and zealous labors." In the ensuing century, the Sisters of Charity of Saint Vincent de Paul provided care and direction and were an omnipresent and reassuring influence at the hospital.

The great strides that have taken place at the Carney Hospital since its founding in 1863 include the first ovariectomy surgery in Boston in 1882 by Henry I. Bowditch, M.D.; the first abdominal surgery in the United States in 1882 by John Homans, M.D.; the first skin care clinic in Boston in 1891; the first Catholic school of nursing in New England in 1892; the first hospital in New England to have permanent chiefs in medicine and surgery with Henry Christian, M.D., named physician in chief in 1907 and John Munro, M.D., surgeon in chief; the first plastic hip operation in the United States performed by W. Russell MacAusland, M.D., in 1950; and the first use of rubber gloves in an operating room by Frederick Johnson, M.D. Each of these milestones ensures Carney Hospital's place in Boston's medical history, even though the hospital moved to Dorchester in 1953. As a member of Caritas Christi, the Health Care System of the Archdiocese of Boston, the hospital looks not just to the future with optimism that it will continue to provide medical attention to patients from all walks of life compassionately and respectfully, but also it remembers its 1863 founding in South Boston, made possible by the generosity of Andrew Carney, an immigrant and "generous friend and protector" of all who pass through the hospital doors.

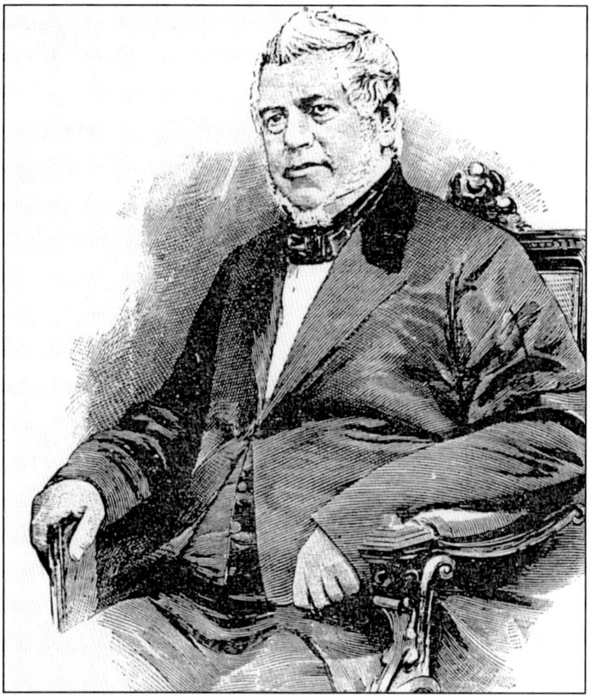

Andrew Carney (1784–1864) was a well-respected man in Boston, who liberally contributed to the founding of the Carney Hospital for "relief to the sick poor... of all religious denominations." Leaving Ballansgh, County Caven, Ireland, in 1816, he arrived in Boston and worked as a tailor before establishing a partnership with Jacob Sleeper in the ready-made clothing firm of Carney & Sleeper in Boston's North End. His generosity was legendary, and he was often referred to as "one of God's best noblemen," as well as a "kind-hearted, whole souled, generous friend and protector."

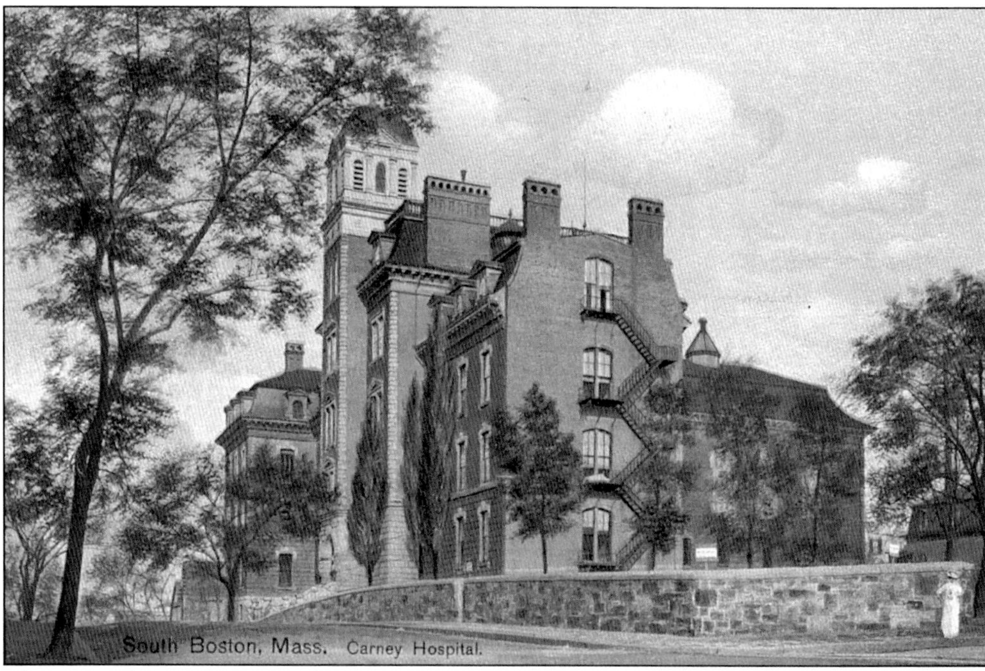


The original Carney Hospital was the former estate of Hall Jackson Howe (1791–1849) on Old Harbor Street. This hospital was designed by Charles Bateman and was built on the rise of Telegraph Hill from Dorchester Street, from which superb panoramic views of Boston and the harbor could be seen. The Carney Hospital provided care for patients from all walks of life and was established as a "hospital where the sick without distinction of creed, color or nation shall be received and cared for." Many outpatients were cared for gratuitously.

Charles J. Bateman (1851–1940) was a noted architect who served as city architect for Boston between 1883 and 1891. A graduate of Massachusetts Institute of Technology, Bateman's work was widely acclaimed, but more to the fact was that "a peculiar feature of Mr. Bateman's work is that while in public office the actual cost of his plans never exceeded his first estimates." His design for the Carney Hospital was as impressive as it was medically important to those it served.

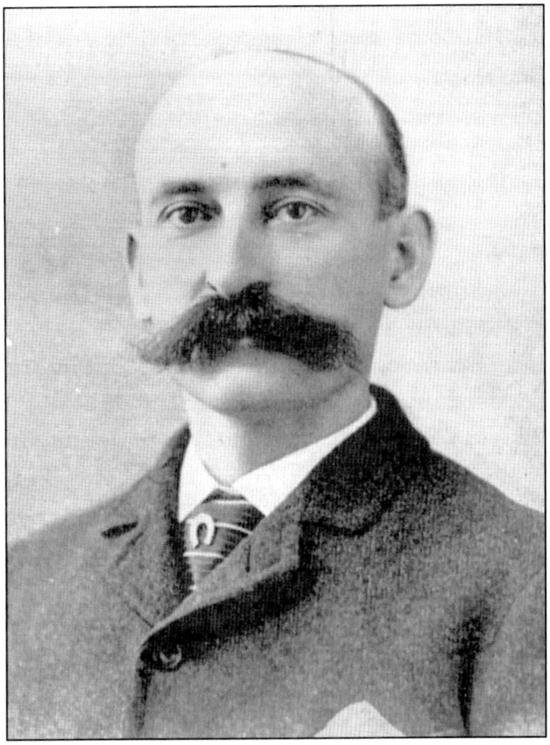

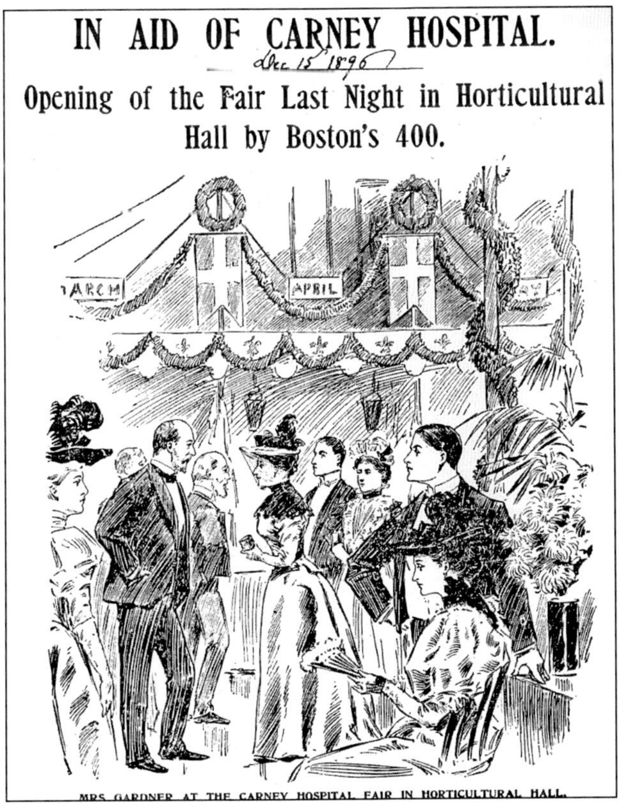

IN AID OF CARNEY HOSPITAL.

Dec 15 1896

Opening of the Fair Last Night in Horticultural Hall by Boston's 400.



MRS GARDNER AT THE CARNEY HOSPITAL FAIR IN HORTICULTURAL HALL.

A gala benefit was held "In Aid of Carney Hospital" on December 15, 1896, at Horticultural Hall in Boston. Mrs. John Lowell Gardner ("Mrs. Jack") can be seen at the fair, which was attended by Boston's 400 in support of Carney Hospital to raise necessary funds to continue the good work of the Sisters of Charity, who had staffed the hospital since 1864. The *Boston Pilot* said of the hospital that "[h]ad the motive of this work been one of gain . . . failure would without doubt have been the outcome, but because devotion to the cause of suffering humanity was the underlying principle it claimed the cooperation of generous-hearted people, and the blessing of God rested upon the hospital."

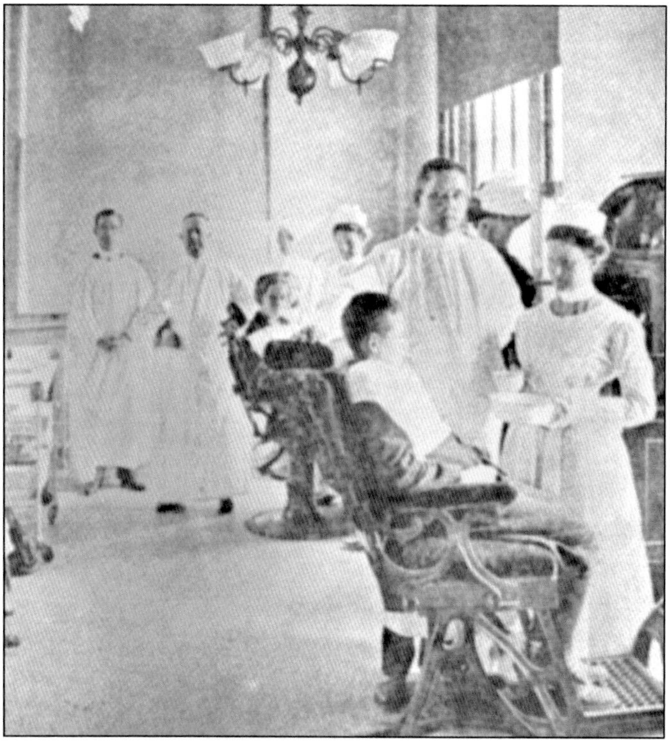

Dentists and assistants pose for a photograph with patients in the Dental Clinic at Carney Hospital in 1913. The clinic was opened in 1912 by Dr. George A. Sullivan for schoolchildren in the outpatient department. (Courtesy of the Carney Hospital.)

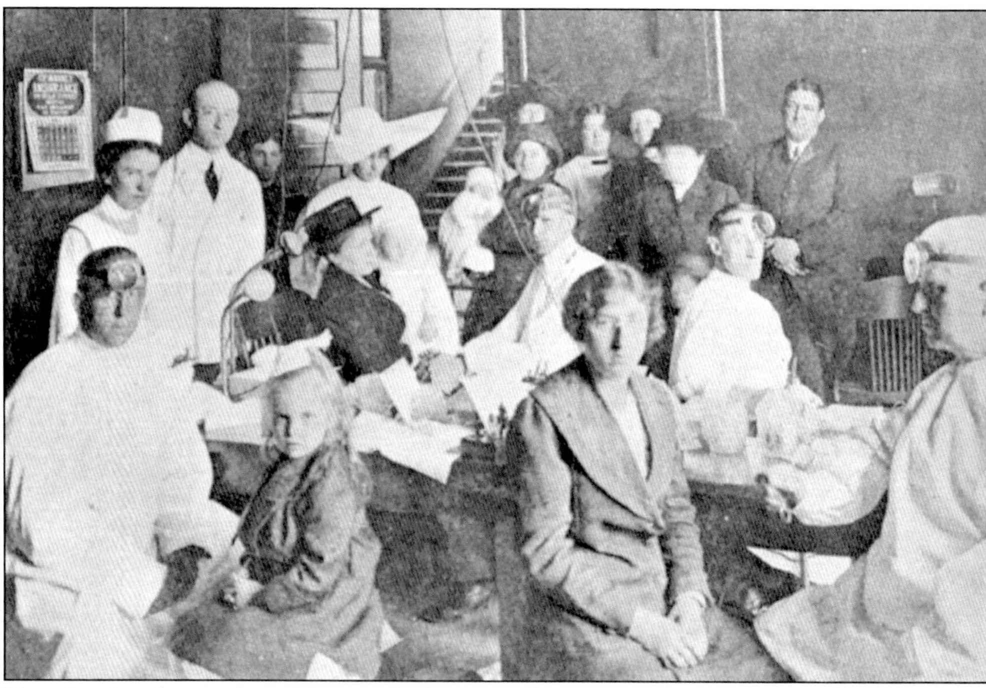

The Otorhinolaryngology Clinic, which treats diseases of the ear, nose, and larynx, was photographed in 1912 with patients waiting to speak with physicians. Notice the Sister of Charity in the center—ever attentive and of great assistance to both physician and patient, the sisters were a vital part of Carney Hospital. (Courtesy of the Carney Hospital.)

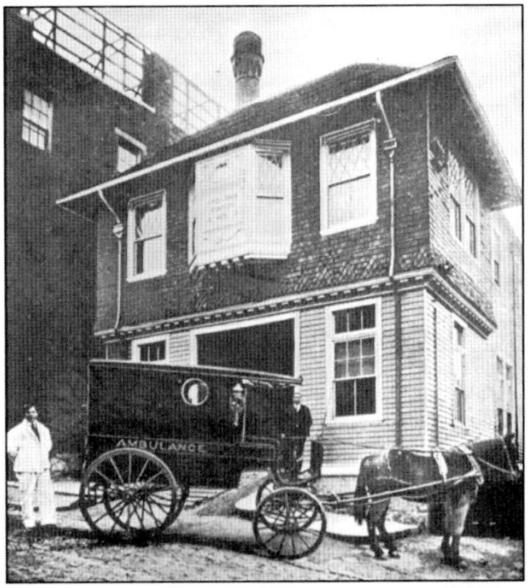


The Ambulance Station was opened in 1899 at Carney Hospital and was located in a distinctive shingle-style building on National Street. There were stables on the first floor. Pictured in 1899, an ambulance driver stands to the left of the horse-drawn ambulance, which was ready to "be dispatched to any point within the city proper for conveyance of cases of accidents or urgent sudden illness (not contagious) to this hospital." (Courtesy of the Carney Hospital.)

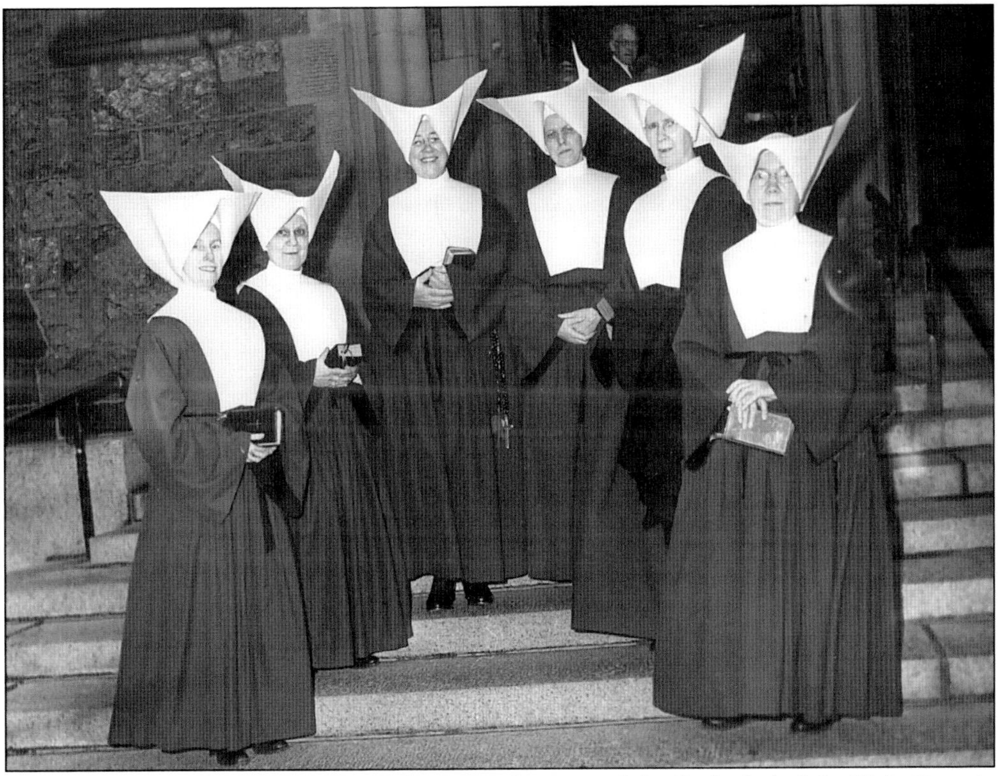

Administrators of the Carney Hospital pose on the steps of the Cathedral of the Holy Cross in Boston's South End in 1963, after a Mass in honor of the centenary of the founding of Carney Hospital. Seen here, from left to right, with the year of their appointment, are Sr. Margaret Finnegan (1958), Sr. Louise Driscoll (1954), Sr. Oliva Cunane (1948), Sr. Mary Paul Chrismer (1942), Sr. Marie Daly (1933), and Sr. Electa Stafford (1928). Earlier administrators included Sister Ann Alexis (1863), Sister Ann Aloysia (1870), Sister Simplicia (1870), Sister Gonzaga (1899), Sister Raphael (1910), Sister Vincent (1919), and Sister Fidelis (1927). (Courtesy of the Carney Hospital.)

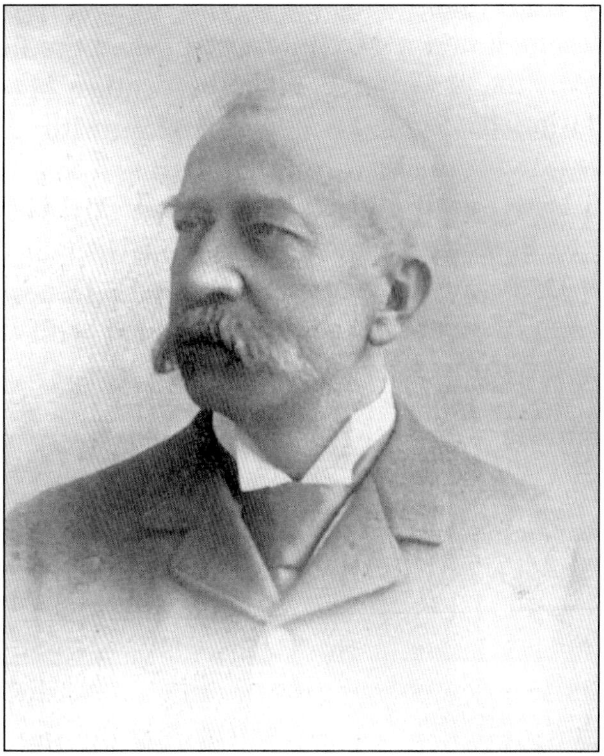

Dr. Francis B. Greenough (1837–1904) was a member of the original surgical staff at the Carney Hospital in 1863. A graduate of the Harvard Medical School, he provided surgical and medical attention to immigrants and others who could not afford this service elsewhere.

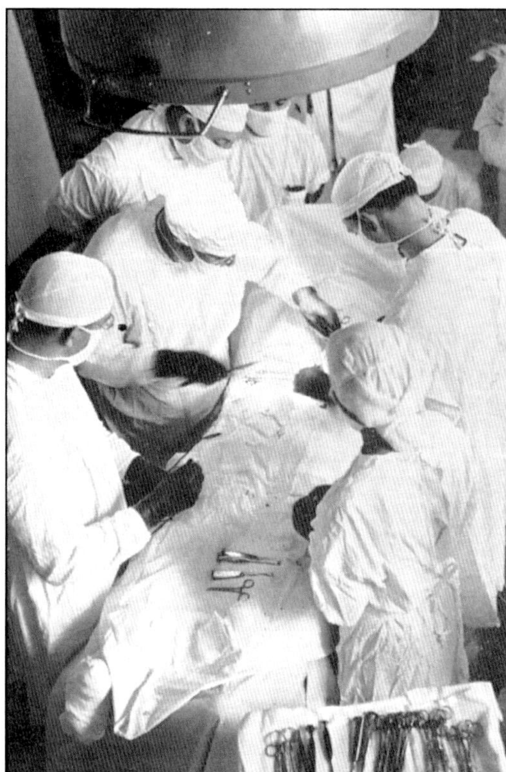

Surgeons perform an operation at the Carney Hospital in 1951. In 1903, the first surgeon in chief and the first physician in chief were appointed at the Carney Hospital; they were the first permanent chiefs ever appointed in New England. The Hippocratic oath states that "I will impart this Art by precept, by lecture and by every mode of teaching." (Courtesy of the Carney Hospital.)

A mother cradles her newborn baby at the Carney Hospital in 1950, where 940 babies were born in that year alone. The Maternity Department was established in 1918. It was said that in 1950 "eighty-five mothers had three or more Cesarean deliveries at the hospital during the preceding ten years. Of these, eight had successfully undergone the operation five times." (Courtesy of the Carney Hospital.)

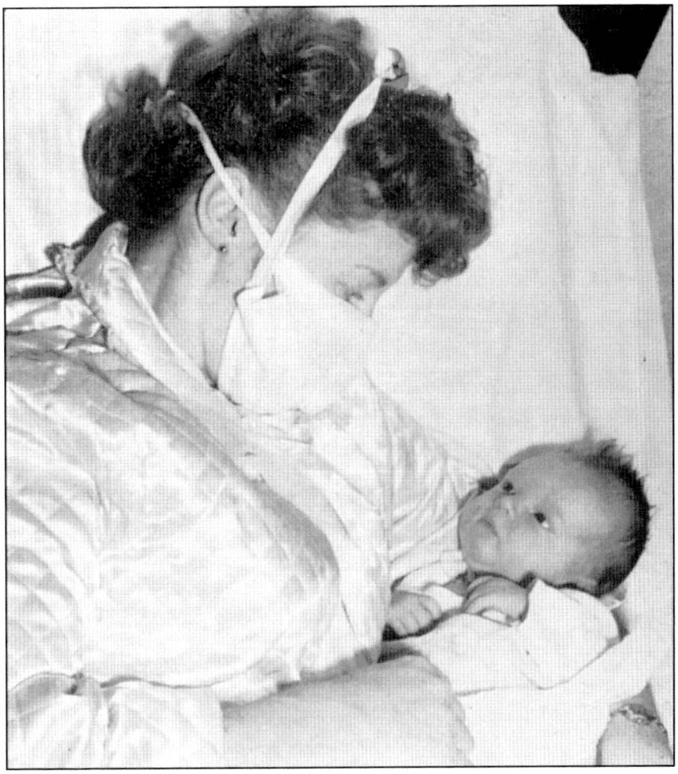

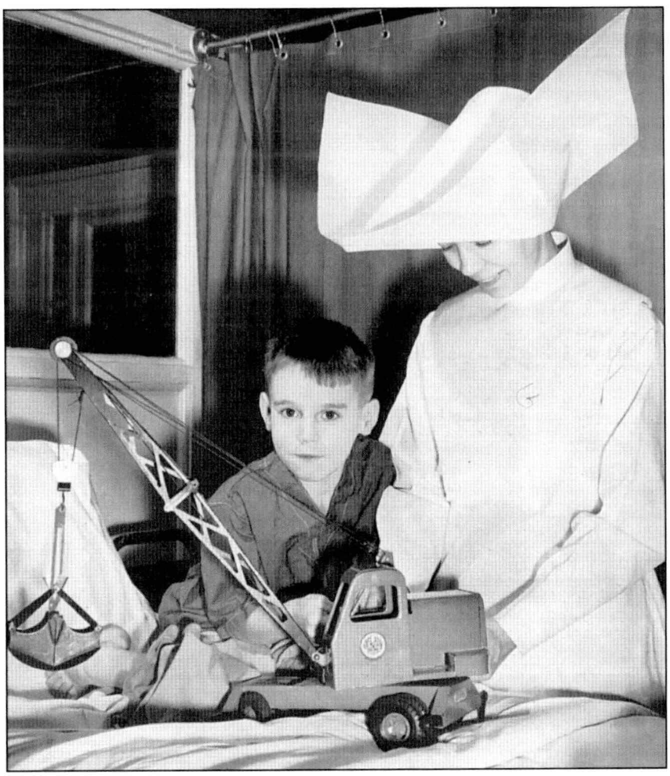

A Sister of Charity admires the toy steam shovel of a young patient at the Carney Hospital in 1951. (Courtesy of the Carney Hospital.)

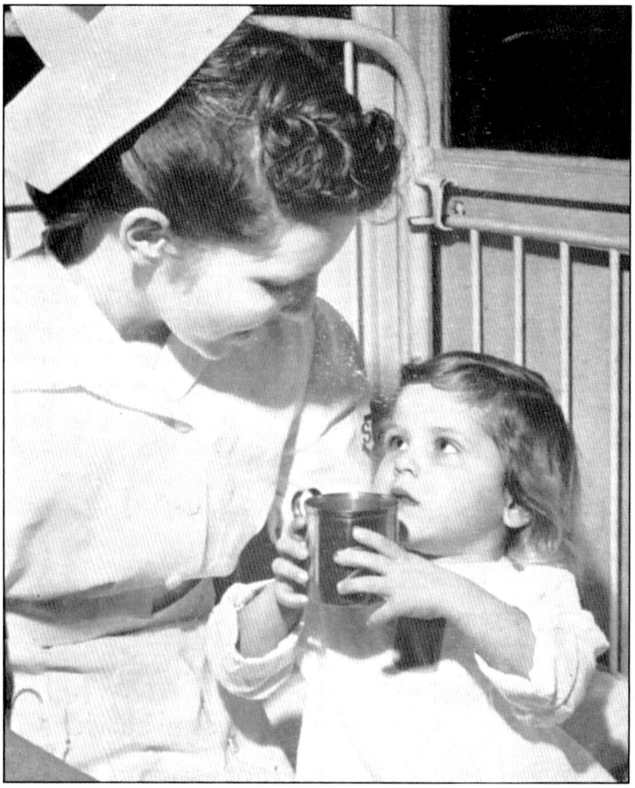

A nurse offers a cup of juice to a young child in the children's ward at the Carney Hospital. The Florence Nightingale pledge said that "With loyalty will I endeavor to aid the physician in his work and devote myself to the welfare of those committed to my care." (Courtesy of the Carney Hospital.)

A Sister of Charity directs a group of neighborhood boys to scrub the brick wall of the Outpatient Building at Dorchester and Old Harbor Streets at the Carney Hospital in 1950. One wonders if the boys had "accidentally" written on the wall with chalk and were scrubbing out their words with soap and water at the direction of the sister. *Mia culpa*, Sister. (Courtesy of the Carney Hospital.)

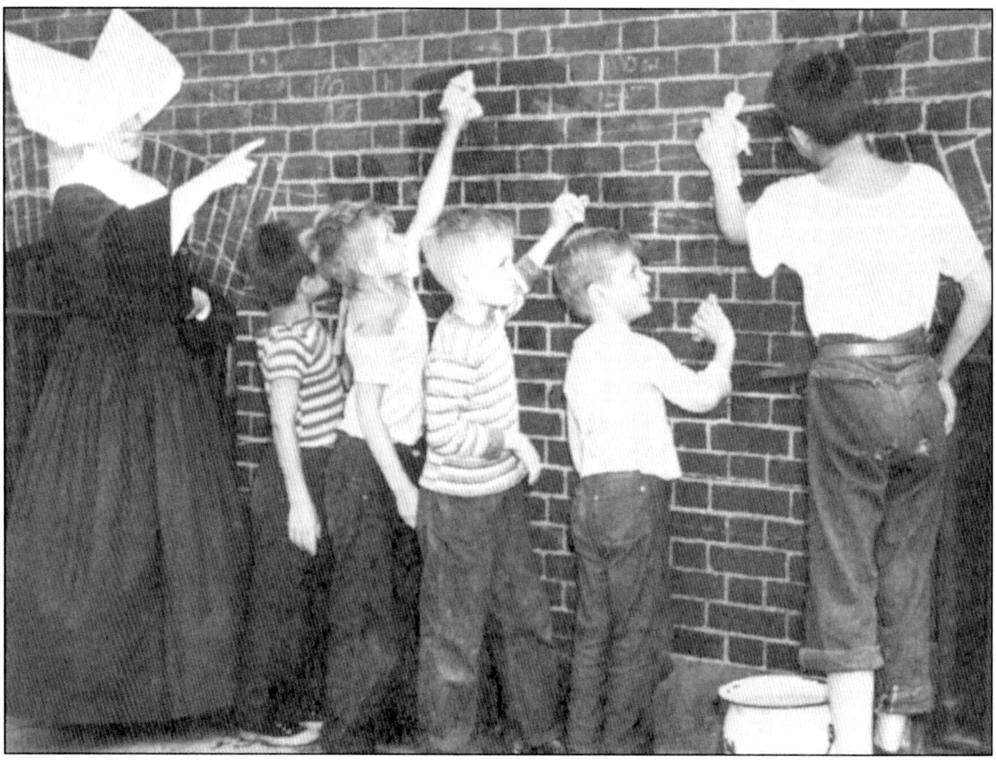

# *Eight*

# Marian Manor

Marian Manor was established in 1954 when Richard Cardinal Cushing invited the Order of the Carmelite Sisters for the Aged and Infirm to take over the buildings of the former Carney Hospital as a nursing home. The Order of the Carmelite Sisters for the Aged and Infirm was founded in 1929 in New York City by Rev. Mother M. Angeline Teresa. The Carney Hospital had moved to the Dorchester Lower Mills in 1953 and the large hospital complex on Telegraph Hill in South Boston was given over to serve the elderly of South Boston, preserving their dignity and ensuring their independence. The new nursing home was called Marian Manor in honor of the 1954 Marian Year.

In the early years, the manor accommodated 100 residents; today, it is able to accommodate nearly 400 residents. The staff, headed today by Sr. Pauline Ross as administrator, is devoted to the ideals upon which the Carmelite Order was founded: personal attention to the physical, temporal, and spiritual well-being of the individual, thereby ensuring a safe, secure, and comfortable environment for the residents, without regard to their religion, race, or ethnicity. Today, Marian Manor has become an integral part of South Boston; the impressive group of buildings on Dorchester Street testify to its tremendous growth from the former Carney Hospital buildings to a modern facility for the care of the elderly.

The manor was enlarged with a West Wing and East Wing, designed by architect Chester F. Wright, providing additional space for residents. In addition, the Immaculate Conception Chapel was dedicated in 1965 and Carmel Hall in 1984. Each of these new additions has ensured that Marian Manor is a place of comfort and security, where senior citizens can enjoy their golden years under the faithful attendance of the Carmelite Sisters.

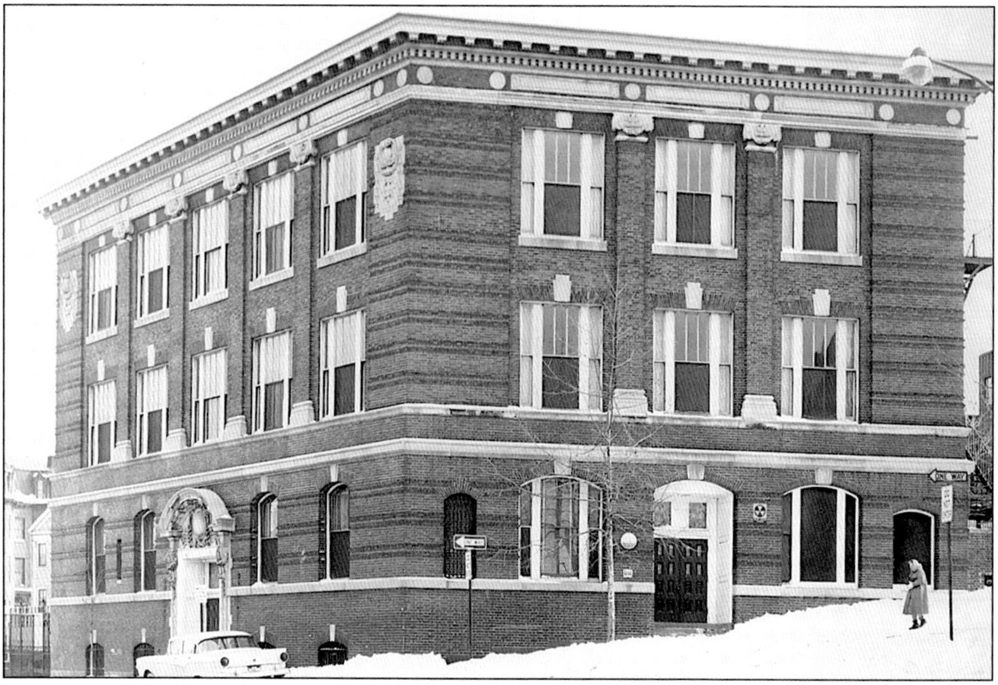

The original building of Marian Manor, formerly the Outpatient Clinic of the Carney Hospital at the corner of Dorchester and Old Harbor Streets, was opened in 1954 as "Marian Villa" by the Order of the Carmelite Sisters for the Aged and Infirm. An impressive red brick and limestone Classical Revival building, it stands at the corner of Dorchester and Old Harbor Streets. (Courtesy of Marian Manor.)

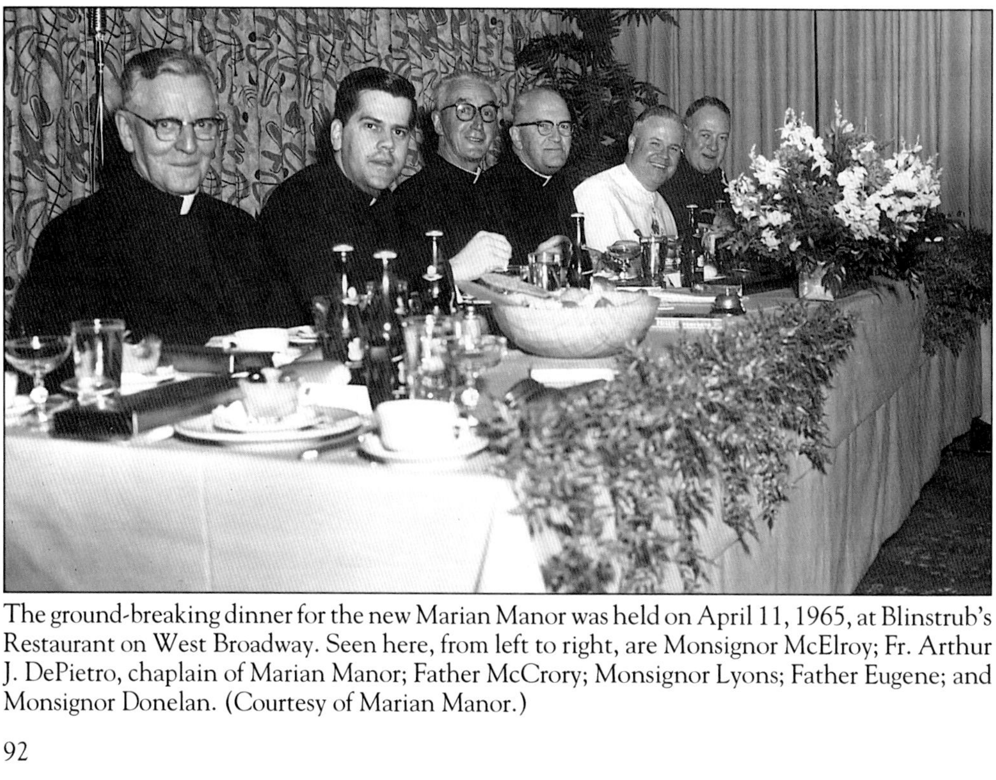

The ground-breaking dinner for the new Marian Manor was held on April 11, 1965, at Blinstrub's Restaurant on West Broadway. Seen here, from left to right, are Monsignor McElroy; Fr. Arthur J. DePietro, chaplain of Marian Manor; Father McCrory; Monsignor Lyons; Father Eugene; and Monsignor Donelan. (Courtesy of Marian Manor.)

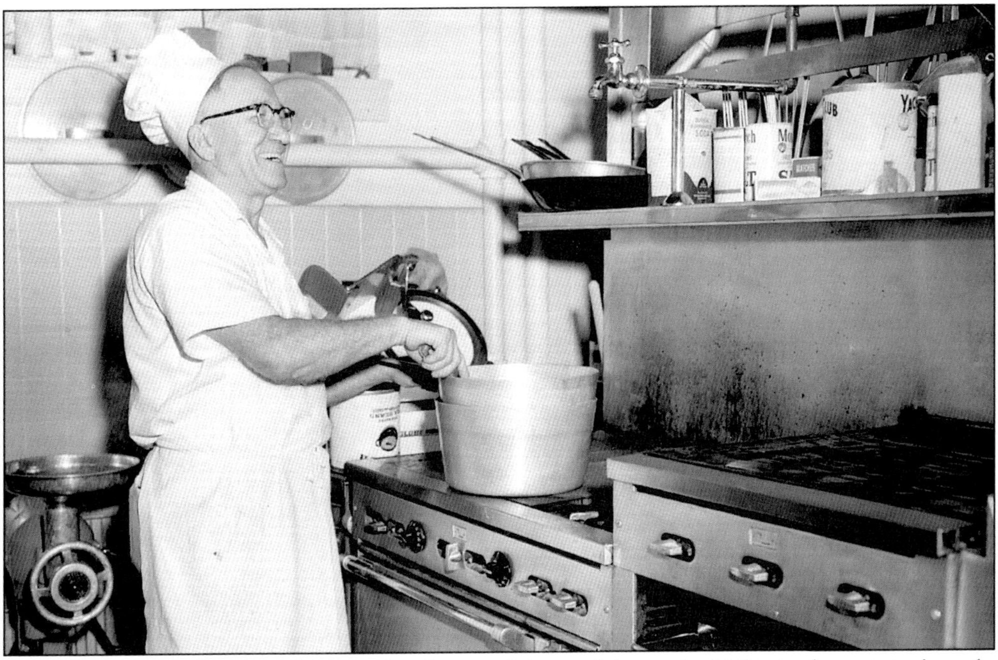

Stirring a pot of soup in the new kitchen at Marian Manor in 1954 is the original cook. This jovial man provided nutritious as well as delicious meals for the residents. (Courtesy of Marian Manor.)

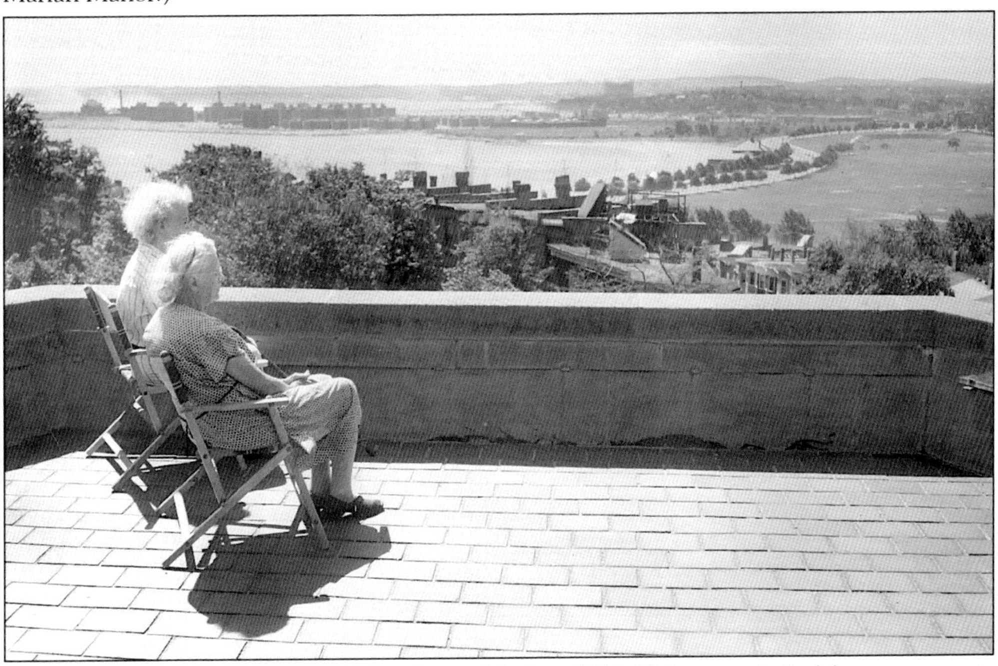

Two residents of Marian Manor rest on the roof deck in 1954. This open-air deck has a panoramic view of Old Harbor, Boston Harbor, and the numerous harbor islands. In the distance, on the left, the Columbia Point Housing Project, now known as Harbor Point, in Dorchester can be seen. Notice in the center distance the Boston Gas Company gas tank on Commercial Point in Dorchester. (Courtesy of Marian Manor.)

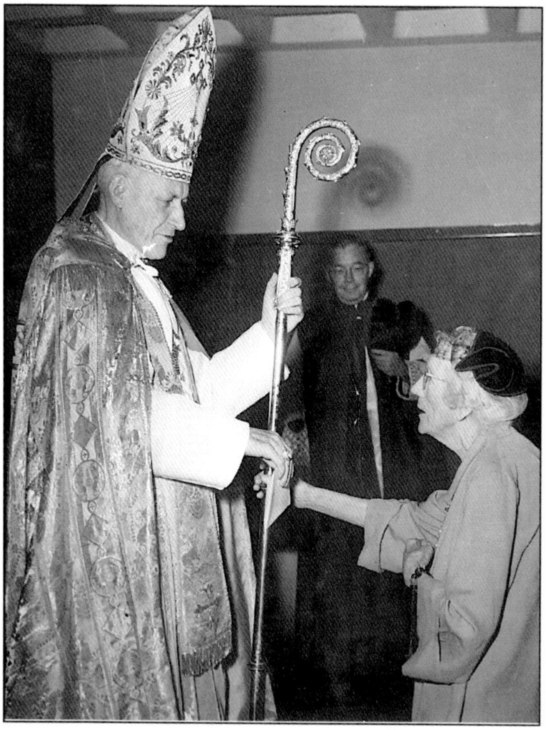

Richard Cardinal Cushing accepts a Spiritual Bouquet from Annie McNamara on the occasion of his 60th birthday, which he celebrated by saying Mass at Marian Manor in 1955. Mrs. McNamara, a resident of Marian Manor, presented His Eminence with a bouquet of 265 rosaries, in addition to vivid and lengthy remembrances of him as a young schoolboy in South Boston. (Courtesy of Marian Manor.)

Richard Cardinal Cushing poses with residents of Marian Manor following Mass, *c.* 1960. The Carmelite Sisters are, from the left to right, Mother Maria Paul, founder Mother M. Angeline Teresa; and Mother Bernadette. (Courtesy of Marian Manor.)

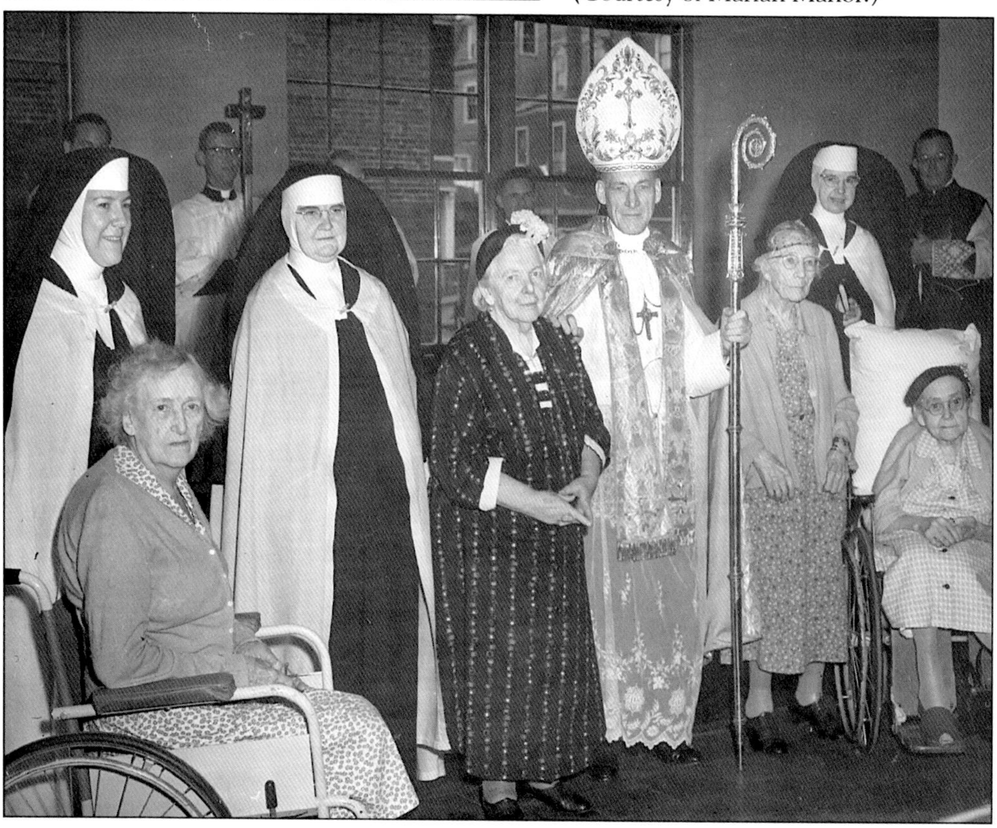

Richard Cardinal Cushing poses with members of the Carmelite Sisters in the convent garden, following the dedication of the statue of Our Lady of Mount Carmel and the Infant Jesus. Hand carved of white marble in Italy, the statue was an elegant and appropriate addition to the manor's garden. The Carmelite Sisters endeavor to create "an environment of a warm, home-like atmosphere in a pleasant setting where the residents can enjoy the final years of life." (Courtesy of Marian Manor.)

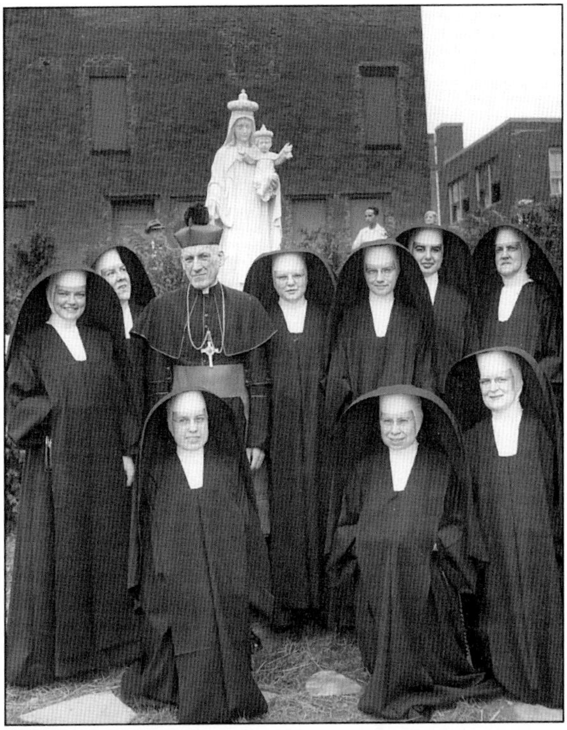

Richard Cardinal Cushing sits with four members of the Carmelites, young girls who volunteered at Marian Manor, as a band entertains residents in the early 1960s. (Courtesy of Marian Manor.)

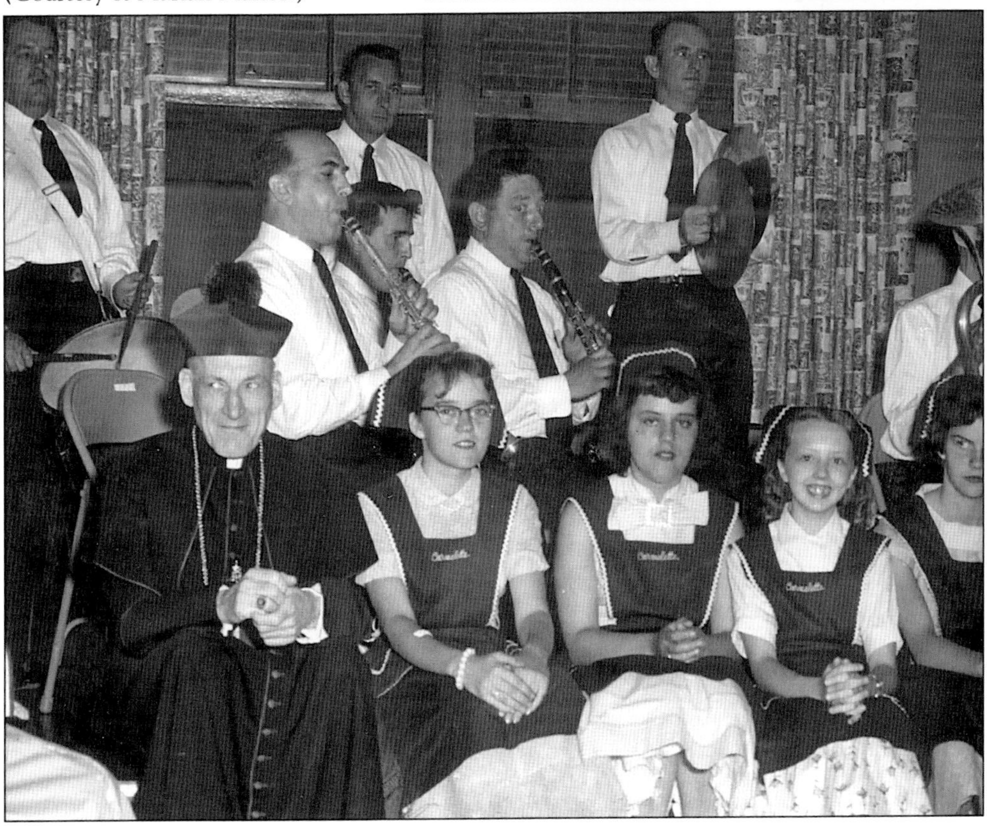

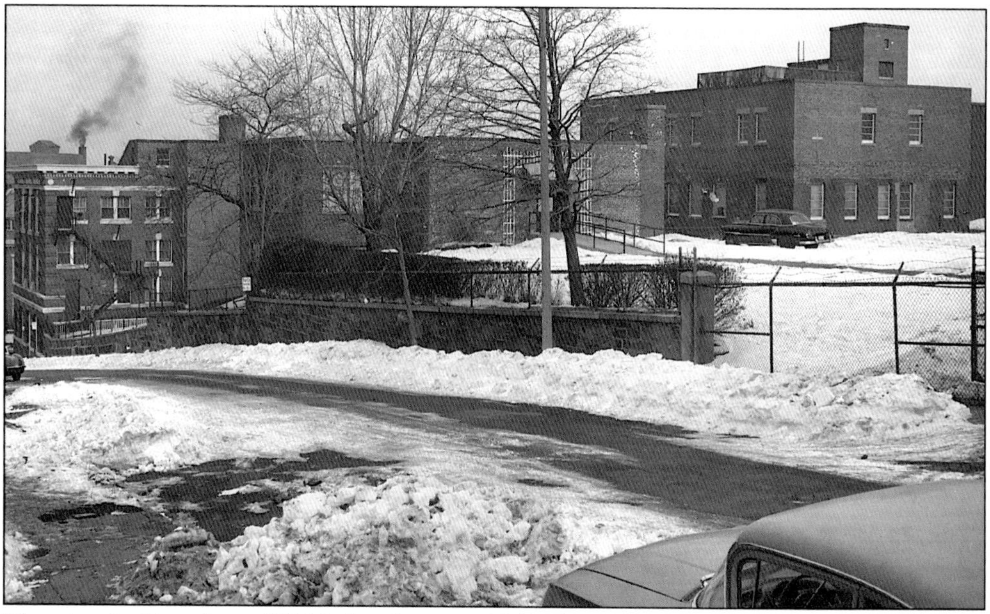

The view looking down Old Harbor Street *c.* 1960, shows the site of the old Carney Hospital where Marian Manor serves senior citizens in its sprawling complex of buildings. From left to right are the Villa Building (now the West Wing), the former Outpatient Building of the Carney, St. Joseph's Auditorium (now St. Joseph's Apartments), and the Marian Manor Convent (now the site of the East Building). Notice the old stone wall from the Hall J. Howe estate, running along Old Harbor Street. (Courtesy of Marian Manor.)

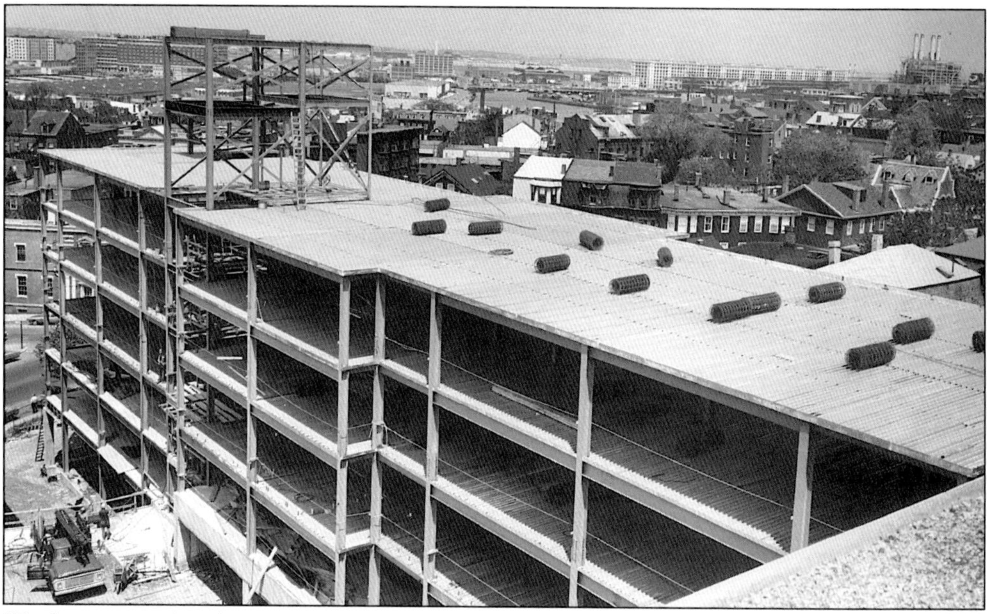

Work was completed in 1967 on a modern facility, known as the North Wing, for residents of Marian Manor. This rooftop scene shows the structure being erected on Dorchester Street with much of the area to the west in the background. The new building greatly added to the amount of available space for new residents of Marian Manor and provided space for a new chapel, a beauty parlor, a dining room, and the main kitchen. (Courtesy of Marian Manor.)

# *Nine*

# South Boston Businesses

After the South Boston Bridge was opened to traffic in 1805, South Boston's prime location attracted numerous commercial and industrial concerns to relocate there throughout the 19th century. Glass companies, iron concerns, and manufactories opened and as the century progressed, they were joined by numerous other commercial concerns.

South Boston's location was advantageous to business, with its wharves along the waterfront, accessibility from Boston by two bridges after 1828, and open land that could be developed for businesses and commercial concerns that were crowded out of the downtown area. From the brickyards of Richard Clapp, which produced thousands of baked clay rectangles used in the frantic building boom of 1810 to 1860, to the numerous flint glass manufactories, including the Suffolk, Phoenix, Mount Washington, and American Flint Glass Companies, these new industries required skilled workers and day laborers. These workers required housing and thus moved to South Boston, where it was said that "growth has been rapid and steady."

The workers who moved to South Boston in the period prior to the Civil War were a cosmopolitan mixture, mostly Western European, with English, Scotch-Irish, Down Easters, Germans, and Irish. However, following the Civil War, the greatest ethnic group in numbers became the Irish; this held true for the next century. Soon, South Boston was home to well-known businesses such as Lawley's Shipyard, the Walworth Manufacturing Company, and the South Boston and Suffolk Breweries. These businesses boosted the local economy, provided employment, and were a stabilizing factor in the community.

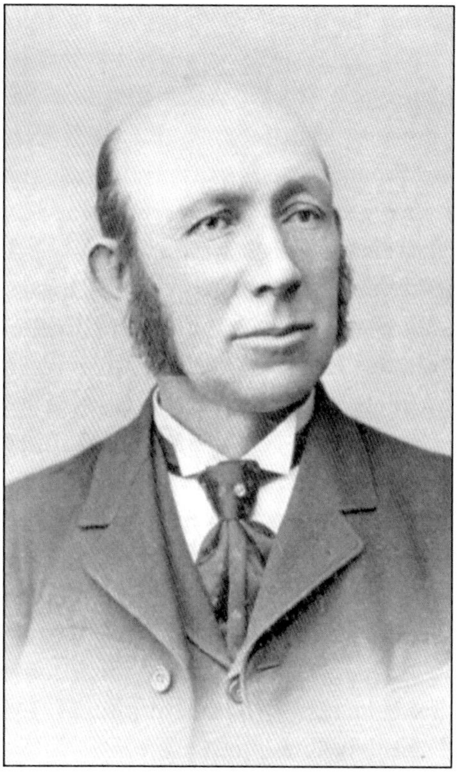

George F. Lawley (1848–1928) was associated with his father, George Lawley, and Thomas Hibbard in boat and yacht building. In 1874, by invitation of members of the Boston Yacht Club, the business moved from Scituate to South Boston, where Lawley's boats and yachts became increasingly famous. Lawley's first location was on East Sixth Street at the foot of P Street, near Columbia Road. The business later relocated to the Lawley Boat Basin at City Point, where numerous vessels were built and about 300 "highly skilled mechanics" were employed during the busy season.

The Basin at Lawley's Yards at City Point in South Boston was the site of such well-known Lawley-built crafts as the sloop yacht *Puritan*, defender of the America's Cup against the *Genesta* in 1885; the famous *Mayflower*; the schooner yacht *Merlin*; and the *Volunteer*, which defeated the *Thistle* in 1887. A machine shop was erected in 1898 and was fully equipped with first-class and high-grade tools—all of which continued the high level of craftsmanship expected from Lawley's.

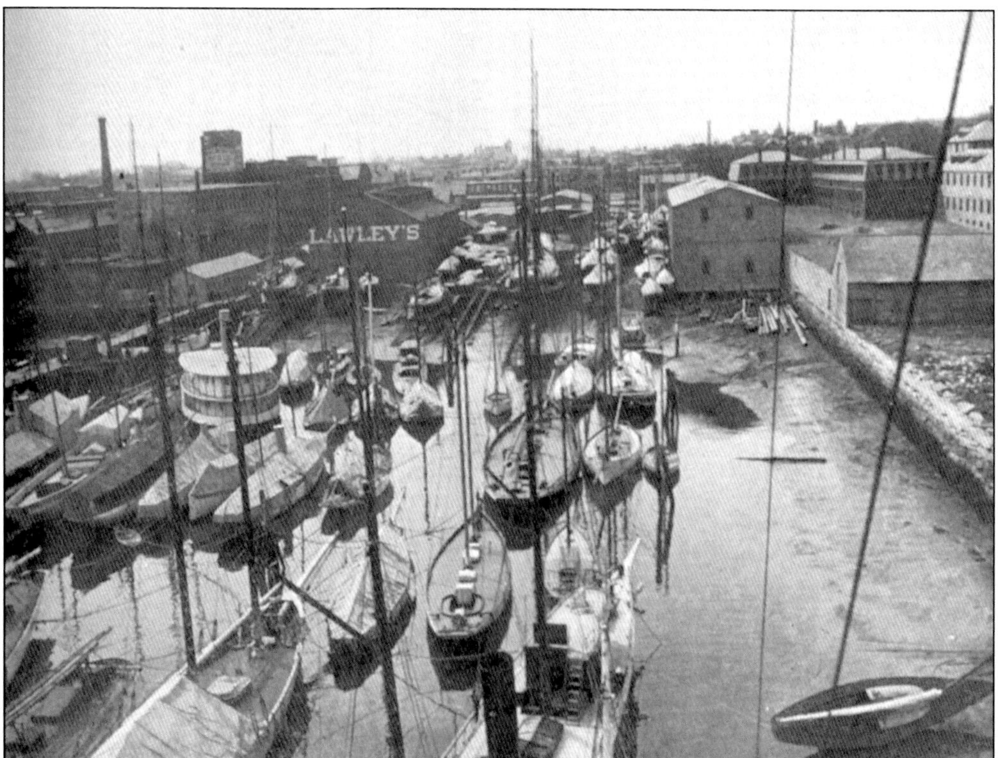

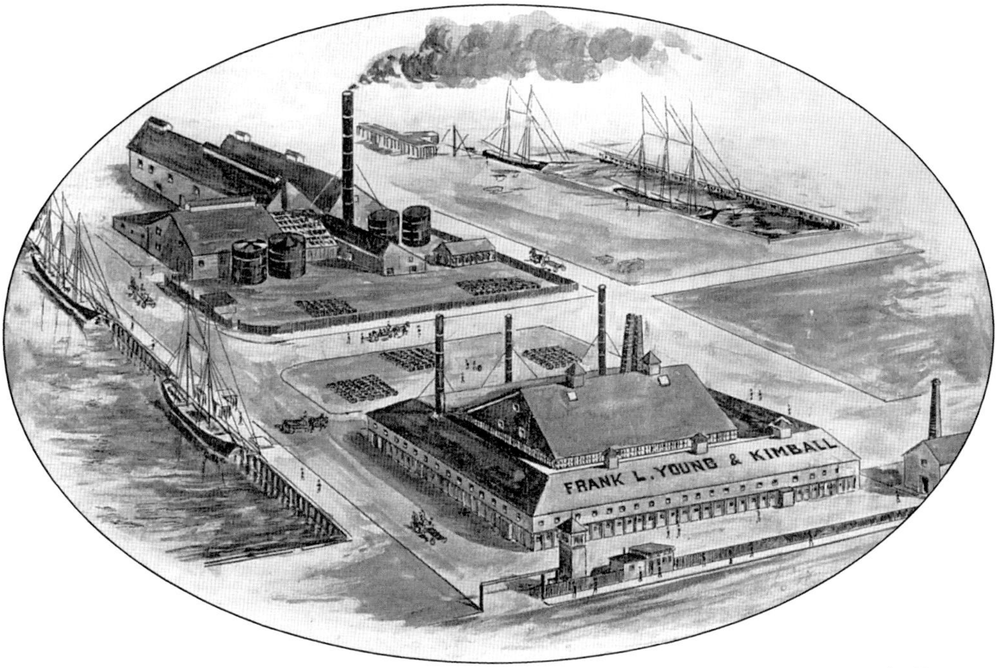


The works of Frank L. Young & Kimball were located on I Street in South Boston. Manufacturers of and dealers in oils, grease, degas, and wax, the 3-acre facility was considered to be, in 1895, "one of the most widely known dealers in . . . [oil] in this country. The wharves alone covered three acres and the factory and storehouses were considered unexcelled facilities."

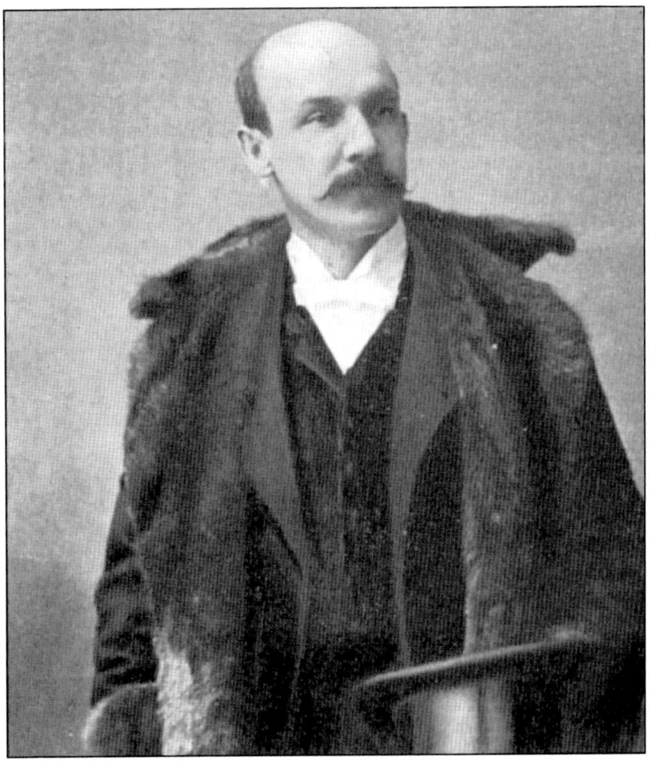

Frank L. Young (1852–1937) was a prominent member of the Boston Board of Trade, and a leader in Boston's oil industry. President of the Oil Trade Association, Young was said to exemplify "that type of strong, self-reliant character which surmounts all obstacles, and, with no aid from external sources . . . achieves a most remarkable and thoroughly deserved success."

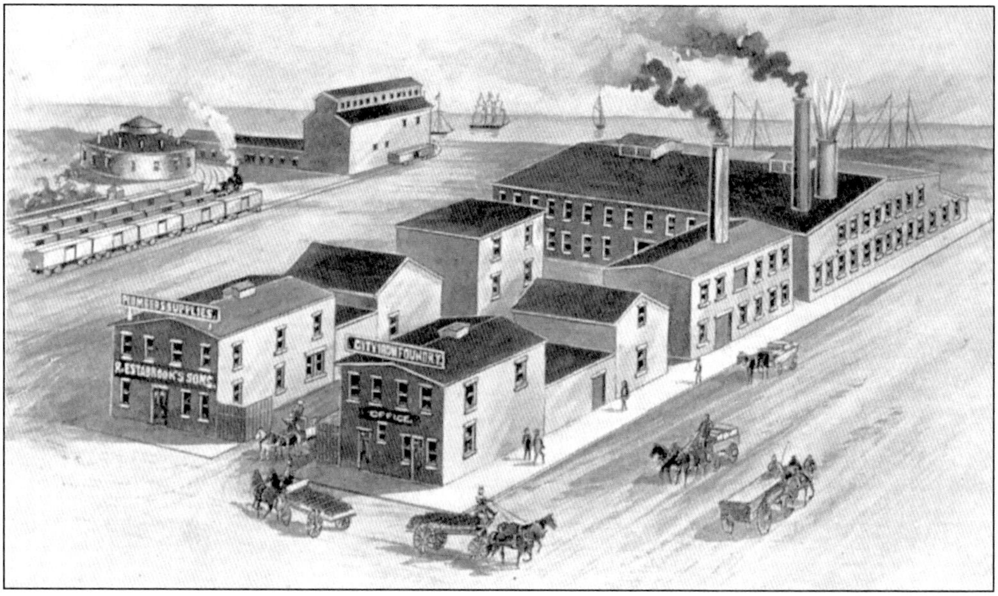


R. Estabrook's Sons, City Iron Foundry, was established in 1874 and was located at West First and C Streets. The company manufactured machinery, boiler and building castings, soil pipe and fittings, bathtubs, and plumbing supplies in general. By the beginning of the 20th century, the three sons of R. Estabrook operated the iron foundry.

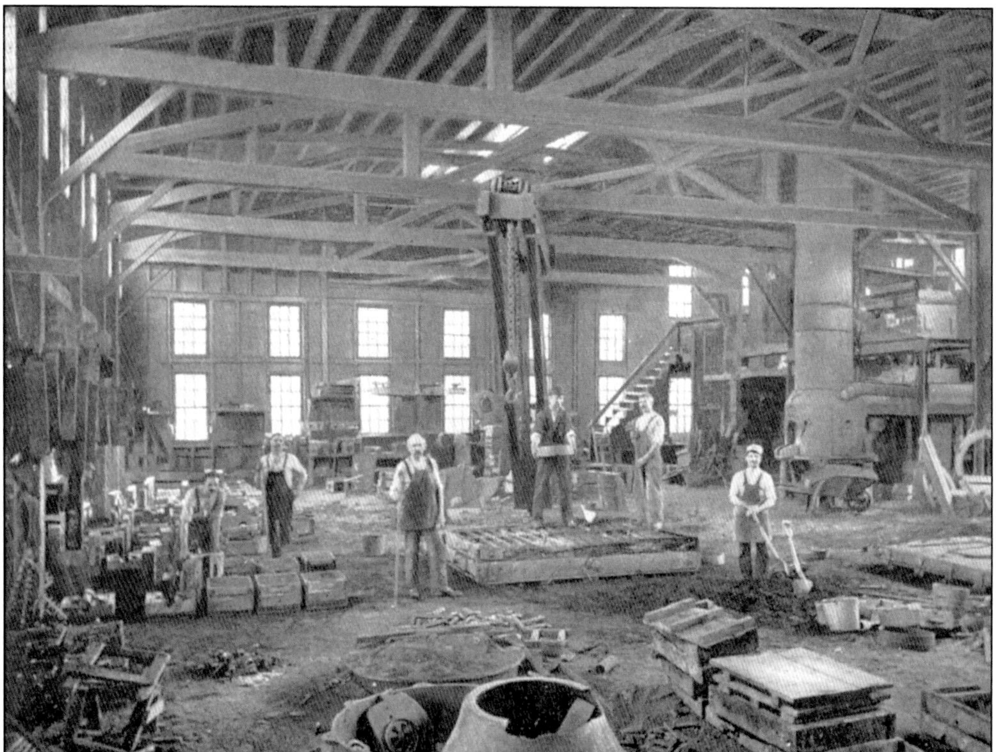

The molding shop of R. Estabrook's Sons, City Iron Foundry, was a vast room where boiler and building castings and brass and copper works were molded by the workmen in the photograph.

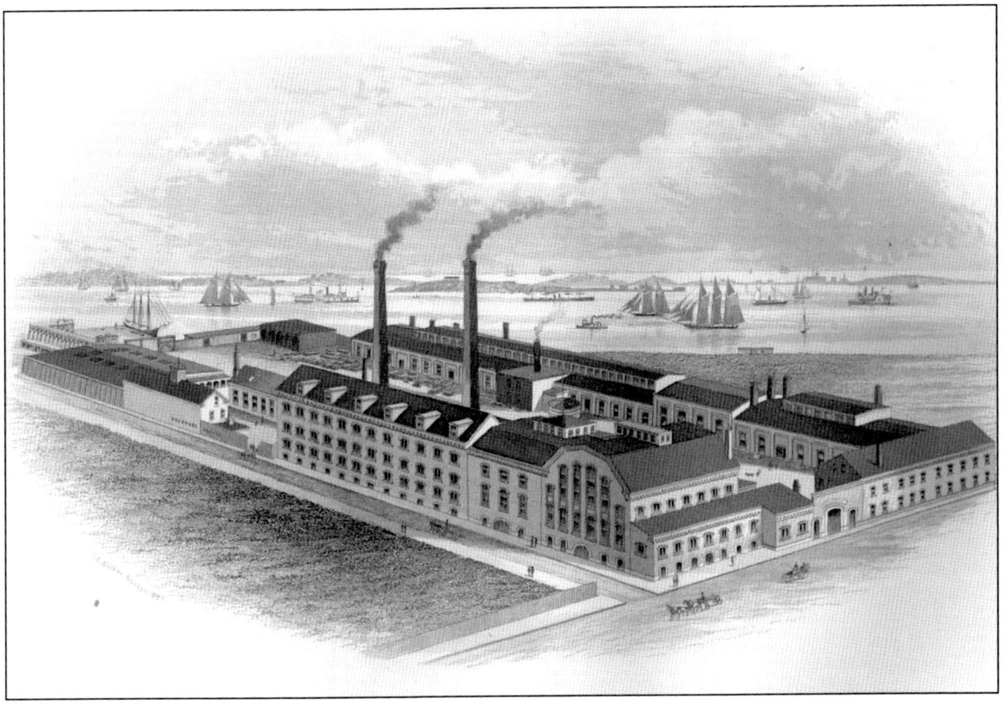

The Walworth Manufacturing Company was established in 1842 and moved to City Point 40 years later, when it was incorporated. In its new location, the company occupied 13 acres of land and employed 1,300 men. Its products consisted of cast iron, malleable iron, brass and steel valves, Walworth die plates, pipe cutters, wrenches, and reamers. Notice the ships in Boston Harbor and the harbor islands in the distance.

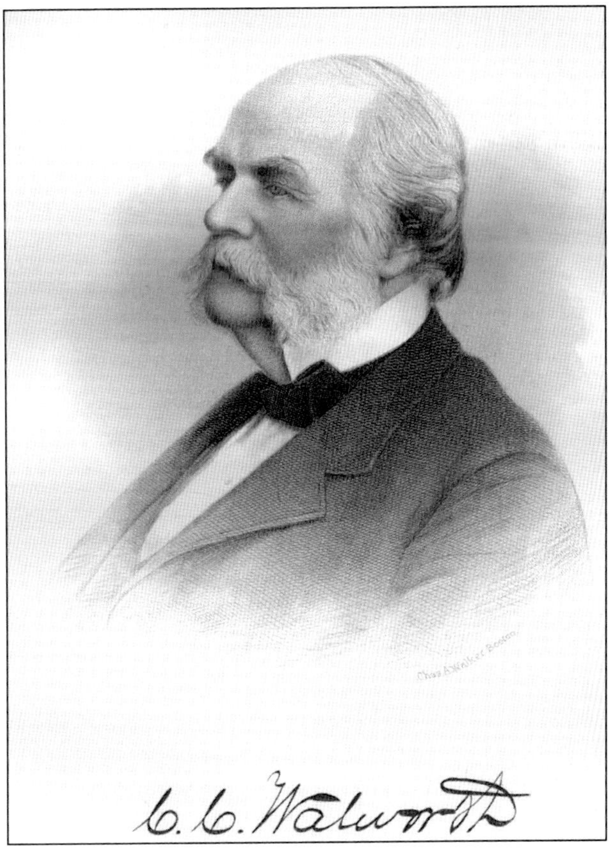


C. Clark Walworth (1815–1894) was president and general manager of the Walworth Manufacturing Company. He was the inventor of the six-spindle tapping machine, a patent radiator, a manifold that reduces the cost over the old-fashioned fittings, the patent screw plate, and a patent safety floor flange. His most important invention was the Walworth sprinkler, which saved millions of dollars worth of property.

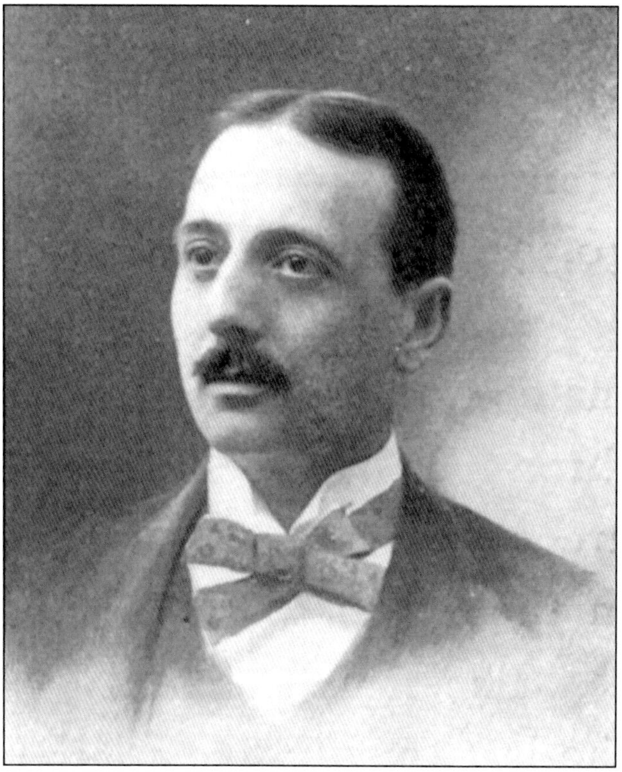

W.B. Holloway was the manager of the New England Branch of the Rochester Brewing Company at 295–305 A Street, near Broadway Station, at the beginning of the 20th century. One of numerous breweries in Boston, this one produced a popular brand of lager beer.

The Rochester Brewing Company was one of many breweries located in South Boston. As early as 1829, the Boston Beer Company produced golden ale at the corner of D and West Second Streets. Other well-known breweries in South Boston included the Suffolk Brewery at Eighth and G Streets. So heady an aroma was created by these breweries that one resident said, "Boy, I smelled the hops!"

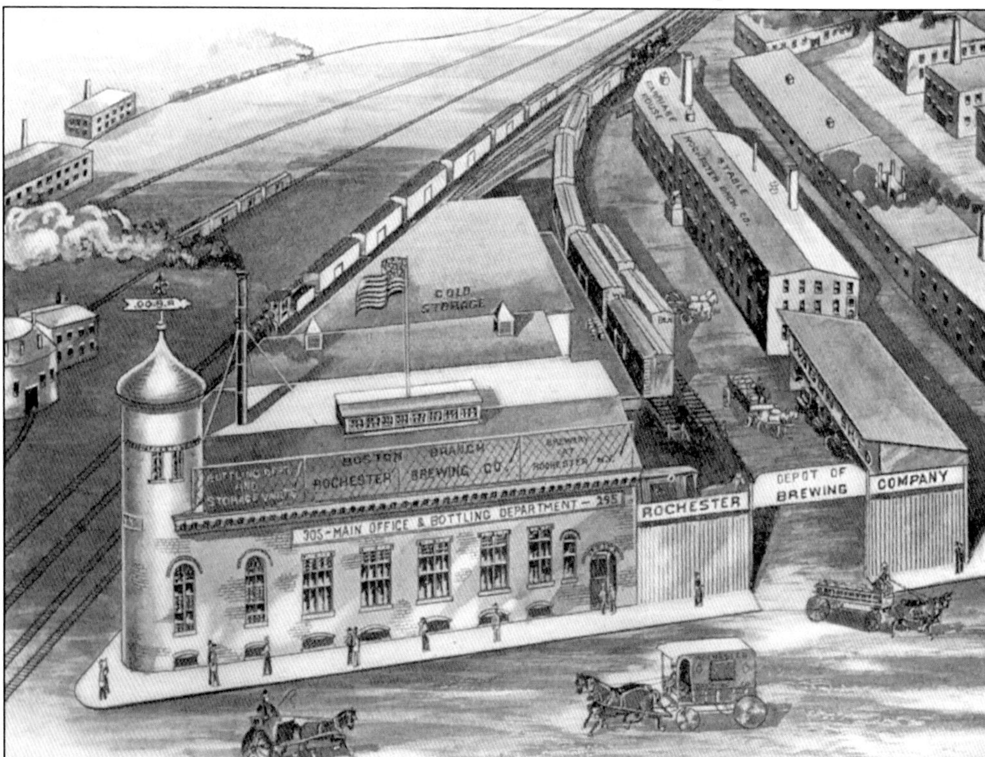

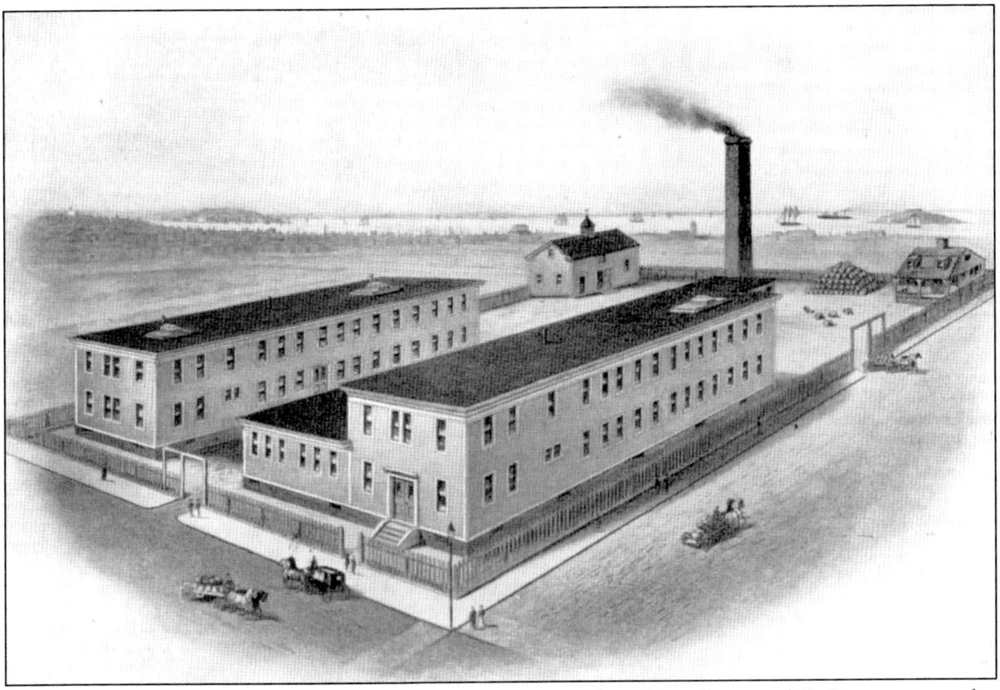

The works of F.E. Atteaux & Company Inc. was located at West First and D Streets, now the site of Shaughnessy & Ahearn. Manufacturers of colors and chemicals, the company's plant was on the edge of the waterfront that was later filled in and known as the Commonwealth Flats.

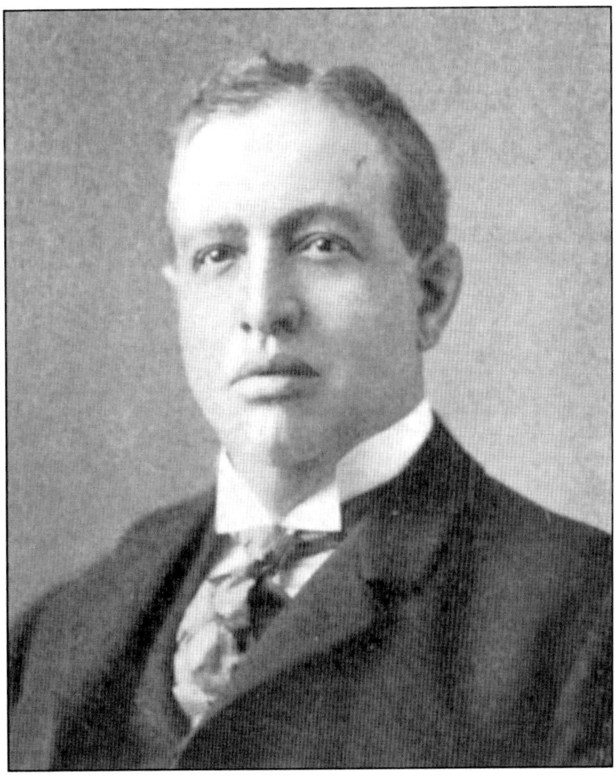

Frederick E. Atteaux was the president of F.E. Atteaux & Company, which imported dyestuffs and chemicals.

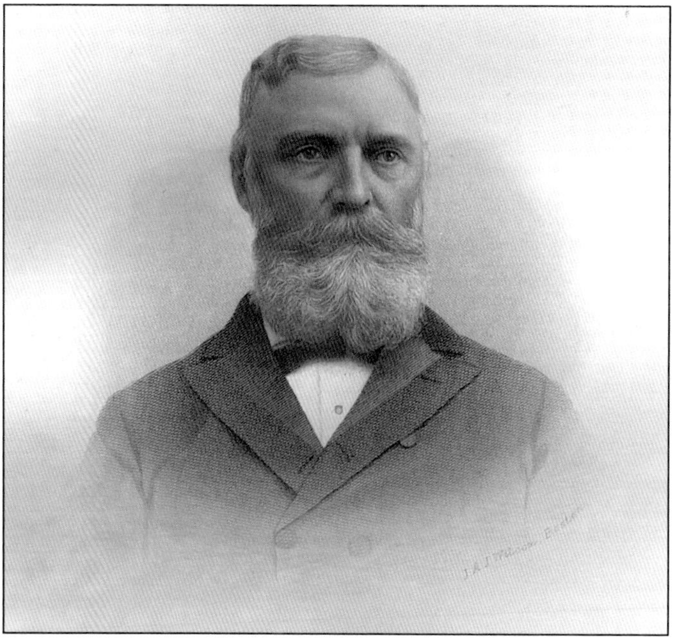

William Prescott Hunt (1827–1911) was president of the South Boston Iron Company, founded in 1827, which produced much of the decorative cast iron used in mid-19th century Boston. The company employed upwards of 250 workmen. Other iron foundries in South Boston included Alger's, Bay State, Norway, Fulton, and Howard Iron Foundries.

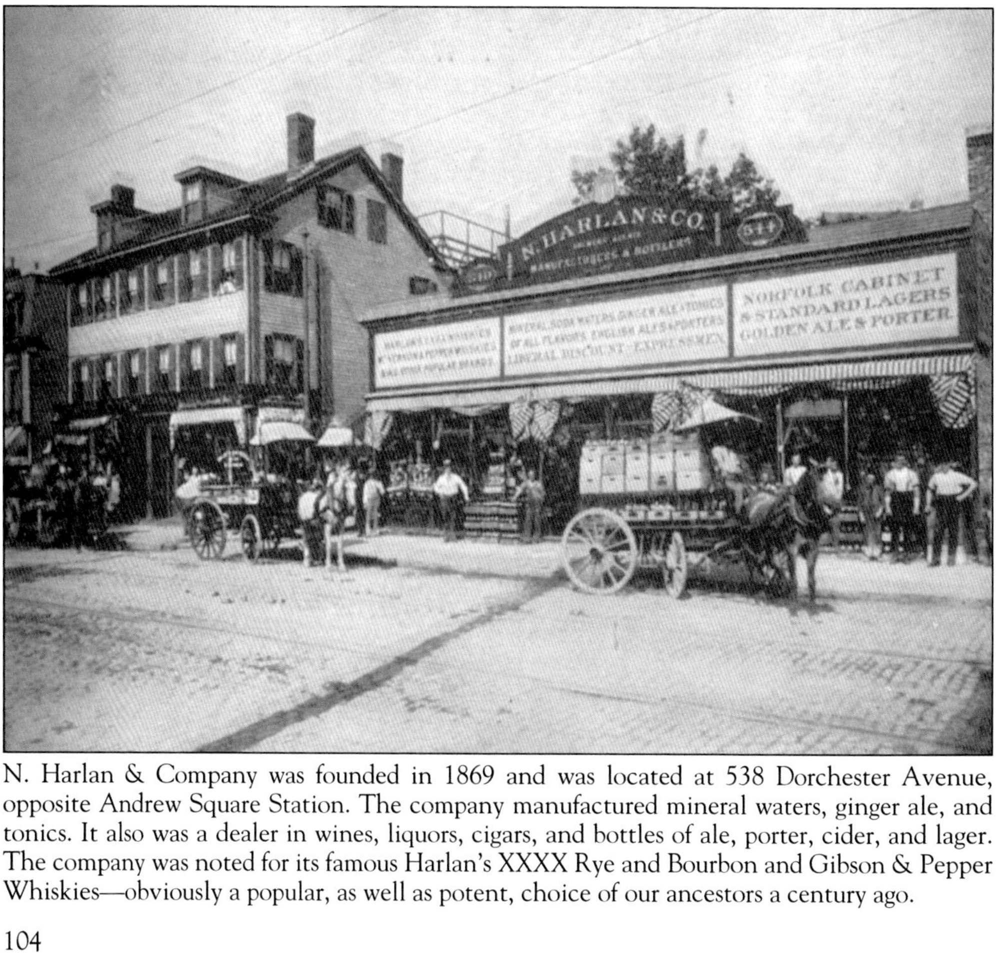


N. Harlan & Company was founded in 1869 and was located at 538 Dorchester Avenue, opposite Andrew Square Station. The company manufactured mineral waters, ginger ale, and tonics. It also was a dealer in wines, liquors, cigars, and bottles of ale, porter, cider, and lager. The company was noted for its famous Harlan's XXXX Rye and Bourbon and Gibson & Pepper Whiskies—obviously a popular, as well as potent, choice of our ancestors a century ago.

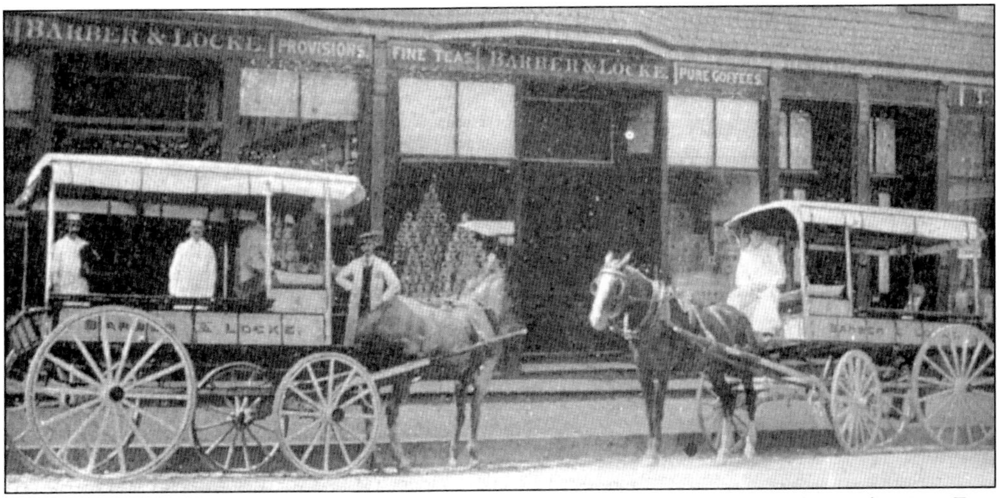

Barber & Locke were dealers in choice groceries and provisions. They were located at 719 East Fifth Street at the corner of N Street. With eight clerks and four horse-drawn delivery wagons, Barber & Locke was known for its promptness in the delivery of orders. The company "made it a standing rule to deal in goods only of the best quality and can name prices that will defy the keenest competition."

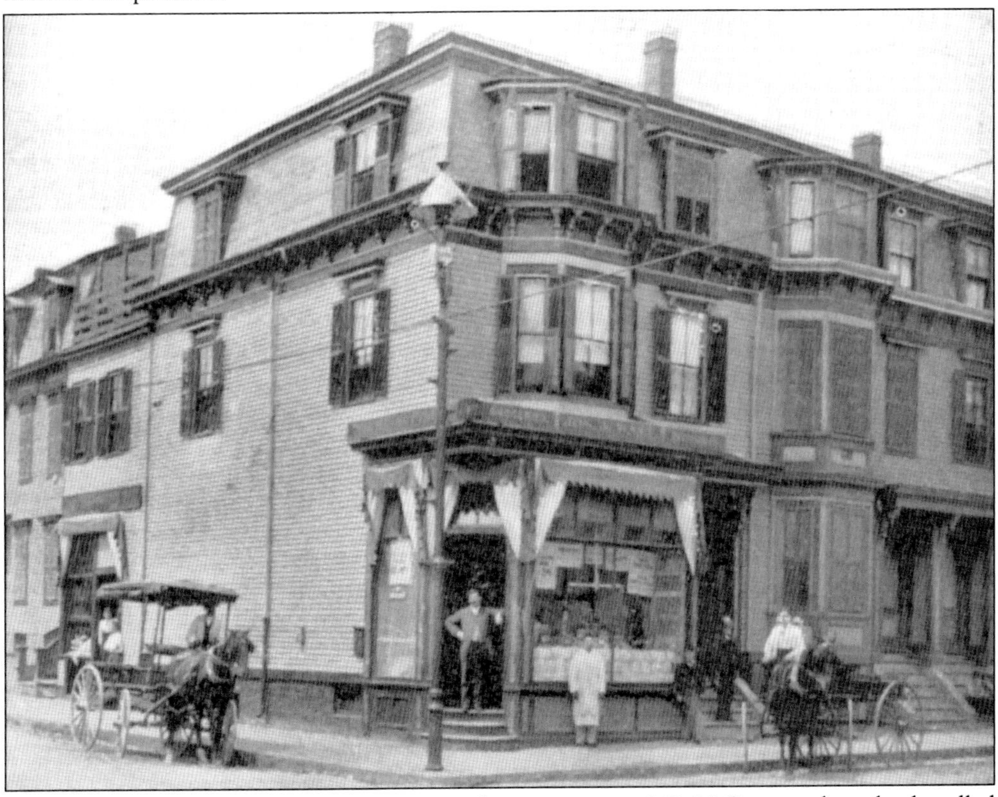
Joseph J. Wall was a dealer in groceries and provisions at 143 M Street, where he handled "only the best goods and his patrons are always assured of receiving the freshest and choicest" available produce, fruits, and vegetables. Wall stands in the doorway; his horse-drawn delivery wagon can be seen on the left.

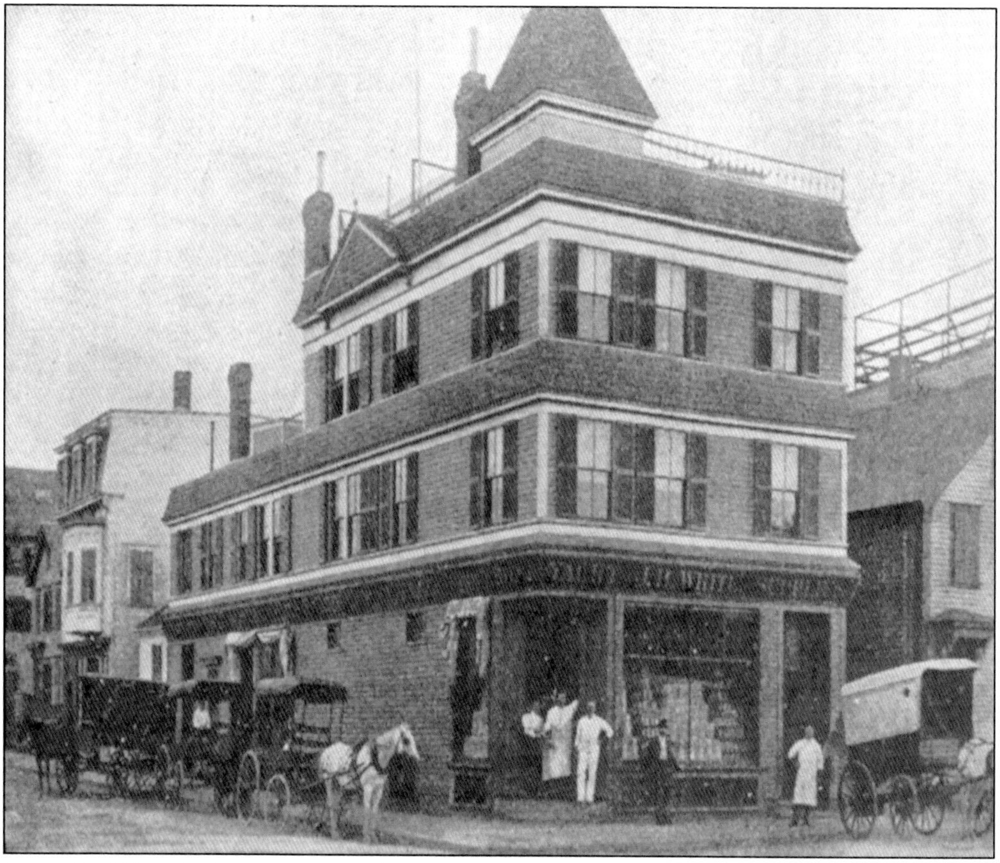

James H. White had a grocery and fancy provision store at the corner of O and East Second Streets. Known for his elegant catering to the various South Boston yacht clubs and to pleasure parties, White was considered "very popular with all his patrons and a courteous, agreeable, pleasant gentleman."

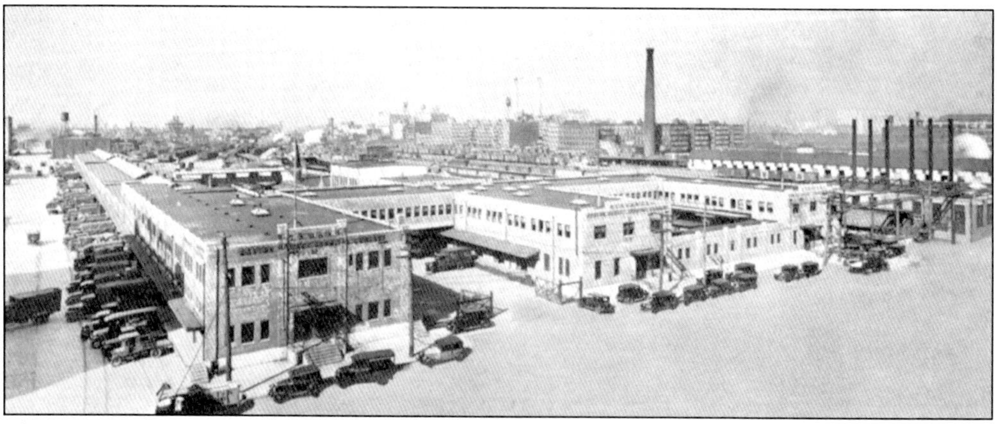

The Boston Market Terminal was opened in 1927 in South Boston. It was known as the "Gateway to All New England." The terminal was located on C Street, between West First and Fargo Streets near the New York, New Haven, & Hartford Railroad, on which the trailers of fruits and vegetables arrived daily. The terminal eventually moved to Everett to join the New England Produce Center in Chelsea in the 1960s.

# *Ten*

# City Institutions

There were numerous institutions that were relocated to South Boston from the city proper in the early to mid-19th century. The House of Correction was founded in 1821 for the "restraint and employment of the idle and vicious poor, for habitual drunkards, beggars and those condemned for petty offenses in the inferior courts of justice." The House of Industry, adjacent to the House of Correction, was "destined for the comfort, support and relief, and, as far as they are competent, for the employment of the virtuous poor, and of those alone who are reduced to seek this refuge from misfortune, or age, or infancy."

Built as identical structures of coarse, rough granite blocks, the institutions were each 220 feet long, 343 feet wide, and 29 feet high. These impressive buildings were "regarded with just pride by the citizens [of Boston], and have been models after which other municipalities have reared, it may be, more elaborate and costly institutions, but that none have more fully and creditably fulfilled the mission for which they have been established." The House of Correction was abandoned in 1902, and all the prisoners were transferred to the new buildings on Deer Island—something "the people of South Boston have been endeavoring since 1847 to be rid of this institution."

Other institutions located at City Point in South Boston included the Massachusetts School for Idiotic and Feeble Minded Youth, the Boston Lunatic Asylum, and the Church Home for Orphan and Destitute Children. By the beginning of the 20th century, 24 acres along East First Street from M to O Streets became Lawley's Shipyard, and afterward it was purchased by the Boston Elevated Railway for use as a lumber mill, materials storage yard, and a coal-handling facility. Today, this prime real estate is used by the Massachusetts Bay Transit Authority as a bus station and holding yard.

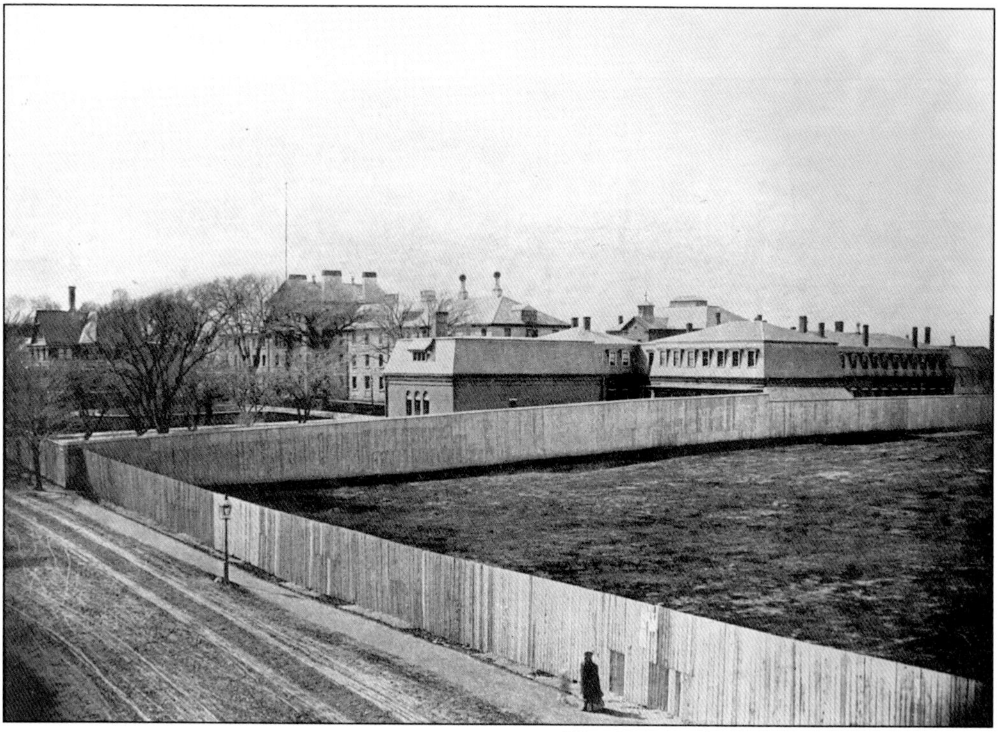

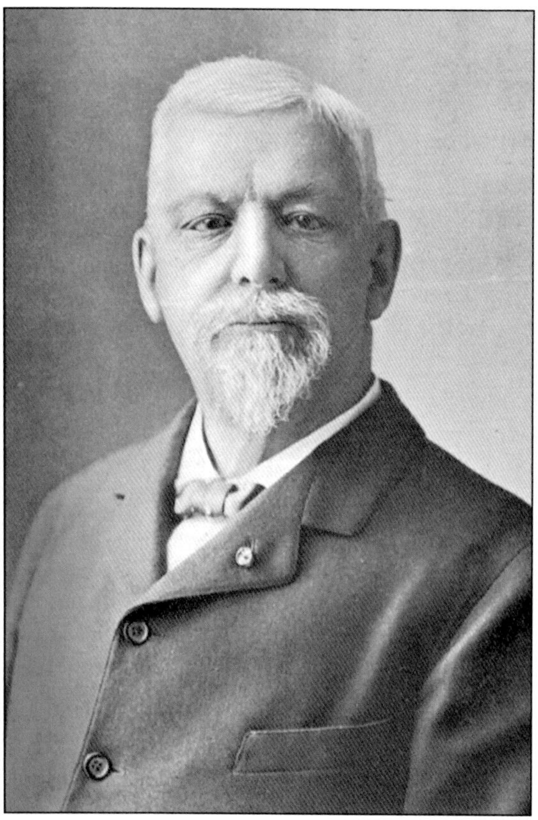

The House of Correction was built in South Boston as "a place of retribution, and not reformation" for both men and women. In many instances, the same persons were committed to this house on numerous occasions, with their crimes ranging from public drunkenness, breaking and entering, assault and battery with a knife, larceny, forgery, and perjury, to assault with attempt to murder. (Courtesy of the Boston Public Library.)

Col. John Chadwick Whiton (1828–1912) served as superintendent of the South Boston House of Correction, where he was considered not just a thorough disciplinarian, but "one of the most able and responsible officials in the public service." The House of Correction was considered an elaborate institution, with a steam engine of 20 horsepower in its workshop, which allowed the inmates to speedily complete their tasks under Whiton's direction.

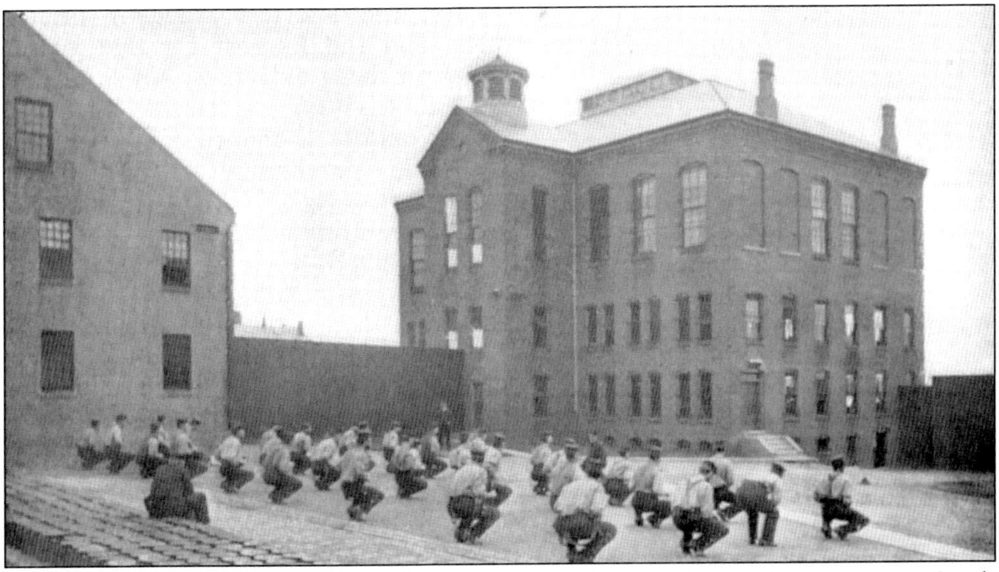

Male prisoners exercise in the woefully inadequate yard at the House of Correction in South Boston. Other than the short time allowed for exercise in the prison yard, they were employed at making shirts and garments on steam-run sewing machines, which were sold to provide income for the upkeep of the prison.

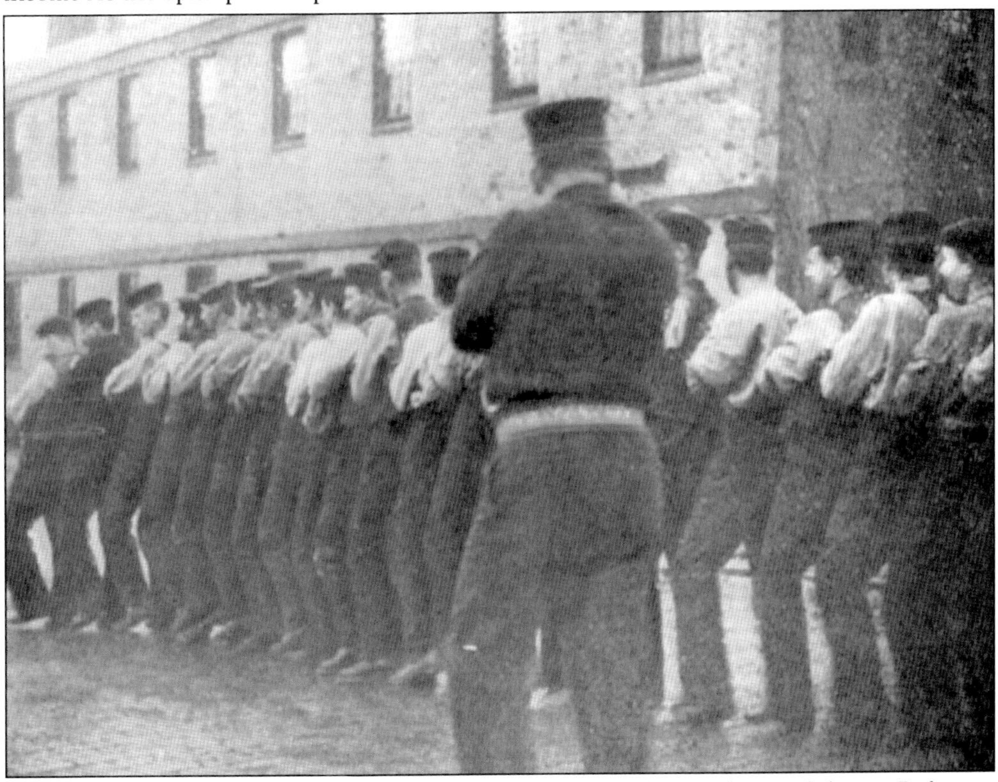

The lockstep was a short march from the inmates' cells to the workshops. Before it became common to do exercises in the prison yard, the lockstep was only exercise that the inmates received.

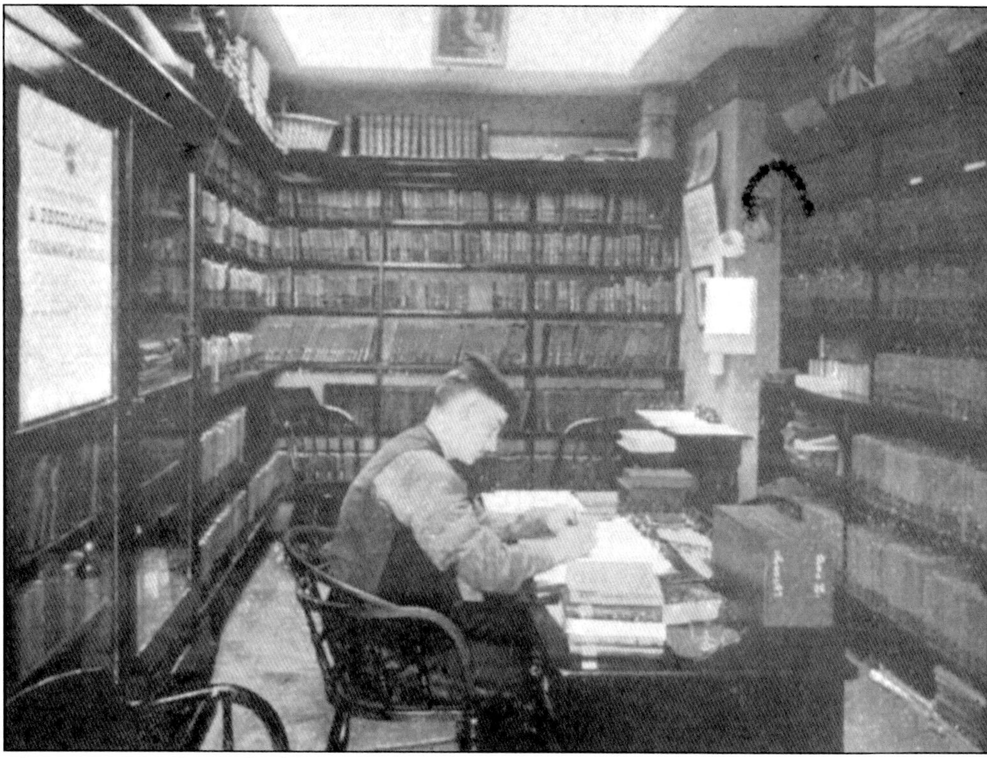

An inmate works in the library at the House of Correction. With a large number of books available to inmates, it was thought that "reformation rather than punishment should be the spirit of an institution of this kind. A man's better nature should be stimulated" rather than suppressed. The inmate should be made aware of hope for the future, as "the state is desirous, primarily, of making him a better man rather than punishing him for his offense."

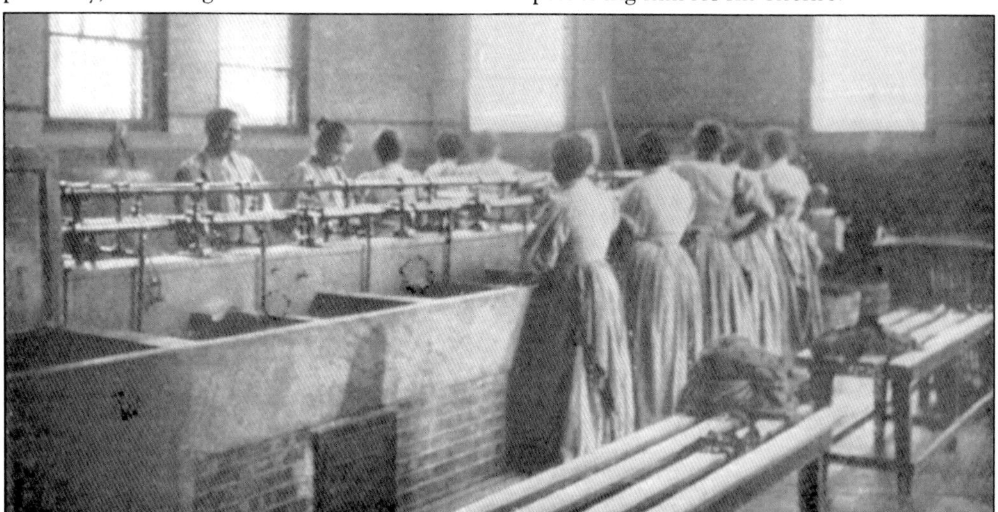

Women inmates worked in the laundry and did all the housework at the House of Correction. "Everything within and about the buildings is kept beautifully neat. Excellent discipline is maintained. The inmates are lodged as well as circumstances permit, well clothed, well fed, and well cared for in sickness. Provision is also made for their spiritual welfare."

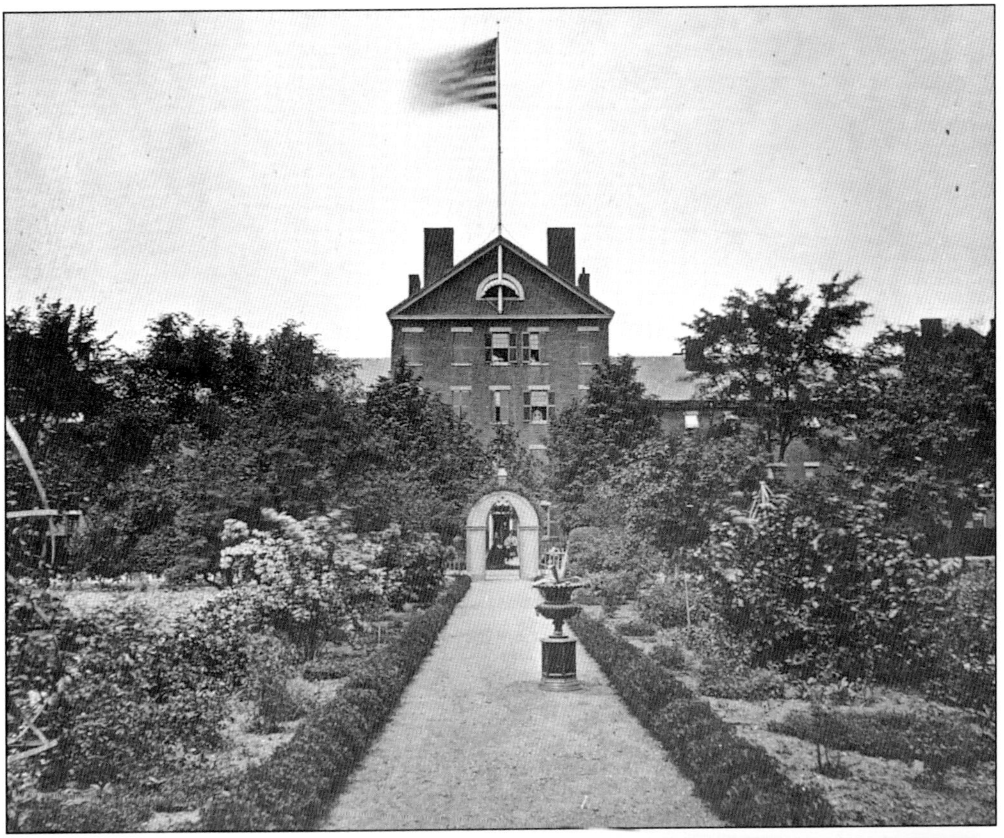

The Boston Lunatic Hospital was located between the House of Correction and the House Industry in City Point, South Boston. It consisted of a central pavilion with two wings of 72 single rooms for patients. The well-maintained garden had a box-edged pathway, with lush flower beds on either side, leading to the elegant brick institution, which flew the Stars and Stripes from a flagpole mounted on its pediment.

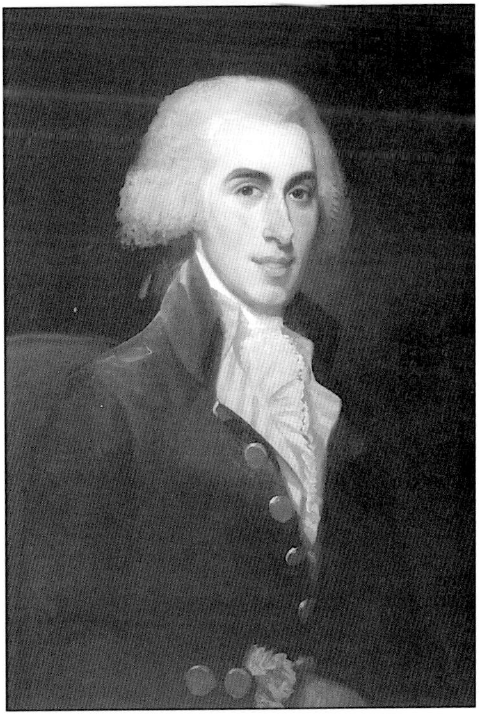

Charles Bulfinch (1763–1844) designed the Boston Lunatic Hospital, the House of Industry, and the House of Correction at City Point in South Boston. A graduate of Harvard College in 1781, he was a "gentleman's architect," who changed the face of Boston—both architecturally and topographically. He served as a chairman of the Boston Board of Selectmen from 1797 to 1818, as well as chief of police. He left Boston in 1819 to work in Washington, D.C., where he rebuilt the capital after the British burned it during the War of 1812.

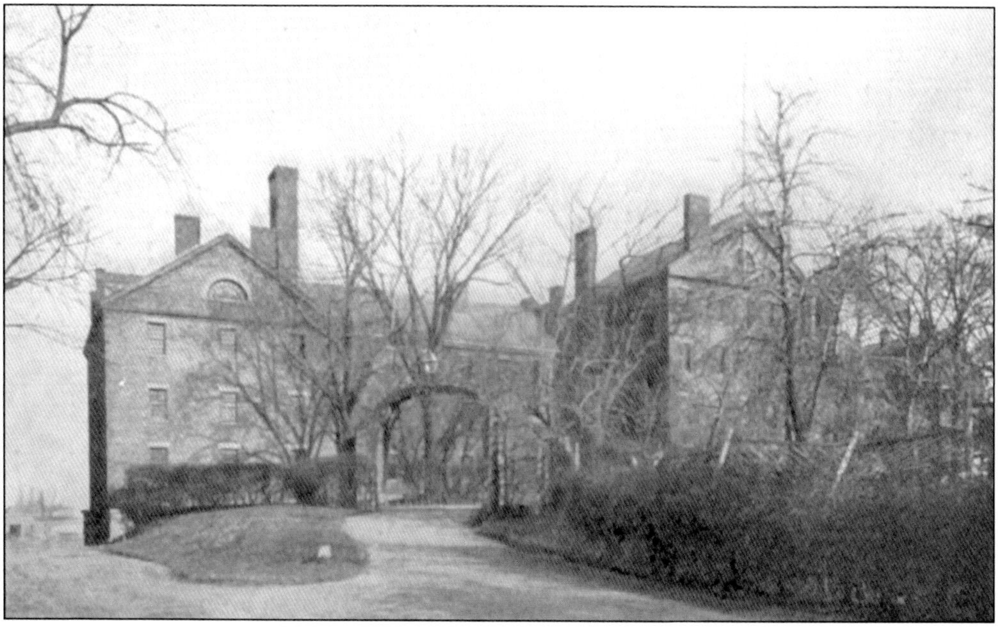

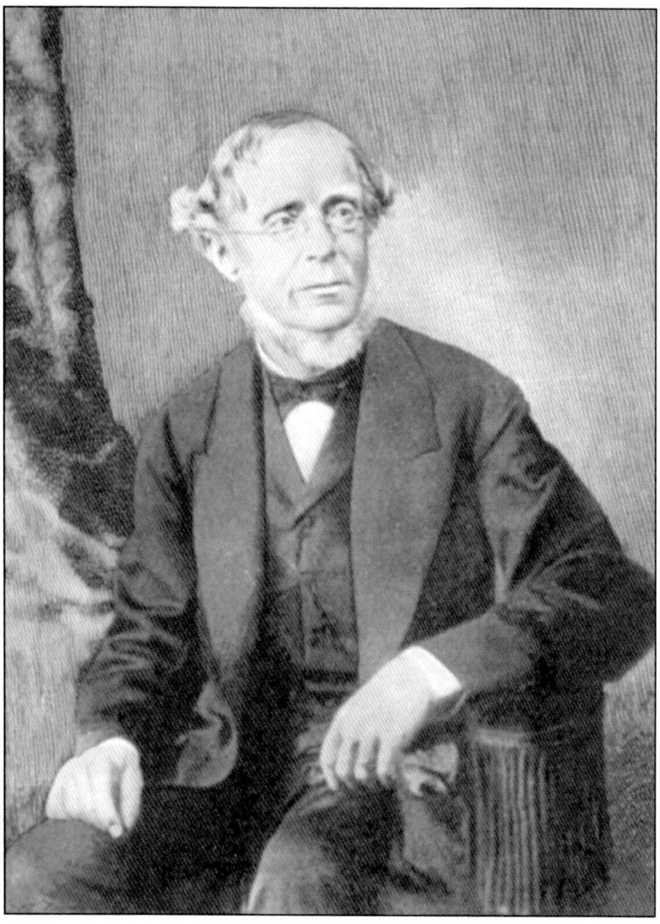

The Boston Lunatic Hospital was located within ample grounds near the ocean in City Point. Opened in 1839, this was the first public institution in Boston for the care and treatment of the insane exclusively. In the 1890s, the hospital moved to the semirural Austin and Pierce Farms in Mount Hope (now Roslindale).

Dr. John S. Butler served as the first superintendent of the Boston Lunatic Hospital. A humane man, he instituted radically new methods in the care of the insane that included compassion and understanding rather than forced coercion.

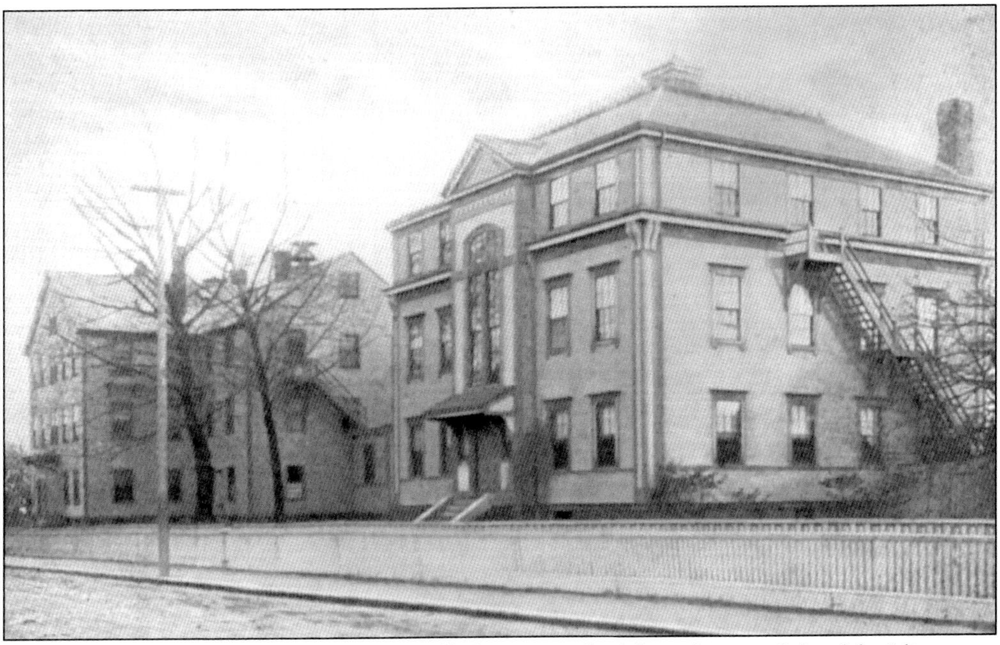

The Home for the Feeble Minded, originally known as the Massachusetts School for Idiots, was an experimental school established in 1848 for "teaching and training idiotic children" through the influence of Dr. Samuel Gridley Howe. Howe "was convinced beyond doubt that idiots were capable of being improved in their bodily habits, in their mental capacities, and in their spiritual natures."

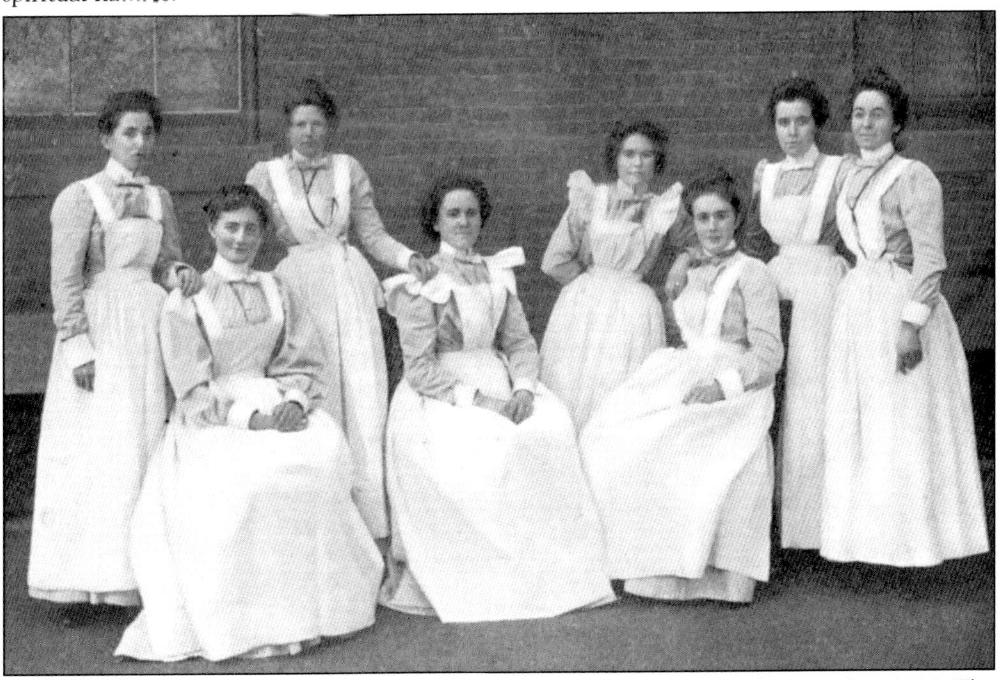

A group of attendants at the Home for the Feeble Minded pose for their photograph c. 1890. The attendants' constant attention provided the children with a safe and nurturing environment in which they could develop skills at their own pace.

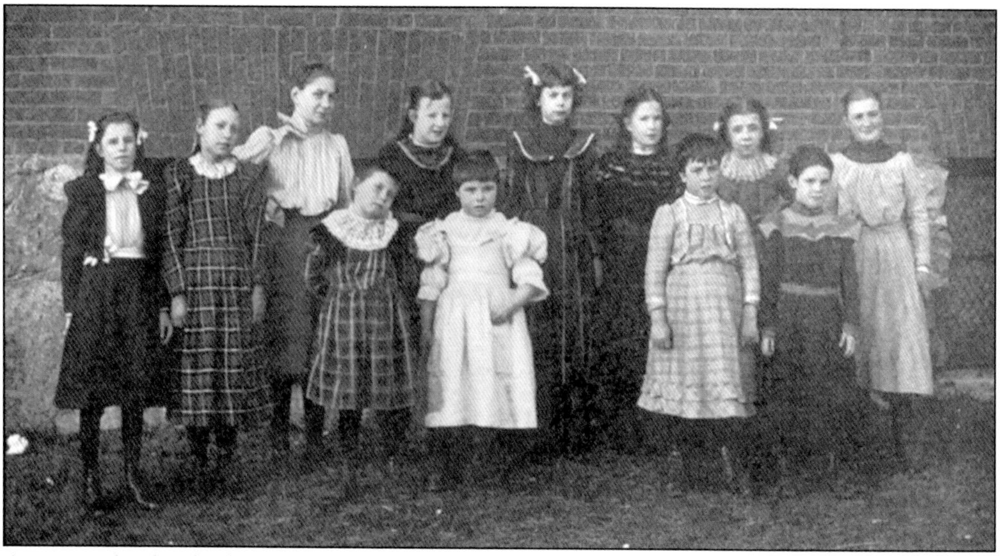

A group of girls who lived at the Home for the Feeble Minded pose for a group photograph c. 1890. It was said by Kate Gannet Wells that there "is no more interesting phase of psychology than that of the development of a low grade, feeble-minded child into an intelligent, self-guiding person, with due regard for the rights of others."

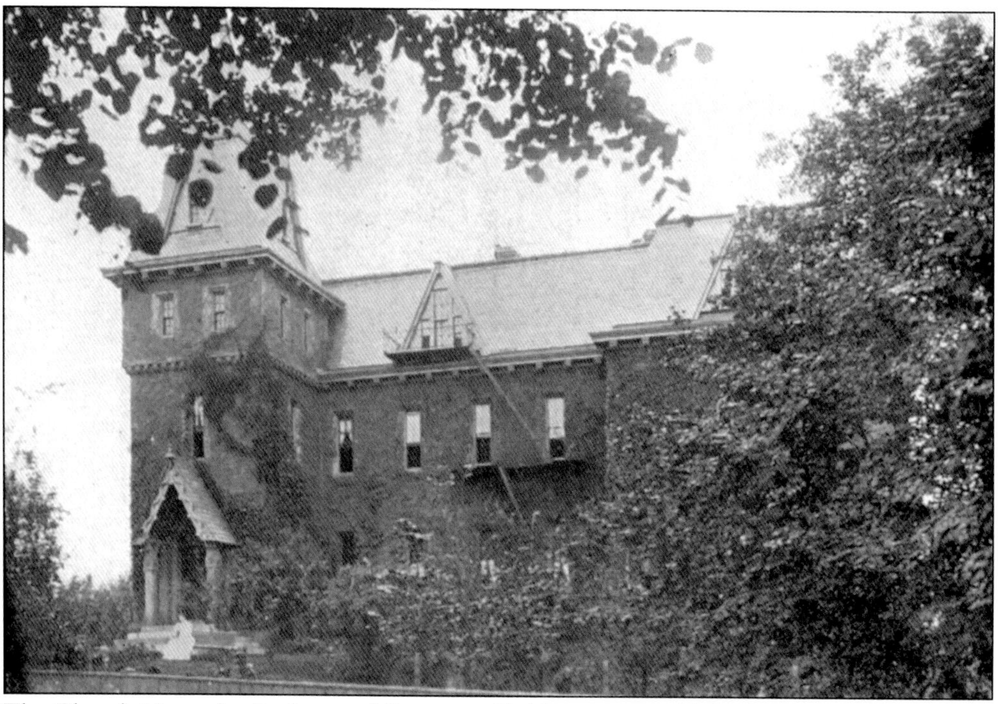

The Church Home for Orphan and Destitute Children was established in 1855 and relocated to the corner of N and Fourth Streets in South Boston in 1858. Under the direction of the Episcopal bishop of Massachusetts, the home received children between the ages of four and six to meet whatever seemed the best advantage of the child. The home was later closed; in 1912, the Sisters of Charity of Nazareth used the building as the Nazareth Grammar and High School, now known as St. Brigid's School. The building was demolished in the mid-1960s.

# *Eleven*

# Marine Park, City Point, and Castle Island

The panoramic views of Dorchester Bay and Boston Harbor from City Point and Castle Island are unsurpassed. They have been a popular destination of Bostonians for well over a century. At the beginning of the 20th century, a wooden footbridge was built connecting City Point to Castle Island. In 1925, the footbridge was replaced by an earthen causeway and in 1932, an automobile road was built there. Since that time, Bostonians have flocked to Castle Island to walk, to picnic, or simply to marvel at the panoramic views of Boston Harbor, which unfold in all directions.

As early as the 17th century, the area of Marine Park between K and L Streets was known as "Pow Wow Point." The Neponset Tribe of the Massachusetts Indians referred to the neck of land as "Mattapanock." The marshes along the beach provided forage for the early settlers' cattle but by the early 19th century, this area began to attract new residents, who built houses near the ocean, but could get to town by the Bay View omnibus. In the late 19th century, the city of Boston began to dredge the beaches and created "the Strand," or what is now called Day Boulevard, along Old Harbor. The laying out of a green belt connecting City Point to the "Emerald Necklace" in Boston was strategic and ensured that, with streetcars, Bostonians would come. One resident said that "City Point was an ideal place for natural scenery and beauty. Its grandeur was beyond compare and one could not wish for better." With shelters for resting and trees for shade, the boulevard has long been a pleasant thoroughfare to walk, day or night.

The castle was built in 1634, rebuilt after a fire in 1674, and rebuilt again in brick in 1701. It was known as Castle William in honor of King William III. In 1799, its name was changed to Fort Independence. It was rebuilt in 1801 with five bastions—the Winthrop on the east, Shirley on the south, Dearborn on the north, Adams on the northeast, and Hancock on the west. The fort was immortalized in Edgar Allan Poe's *Cask of Amontillado*, the story of the Massie-Drane duel at Castle Island on Christmas Day 1817.

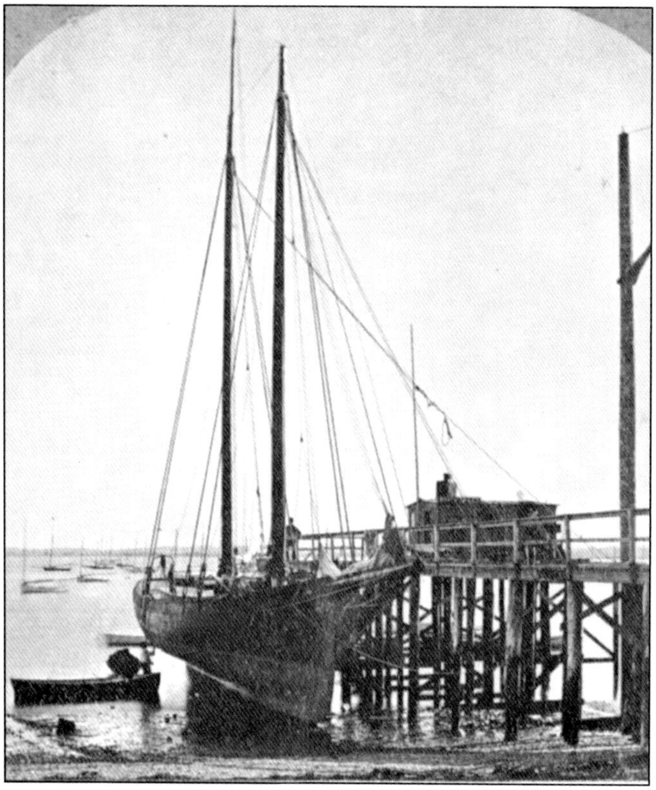

A schooner is docked beside a pier at Old Harbor in South Boston at low tide, while repair work is done to its underside. Numerous boats were repaired at low tide, especially along this stretch of beach in South Boston, unless a dry dock was available elsewhere.

A well-dressed woman walks on the beach at Bay View at the beginning of the 20th century. This stretch of beach was a popular destination for Bostonians, who arrived by foot, by bicycle, and by streetcar to swim, to wade, or just to enjoy a warm sunny afternoon at the beach. Thompson Island is visible in the distance, beyond the pleasure yachts at anchor in Old Harbor.

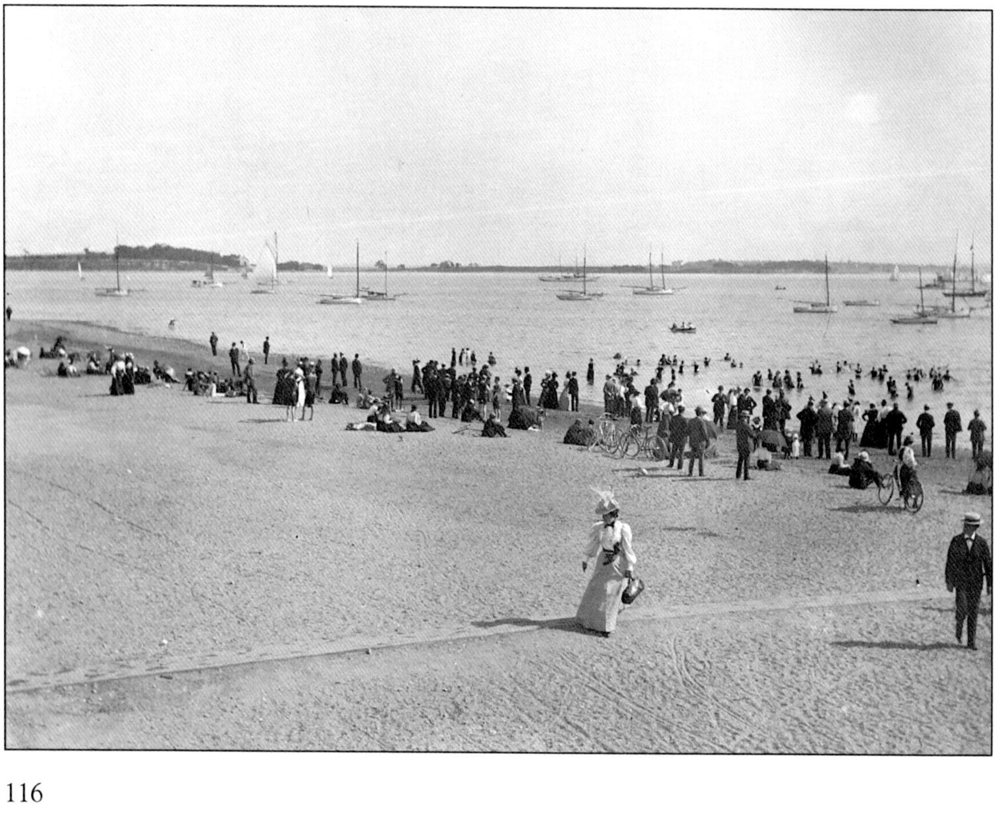

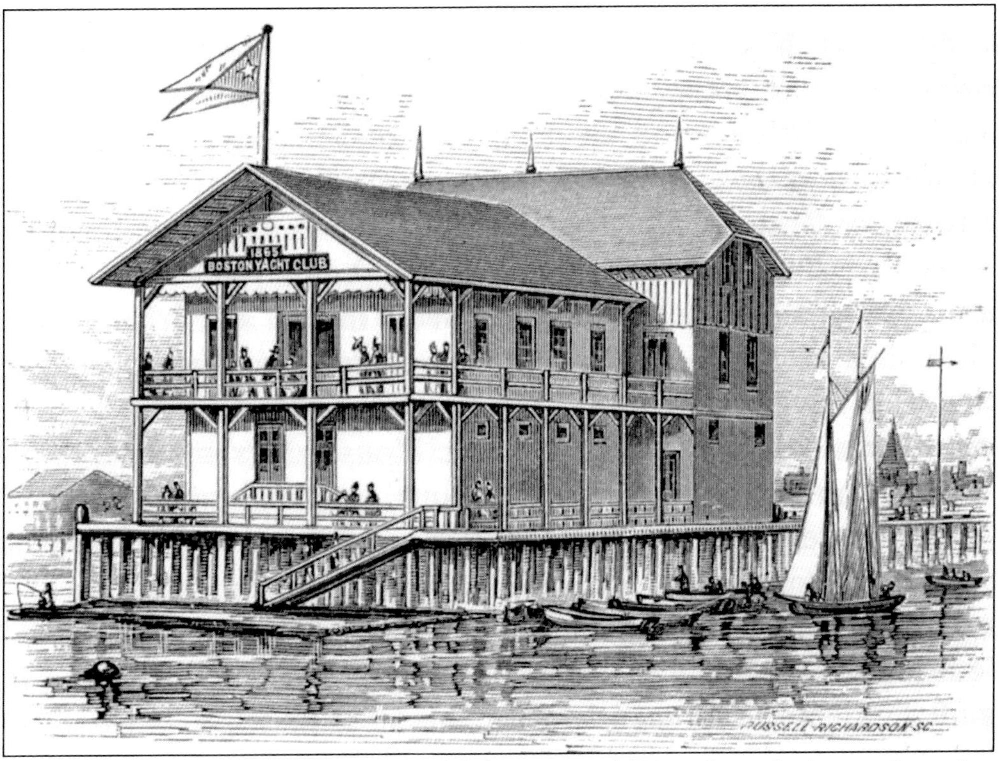


The fanciful stick-style Boston Yacht Club house cost $500 and was built on pilings that projected into the harbor. Organized in 1866, the Boston Yacht Club is the oldest organization of its kind in Boston (although it is now located in Marblehead) and the first yacht club to be chartered in Massachusetts. Other yacht clubs were the South Boston (1868), the Puritan Canoe (1887), the Mosquito Fleet (1888), the Columbia (1896), and the Boston Harbor Yacht Club (1962).

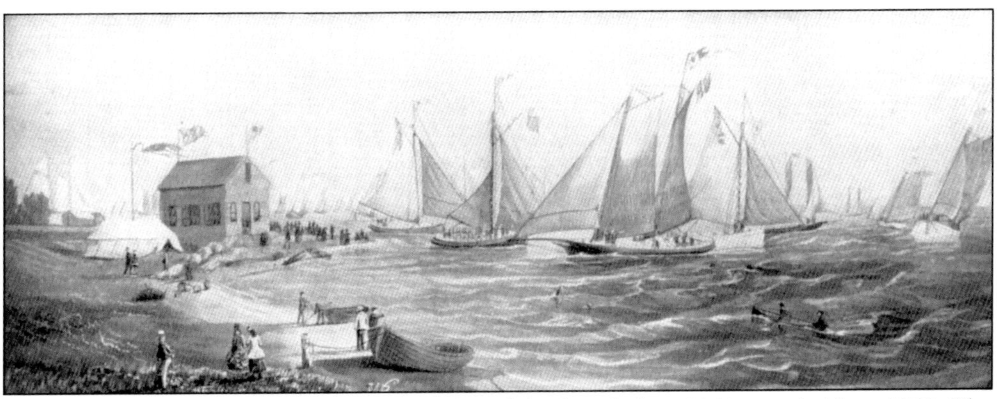

The first review of the South Boston Yacht Club, founded in 1868, was held in 1868. The yacht club had been started by a "party of gentlemen [who] banded themselves together for the purpose of starting a yacht club, and incidentally to promote a social feeling among yachtsmen." This painting, by J. Pierce, depicts various yachts off the coast at the foot of K Street in Bay View. Notice the original clubhouse, the small wood-frame building on the left.

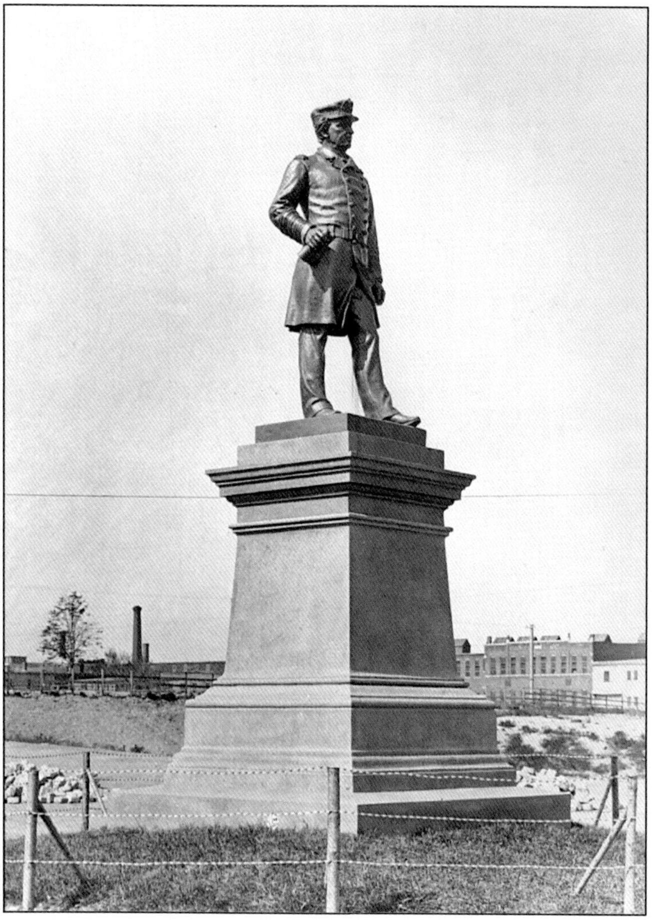

Henry Hudson Kitson designed this statue of Adm. David Glasgow Farragut (1801–1870), which was unveiled by Annie Flood, the daughter of Ald. Thomas Flood, on June 28, 1893, during the Farragut Day celebration in South Boston. It was said of this statue of the "Hero of Mobile Bay" that it "will easily rank with the best statues we have" in Boston. (Courtesy of the Boston Public Library.)

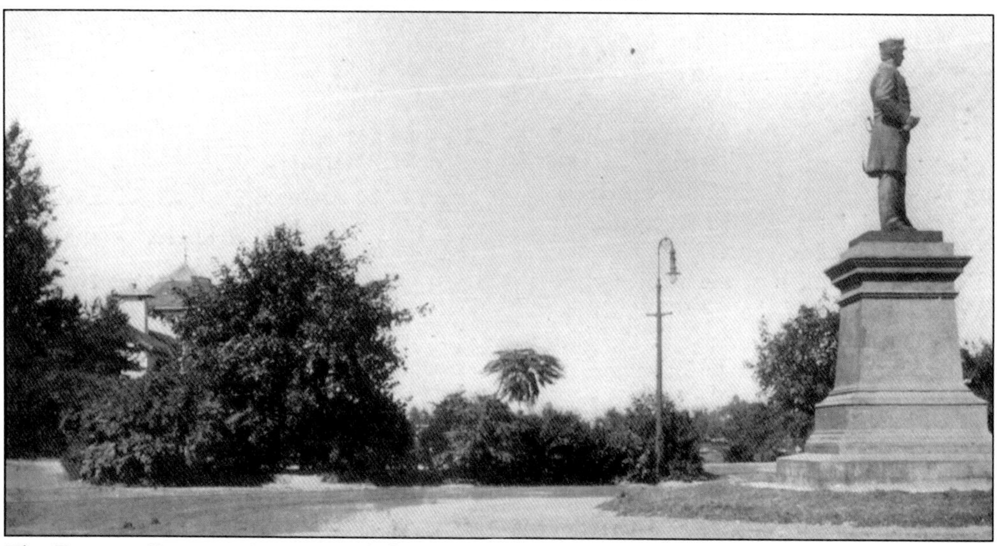

The Farragut Statue at Marine Park faces east and stands on a circle embellished with flowers at the end of East Broadway. The old aquarium, built in 1912 and designed by William Downer Austin, can be seen just beyond the trees on the left. It is now the site of the tennis courts.

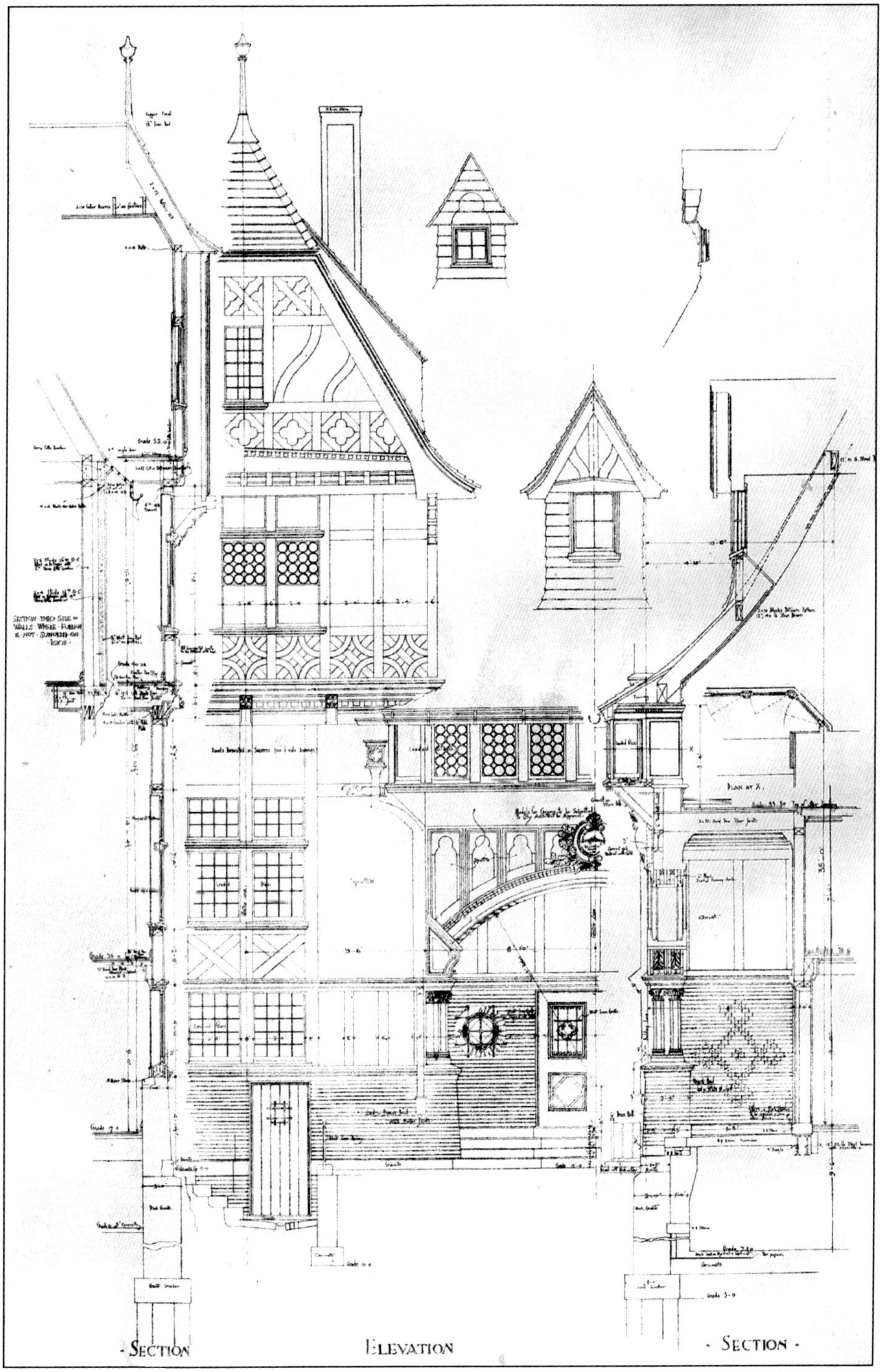


This detailed working drawing of the parts of the Head House of Pier shows Edmund March Wheelwright's design in intricate and fanciful detail. This elevation shows the details of brickwork, pine half-timber work, leaded glass windows, copper drainpipes, and fanciful dormers—all of which combined to make a spectacularly unique building.

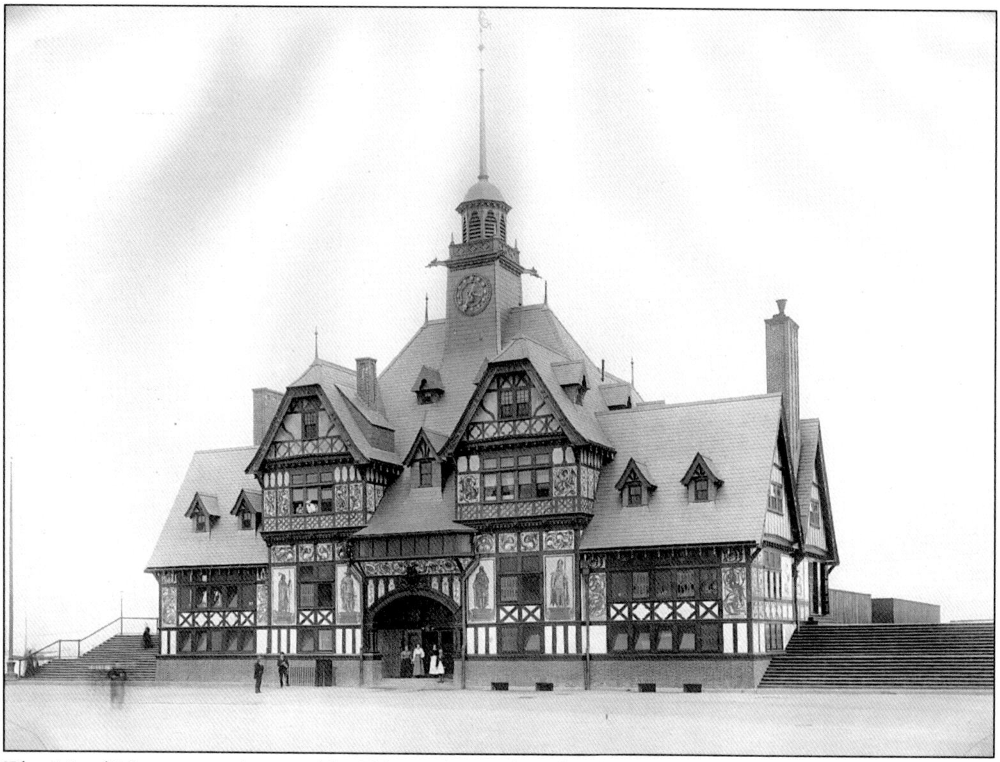

The Head House was designed by Edmund March Wheelwright and was built at City Point in South Boston. Located on Day Boulevard at the entrance to Marine Park, it was built "to give accommodation for sea bathing, and to serve as a restaurant for the frequenters of the pleasure pier." Designed in the half-timbered work of northern Germany, it was considered "charming in its picturesque and fanciful character and yet impressive in its dignity." Notice the broad flights of steps on either side of the Head House, which lead to the promenade that extended into the harbor from the rear, and the four life-sized panels on the facade, depicting *Massachusetts Bay*, *Plymouth Bay*, *The Merrimac*, and *The Charles*.

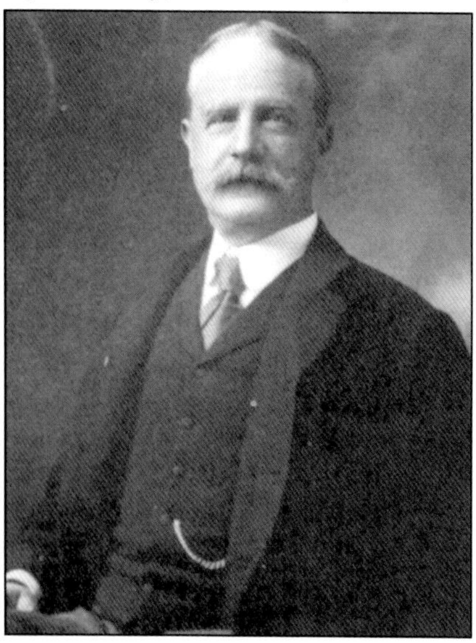

Edmund March Wheelwright (1854–1912) was city architect for the city of Boston from 1891 to 1895. As an architect, in partnership with Parkman B. Haven in the firm of Wheelwright & Haven, he was quite accomplished and "set a high level for municipal architecture in the United States." While designing the decorative scheme of the Head House, which was executed by Max Bachman, Wheelwright created an impressive example of the half-timbered work of northern Germany in City Point. He modeled the Head House after a building erected by the German government in 1893 at the Columbian Exhibition in Chicago. The Head House was destroyed by fire in 1942.

This close-up of the facade of the Head House shows the profusion of detail, with banks of leaded glass windows, carved exterior details, and projecting dormers from the enormous roof of dark Monson slate. The figures on either side of the door are of the *Merrimack River*, on the left, and the *Charles River*, on the right. There were also four smaller panels of four rivers—*The Mystic*, *The Weymouth*, *The Ipswich*, and *The Neponset*.

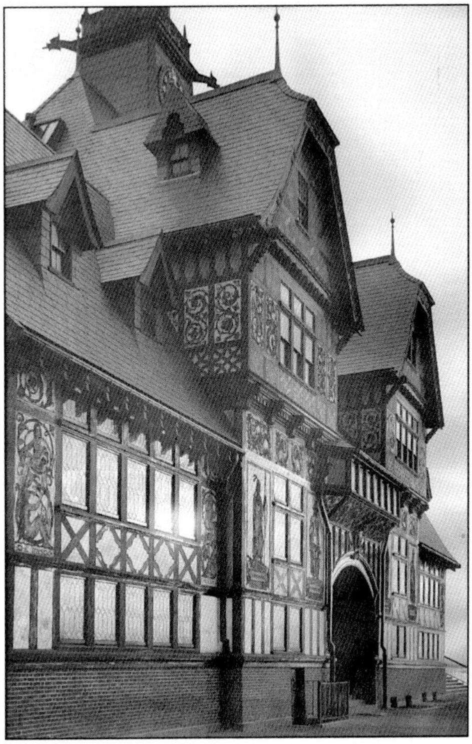

The entrance to the Head House had a wide archway that was surmounted by the ancient seal of the Bay Colony and heavily detailed decorations, such as the figures of *Massachusetts Bay*, a Puritan magistrate holding the Charter of the Colony, on the left, and *Plymouth Bay*, a Pilgrim holding the Bible, on the right. The entrance led to a large, heavily-beamed room, arranged for the bathers. The fanciful carved decoration of figured arabesques, with dolphins and other sea monsters, titans, frolicking mermaids, leaded glass windows, and a mock Tudor half-timbered exterior finish, made for a splendid design.

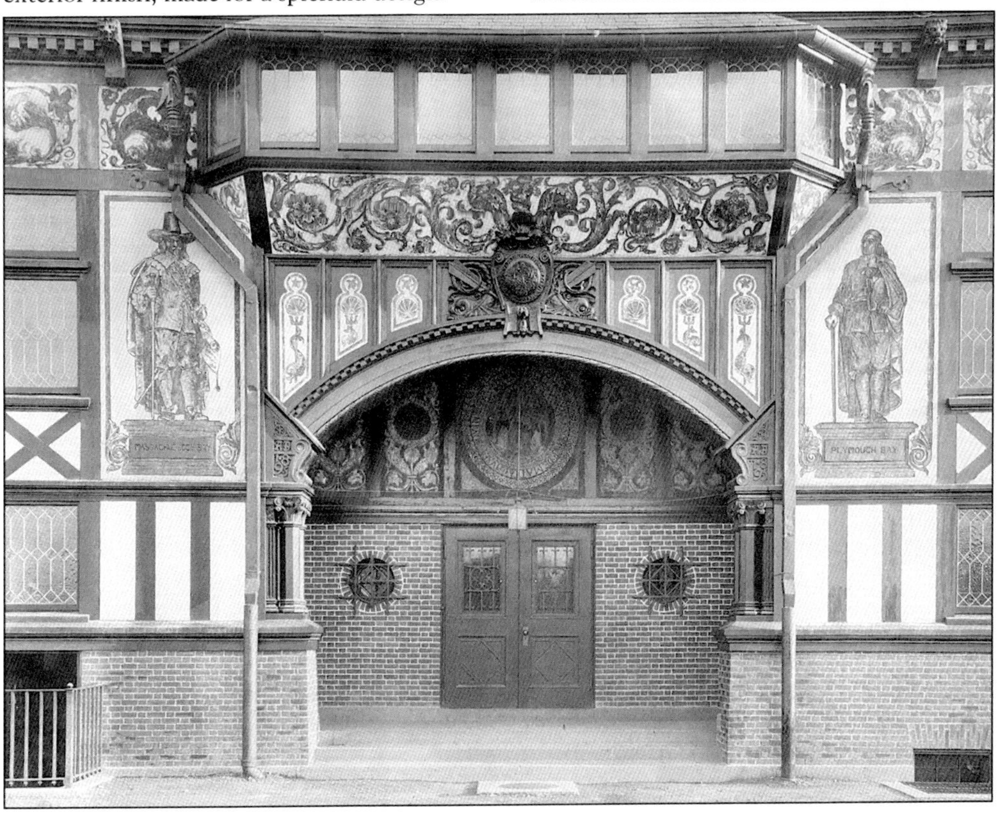

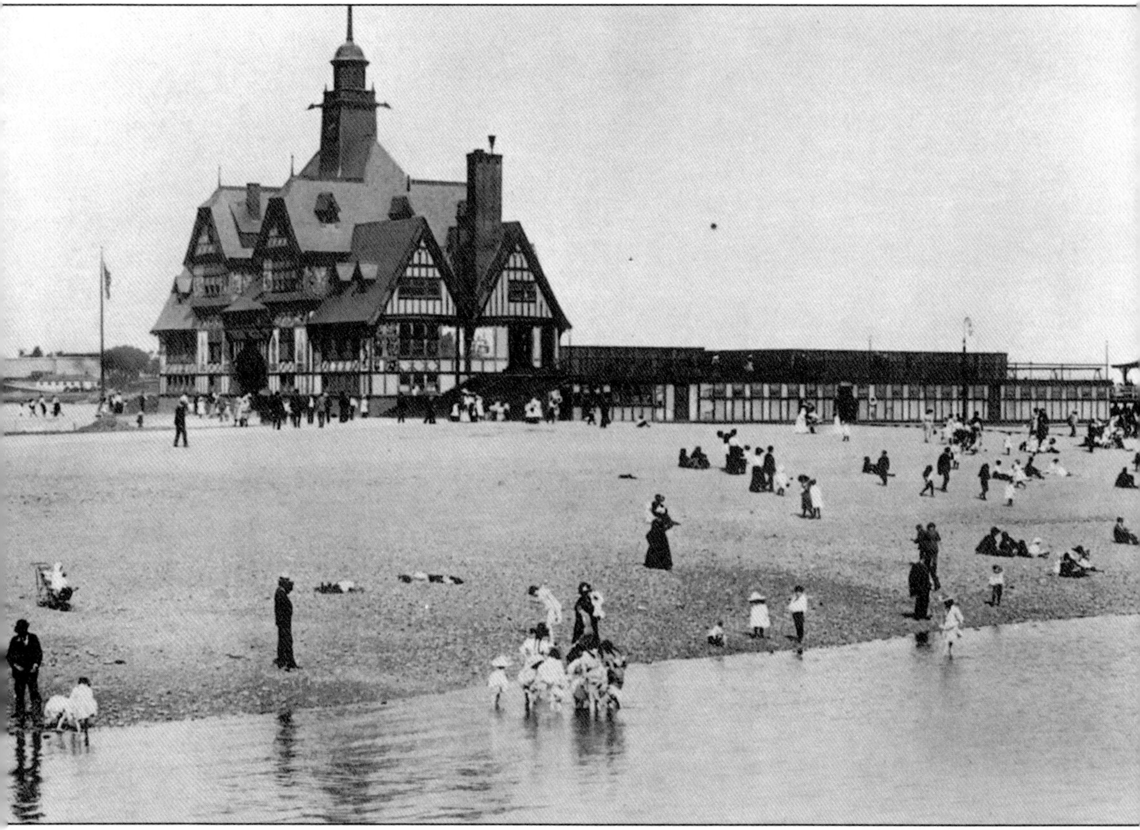

The Head House and the Great Pier at City Point in South Boston was a popular destination of Bostonians a century ago. It was said that "with its resting-places and its beautiful view, it is a healthier place than any horse-car but it takes five cents to reach it if one does not live by." In this *c.* 1900 view, people sun themselves or wade in the water, while others promenade along

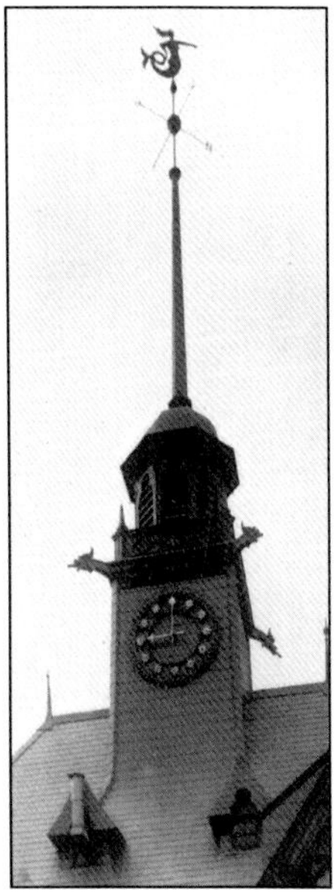

*Left:* The soaring spire of the Head House surmounted the cupola and was capped with a copper weather vane, in the design of an exuberant mermaid. The graffito decoration was scratched into wet cement and was designed by Wheelwright, along with the projecting dragon heads, making for a visually fascinating cap to the roofline.

*Opposite:* Charolotte L. Schicks and her doll enjoy digging in the sand on a sunny afternoon at City Point at the beginning of the 20th century. Others enjoy walking along the beach. (Courtesy of Joan B. Almeida.)

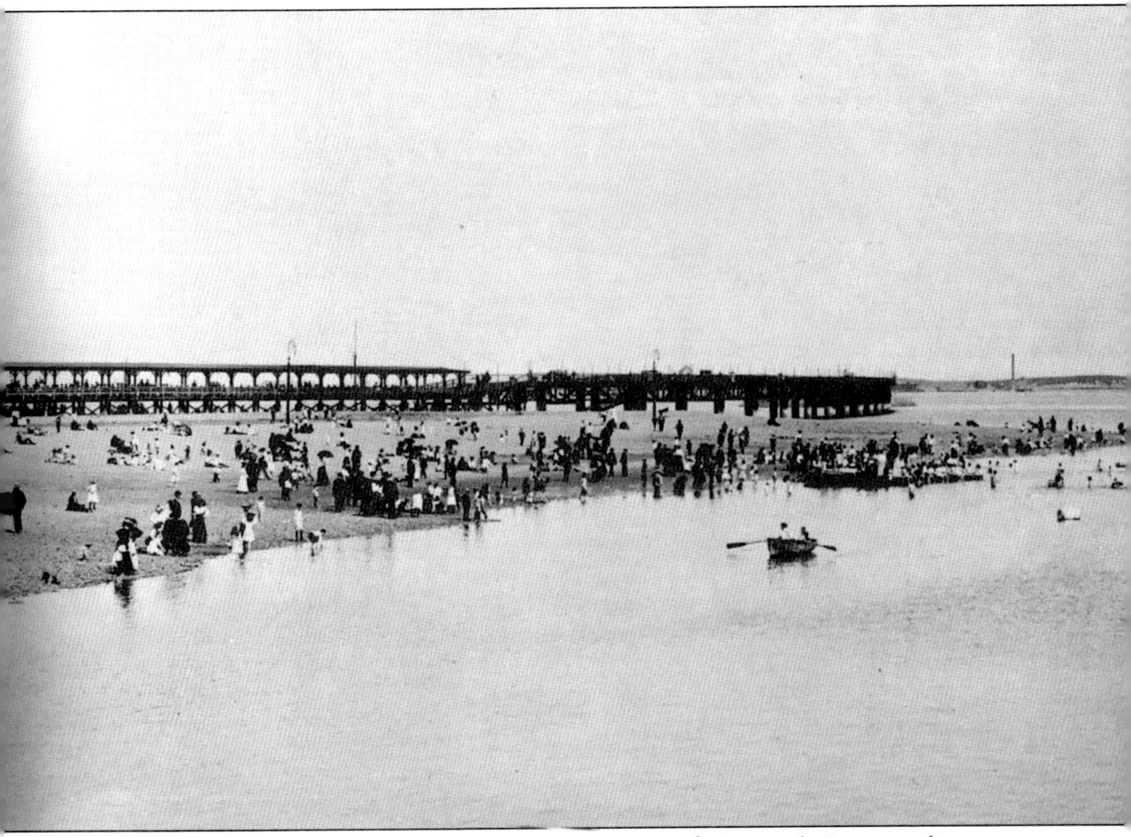

the beach. There were 500 individual lockers at the rear of the Head House, and a separate system of toilet rooms connected with the bathhouses for the multitudes of Bostonians who flocked to City Point on summer weekends. Visible on the far right is Spectacle Island, where Nahum "Boney" Ward rendered horses into glue.

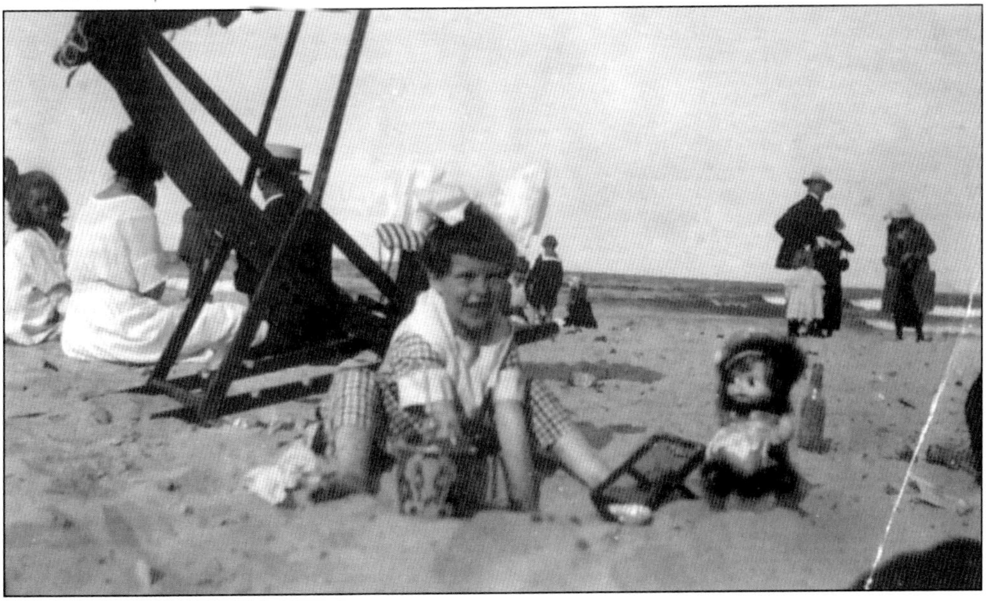

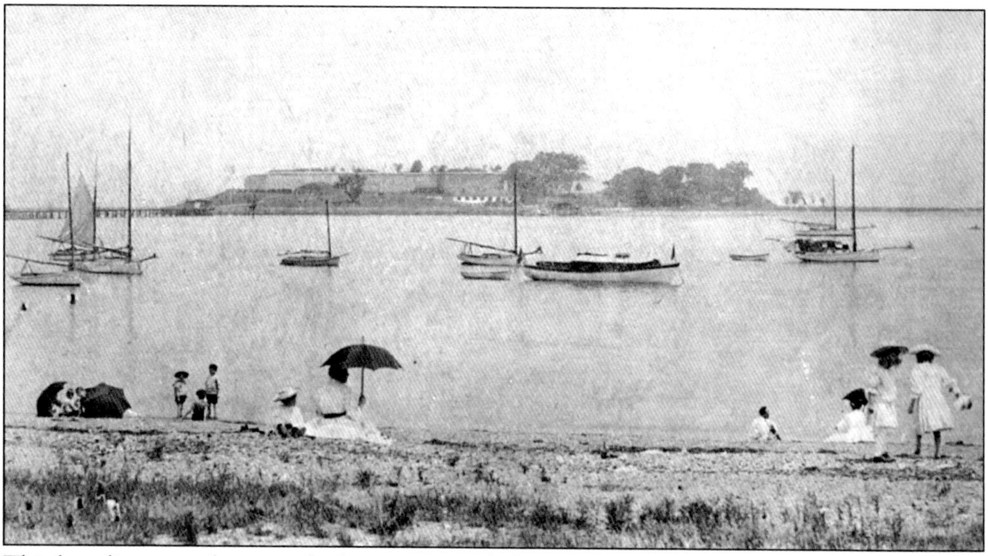

This bucolic scene shows sunbathers, some with large parasols to shade them from the sun, on the beach at City Point. Small boats are lying at anchor in Pleasure Bay; Fort Independence on Castle Island can be seen in the distance. As James Freeman Clark said, "Every sunrise in New England is more full of wonders than the Pyramids. Why go to the Bay of Naples when we have not yet seen Boston Harbor."

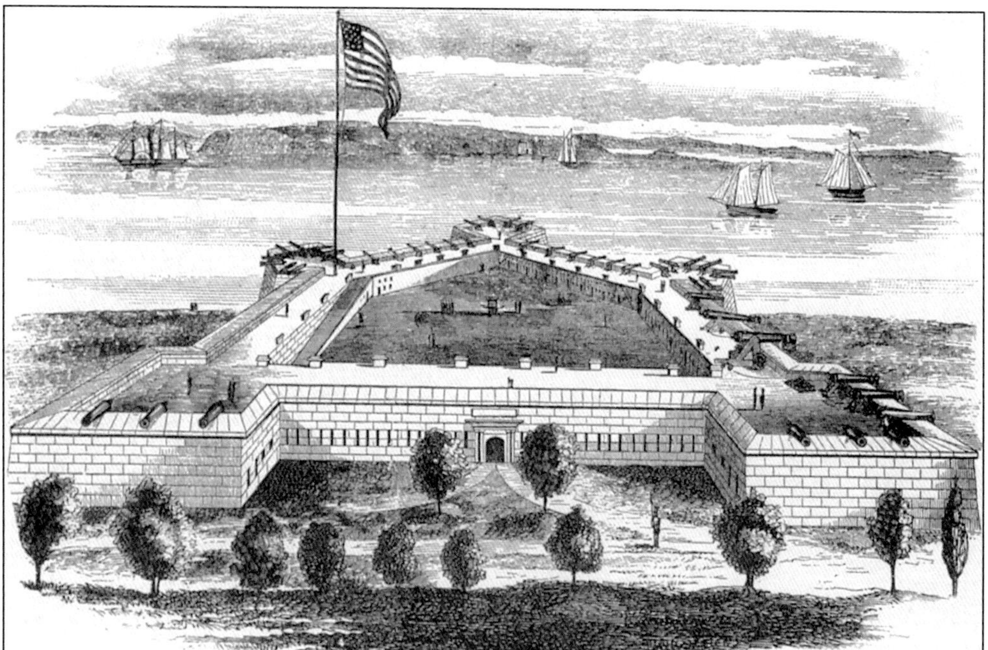

Fort Independence, from an etching in *Gleason's Pictorial Drawing Room Companion* of 1850, was completed in 1833 by Col. Sylvanus Thayer, who remodeled the fort as a "tower of strength and garrisoned by 400 men." Today, on any summer day, cars are parked for miles along William J. Day Boulevard and at the small parking lot at Castle Island, which continues to be a major attraction for Bostonians. The first bridge connecting Castle Island to City Point was built in 1890 by William L. Miller.

The schooner *Bessie* was photographed off Fort Independence, Castle Island, at the beginning of the 20th century. This peaceful scene shows the island with a graceful schooner passing its eastern shore.

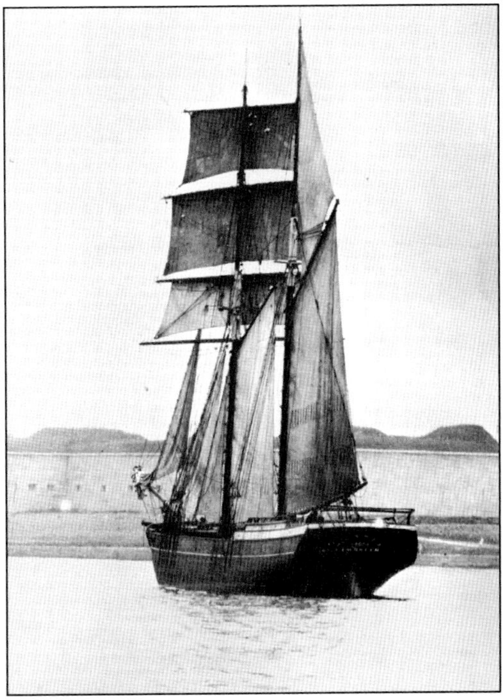

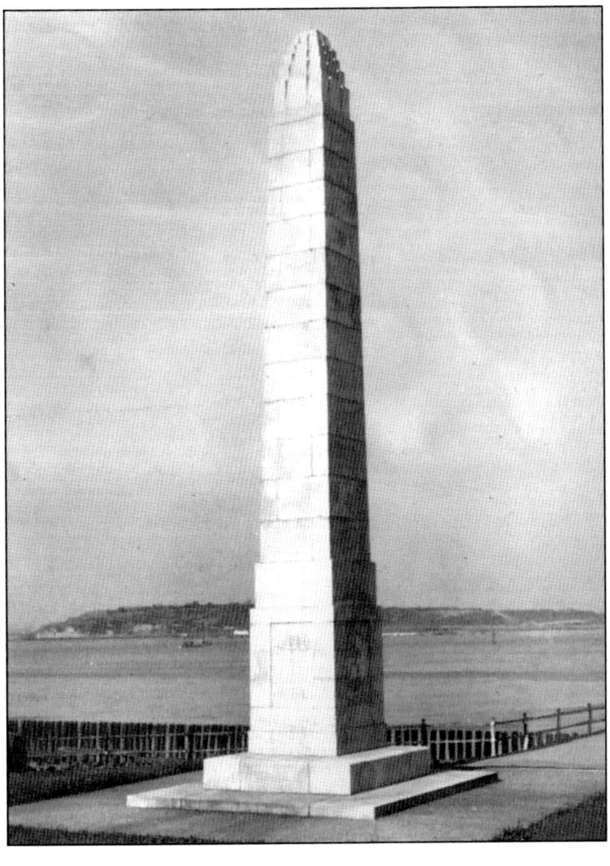

Designed by William T. Aldrich, this obelisk to the memory of Donald McKay (1810–1880) was erected in 1933 on the eastern shore of Castle Island. McKay, considered the greatest clipper ship designer, was a "master-builder whose genius produced ships of a beauty and speed before unknown which swept the seven seas. Made the American Clipper Ship famous the world over and brought renown and prosperity to the City of Boston." A medallion of McKay, sculpted by Philip Sears, was placed on the obelisk, facing the water and his shipyard on Border Street in East Boston, just across the harbor.

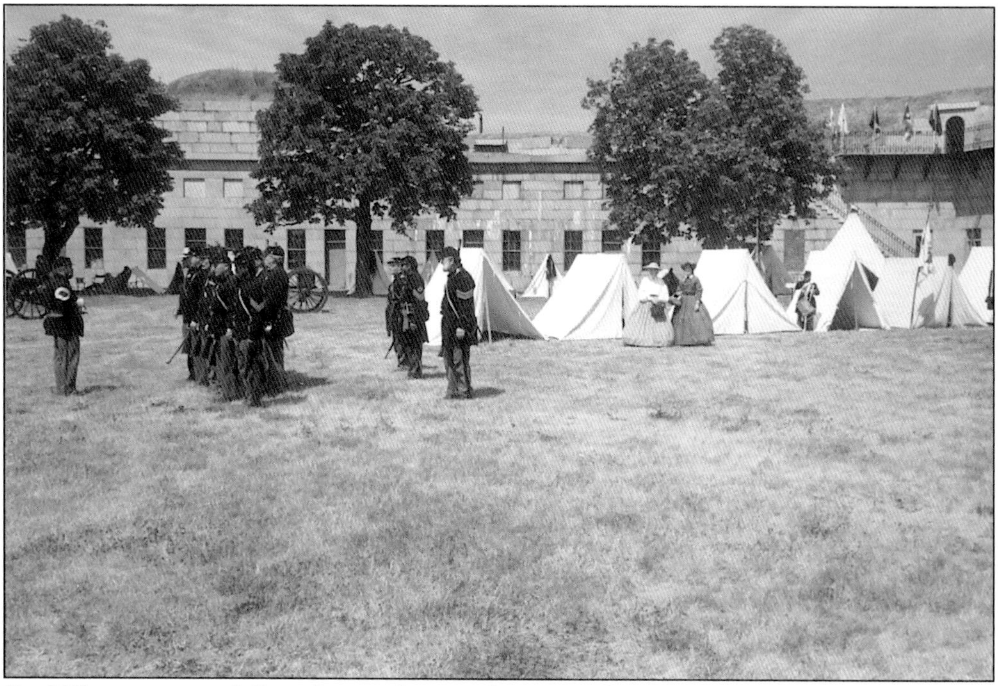

Civil War reenactors drill on the parade ground at Fort Independence, while their "womenfolk" stand near the tents. (Courtesy of Helen Hannon.)

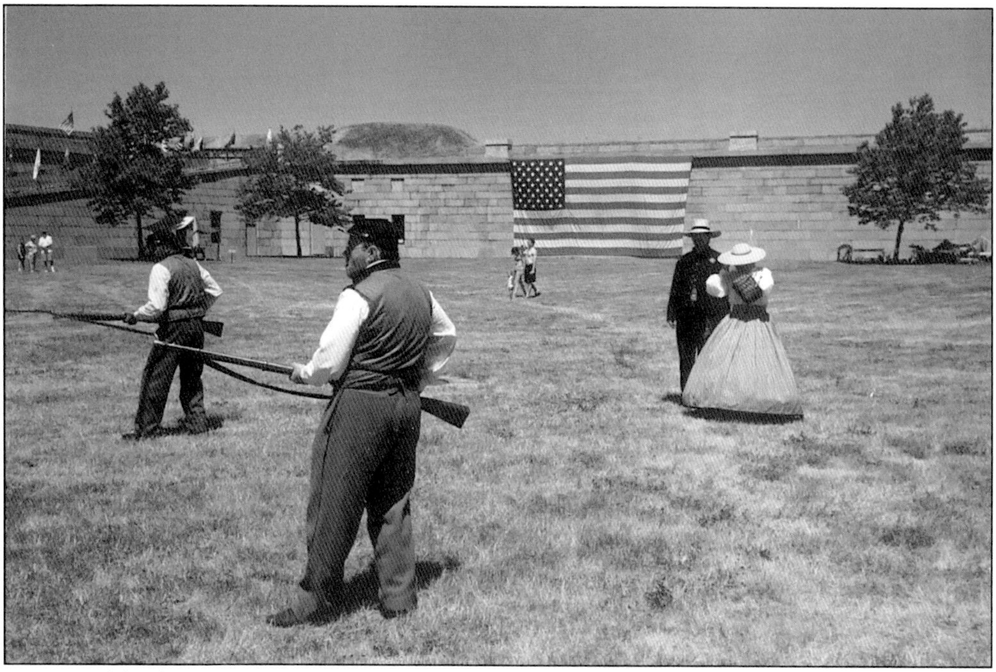

Encamped for the weekend, these reenactors drill on the parade grounds at Fort Independence, Castle Island, in July 1999. (Courtesy of Helen Hannon.)

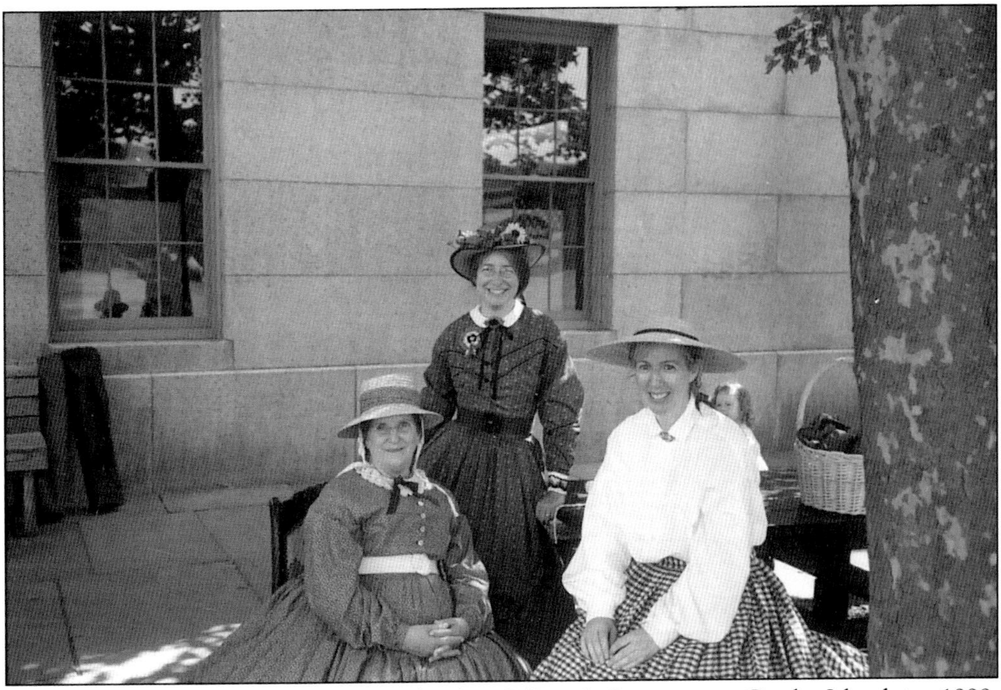

These smiling reenactors pose outside the Officers' Quarters at Castle Island in 1999. They are, from left to right, Cynthia Brown, Laura Eisener, and Helen Hannon. (Courtesy of Helen Hannon.)

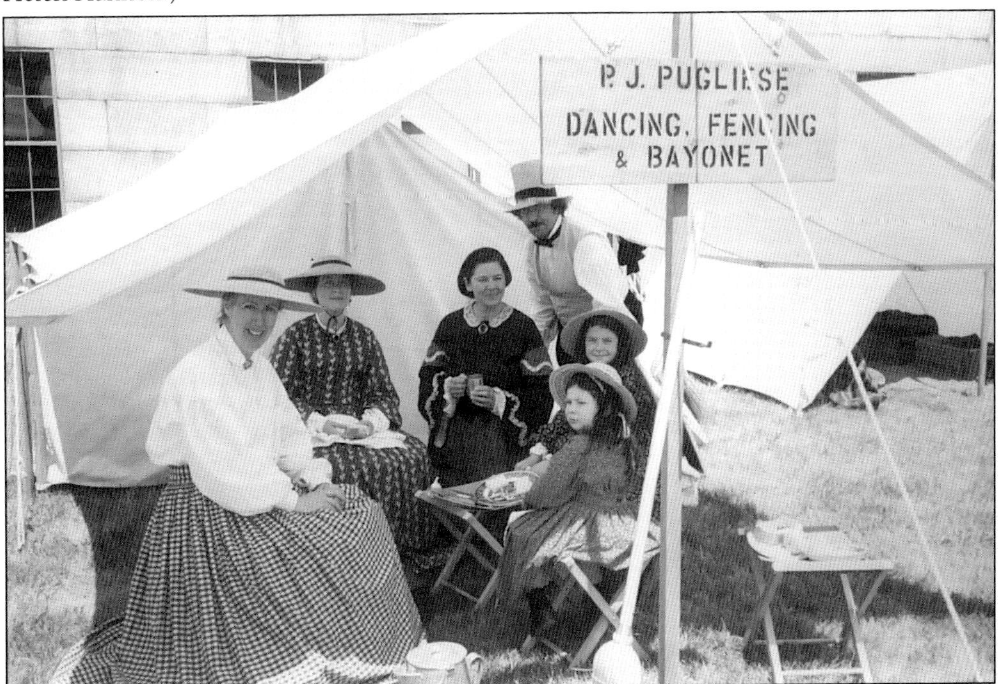


Relaxing in their tent after a warm summer afternoon during a reenactment weekend at Castle Island in July 1999 are, from left to right, Helen Hannon, Barbara Pugliese, Jan Turnquist, Patri Pugliese, Julia Pugliese, and Antonia Pugliese. (Courtesy of Helen Hannon.)

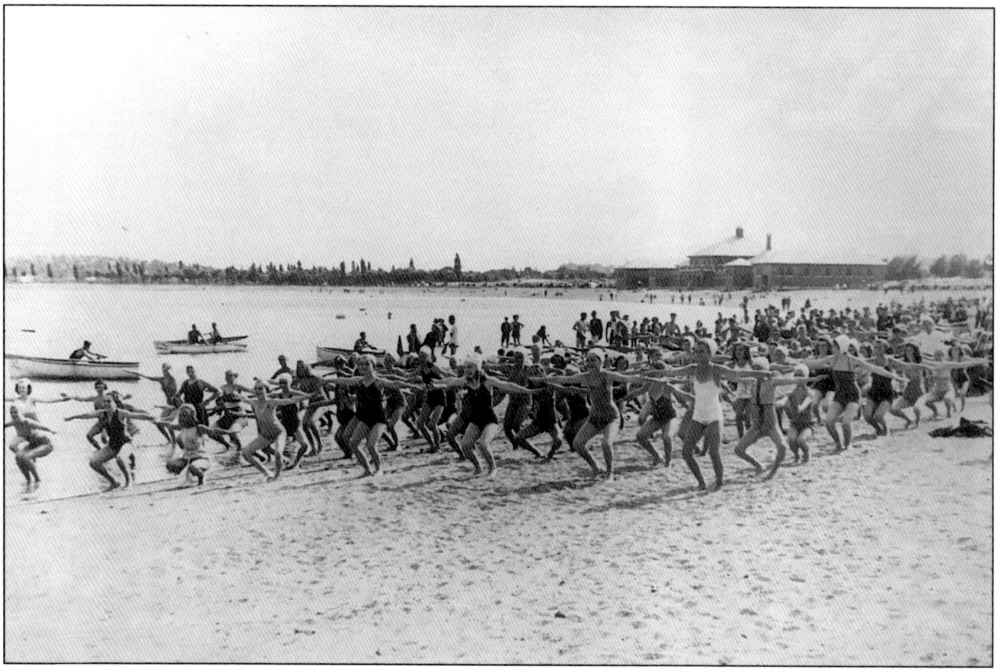

Women perform calisthenics on Carson Beach *c.* 1930. Notice the Carson Beach Bathhouse in the distance and, across the water, the open area of Columbia Point before it was developed for the Columbia Point Housing Project, now Harbor Point. (Courtesy of the Boston Public Library.)

# ACKNOWLEDGMENTS

This second volume of photographs of South Boston is in response to the overwhelming acclaim from those of us who appreciate the history and development of this neighborhood of Boston. This book is the effort of many people who loaned photographs, offered advice, and proved of great support. I urge you to share your photographs and memories with me to continue the *Images of America* series. Thank you to the following: Joan B. Almeida; Joseph April, director of development at Marion Manor; Anthony Bognanno; George Bruger; Paul and Helen Buchanan; the Carney Hospital; Cedar Grove Cemetery; Frank Cheney; Paul A. Christian, department chief, Boston Fire Department; Elise Ciregna and Stephen Lo Piccolo; Mary W. Clarke; Edie Clifford; Elizabeth Curtiss; Dexter; Paula Fleming; Edward W. Gordon; Robert Guthrie, Perkins School for the Blind; John Hannafin; Helen Hannon; James Z. Kyprianos; Mary Linn; Gerard Logan; Diane Loupo, Carney Hospital; Bernard Margolis, director of the Boston Public Library; Dan and Betty Marotta; Judith McGillicuddy; Susan Navarre, Forest Hills Cemetery; Cheryl Needle; William Noonan, Boston Fire Department; Susan W. Paine; Rev. Michael Parise; Sr. Pauline Ross, administrator of Marian Manor; Dr. William Reid, president of the South Boston Historical Society; Dr. Dennis Ryan; Anthony and Mary Mitchell Sammarco; Rosemary Sammarco; Sylvia Sandeen; Robert Bayard Severy; Sal Sorbello; Amy Sutton, my editor; Kim Tenney, Fine Arts Department, the Boston Public Library; Anne and George Thompson; William Varrell; the Victorian Society, New England Chapter; and Lewis Whitlock.